T0317053

'John Stott's remarkable and visionary embrace of both the biblical imperatives for caring and the need to translate them into practical action, particularly in the Majority World where the impacts of both climate change and biodiversity loss are most directly felt, was deeply significant. He took pains to be well-informed and to keep his views under constant revision as both science and biblical theology progressed in response to an unfolding set of ecological crises. In addition, he gave generously of his time to many all over the world who were discovering what their own commitment to Christian callings to care for God's earth might mean. This book charts John Stott's creational journey, one that was made with great rigour and precision. It serves not simply as an account of a rapidly developing set of convictions but also as a model for how authentic Christian leaders can empower the whole church when they live in community and deep humility.'
Peter Harris, co-founder, A Rocha, London, UK

'What a treasure trove this book is! What a testimony to the prophetic foresight of John Stott in urging Christians to be thoroughly and biblically committed to loving, studying and caring for God's creation, long before environmental and climate crises came to dominate our consciousness and trouble our consciences. And what a gift to have all these riches of John Stott's (so quotable!) writing and preaching gathered in one place, within such a helpful historical interpretative framework. May its message still speak as powerfully as the man himself once did.'
Christopher J. H. Wright, Global Ambassador and Ministry Director, Langham Partnership, London

'In 2021, Stott still speaks "a word in season" to every disciple of Jesus. In this 108,000-word feast, we are invited to explore the deep biblical application of the command of Jesus (Luke 10:25–28) in how we care for creation. This embodied obedience, and Stott's brilliant questions, hold together his deep love of Scripture and the biggest need in the world today. It creates new imagination for everyone who desires to be a faithful disciple and a leader in the world.'
The Reverend René August, The Warehouse, Cape Town, South Africa

'In *John Stott on Creation Care*, Sam Berry and Laura S. Meitzner Yoder have given the creation care movement and the entire church family a wonderful gift. Many of us were aware of John Stott's commitment to creation care, but few of us knew how much he had written and how deep were his thoughts on the subject. This exhaustive collection of Stott's writings about creation care, along with key commentary from many others, gives clear insight into how his thinking developed in this area over time. It also provides a solid biblical and theological foundation for the "good doctrine of creation" that Stott called for. This book needs to be in every pastor's library and read by every person preparing for church ministry – and the rest of us as well.'
Edward R. Brown, Executive Director, Care of Creation, Lausanne Catalyst for Creation Care and Lausanne/WEA Creation Care Network Coordinator, Madison, Wisconsin, USA

'John Stott was known for his unimpeachable character, winsome personality and rich theological clarity. What a gift to be able to sit at his feet once again through this new volume on the vital subject of creation care. The authors and contributors have done excellent work framing, commenting on and expounding Stott's work. Whether a sermon, excerpt or lecture, each chapter gleams with his characteristic lucidity and passion. Readers will be delighted to learn about his enthusiasm for wildlife, especially birds, his respect for Charles Darwin, and insistence on the ethical imperative of a simple lifestyle. His is not a secular environmentalism with a little God-talk added on, but a distinctly Christian environmentalism born of faith in the triune Creator God, whom we know and worship by caring for his creation. Throughout, we hear fervent appeal to embrace creation care as the responsibility of every Christian and a central part of the Church's mission. I pray that we will heed his call.'
The Reverend Canon Emily H. McGowin, Assistant Professor of Theology, Wheaton College, Illinois, USA

'This book puts front and centre the cultural mandate as part of what we now call "integral mission", alongside the Great Commission and the Great Commandment. This collection of John Stott's teachings on creation care shall, hopefully, move readers to be concerned about culture and the environment as an important and a most urgent missional task for churches.

I live in a country that is resource-rich and one of the world's densest in terms of biodiversity, yet it has become poor and disaster-prone because of bad governance – over-developed and over-populated. The disasters we live with have intensified fears about the "end times", but this book cogently argues for an alternative picture of the "apocalypse" – a "new heaven and a new earth" as the people of God show up in its remaking. "We are not going to be saved *out of* the earth," it says, "but saved *along with* the earth."'
Melba Padilla Maggay, writer, speaker, social anthropologist and President, Institute for Studies in Asian Church and Culture, the Philippines

'This book offers a thoughtfully assembled account of Stott's decades-long commitment to restoring the doctrine of creation to evangelicalism. His wry and searching observation that "human beings find it easier to subdue the earth than they do to subdue themselves" runs like a faithful thread through his consistent scriptural engagement with growing environmental crises. The collection carefully frames Stott's writing with accounts of a man who was willing to change his mind, who pursued self-restraint and who sincerely loved the diversity and beauty of the life he encountered, both human and non-human. In an era where the toxic culture around many evangelical leaders has, rightly, been exposed, this tribute to a leader of real integrity and vision is welcome and timely.'
Hannah Malcolm, Anglican ordinand and editor, *Words for a Dying World: Stories of grief and courage from the global church*

'I welcome this exposure and articulation of the spiritual and intellectual journey of one of the most influential theological leaders of the modern church, John R. W. Stott. Stott influenced many to think and act as biblical Christians in a modern world. It is fascinating to see how his understanding developed towards greater involvement in creation care. Our guide, Professor Sam Berry, a great British genetic scientist, has curated Stott's intellectual journey and Laura S. Meitzner Yoder has highlighted that work brilliantly in a volume that increases our theological and scientific appreciation of God's created world and the global creation care movement they influenced.

Las G. Newman, Global Associate Director for Regions, Lausanne Movement, Kingston, Jamaica

'I listened to John Stott's presentation on the Snowy Owl while doing a course at the London Institute for Contemporary Christianity. I never labelled him as an environmentalist, and he wasn't – he was a Christian whose life was so rooted in Scripture, that his love for and stewardship of the rest of creation was part of his daily life. He was also willing to be challenged and changed in his understanding and interpretation of Scripture. His understanding of stewardship of creation also evolved and this book is an excellent collection, documenting this journey. Whatever stage we are at in our own journey – whether sceptical, exploring, interested or passionate – this will inspire, inform, invigorate and illuminate our understanding. This book is not an appeal to start caring for creation or a mere reaction to the ever-growing environmental crises, but a collection of inspiring biblical reflection that will also influence how and why we worship God.'

Kuki (Lalbiakhlui) Rokhum, Director of Training and Mobilization, Evangelical Fellowship of India Commission on Relief, Delhi, India

'John Stott's *The Radical Disciple* was the first Christian book I read. I was a teenager and knew nothing about Stott or the global significance of his ministry, but the chapters on creation care and simplicity had a profound impact on me. As a young person passionate about climate justice and very much figuring out faith, those chapters painted a compelling picture of how following Jesus impacts the way we live and consume. I would highly recommend *John Stott on Creation Care* to anyone looking for a solid biblical foundation from which to engage in climate justice.'

Josh Smedley, CEO, Just Love, Durham, UK

'John Stott was a giant of his time, but I didn't know that he was a birdwatcher, nor that this interest enabled him to encounter, through Scripture, a clear mandate to care for creation. The late Sam Berry, himself a giant of a man in the interface between ecology and Christianity,

has left a valuable legacy by drawing together Stott's writing about creation care being a core part of Christian discipleship. Despite the vintage of some of Stott's texts, this book has a freshness and an ability to speak prophetically at this time of climate and biodiversity emergency.'
The Rt Revd Graham Usher, Bishop of Norwich, UK, and Church of England Lead Bishop for the Environment

'*Read this book outside!* And follow Jesus' exhortation and Stott's example, observing the birds and the lilies of the field. Read it outside, and pause between sections or chapters to reflect and to really see what and who is going on around you . . . We know now, even more than Stott did, just what a desperate state our world is in and the terrible destruction that we have wrought on it, and we need to act. We cannot read his words, as we cannot read the Scriptures, and fail to take action.'
Ruth Valerio, from her foreword

JOHN STOTT
ON CREATION CARE

R. J. (Sam) Berry with Laura S. Meitzner Yoder

INTER-VARSITY PRESS
36 Causton Street, London SW1P 4ST, England
Email: ivp@ivpbooks.com
Website: www.ivpbooks.com

© R. J. (Sam) Berry and Laura S. Meitzner Yoder, 2021

R. J. (Sam) Berry and Laura S. Meitzner Yoder have asserted their rights under the Copyright, Designs and Patents Act 1988 to be identified as Authors of this work.

All rights reserved. No part of this publication may be reproduced, stored in a retrieval system, or transmitted, in any form or by any means, electronic, mechanical, photocopying, recording or otherwise, without the prior permission of the publisher or the Copyright Licensing Agency.

Scripture quotations marked KJV are taken from the Authorized Version of the Bible (The King James Bible), the rights in which are vested in the Crown, and are reproduced by permission of the Crown's Patentee, Cambridge University Press.

Scripture quotations marked NIV 1984 are taken from the HOLY BIBLE, NEW INTERNATIONAL VERSION. Copyright © 1973, 1978, 1984 by International Bible Society. Used by permission of Hodder & Stoughton Publishers, a member of the Hachette UK Group. All rights reserved. 'NIV' is a registered trademark of International Bible Society. UK trademark number 1448790.

Scripture quotations marked NIV 2011 are taken from The Holy Bible, New International Version (Anglicized edition). Copyright © 1979, 1984, 2011 by Biblica. Used by permission of Hodder & Stoughton Ltd, an Hachette UK company. All rights reserved. 'NIV' is a registered trademark of Biblica. UK trademark number 1448790.

Scripture quotations marked RSV are from the Revised Standard Version of the Bible, copyright © 1946, 1952 and 1971 by the Division of Christian Education of the National Council of the Churches of Christ in the USA. Used by permission. All rights reserved.

Acknowledgments for Scripture quotations have been given and versions and years noted in the text where known. As the authors of various sources may have included their own translations or quoted from memory, it has not been possible to include version details for all Scripture quotations.

All royalties will be donated to A Rocha International, a Christian organization that engages communities in nature conservation.

First published 2021

British Library Cataloguing-in-Publication Data
A catalogue record for this book is available from the British Library.

ISBN: 978–1–78974–364–7
eBook ISBN: 978–1–78974–365–4

Set in 11/14pt Minion Pro
Typeset in Great Britain by CRB Associates, Potterhanworth, Lincolnshire
Printed in Great Britain by TJ Books Limited

Inter-Varsity Press publishes Christian books that are true to the Bible and that communicate the gospel, develop discipleship and strengthen the church for its mission in the world.

IVP originated within the Inter-Varsity Fellowship, now the Universities and Colleges Christian Fellowship, a student movement connecting Christian Unions in universities and colleges throughout Great Britain, and a member movement of the International Fellowship of Evangelical Students. Website: www.uccf.org.uk. That historic association is maintained, and all senior IVP staff and committee members subscribe to the UCCF Basis of Faith.

For those who joyfully labour
in faith and hope
for things not yet seen

This book is 100% recyclable. The paper used is Forest Stewardship Council certified
from sustainable sources and it is printed with environmentally friendly inks.
In addition the boards, endpapers and jacket are made from 100% recycled paper.

Contents

Contents

About the authors

Robert James (Sam) Berry, MA, DSc, FRSB, FRSE (1934–2018), was Professor of Genetics at University College London (1978–2000). He was formerly President of the British Ecological Society, the European Ecological Federation, the Linnean Society and Christians in Science. In 1992, he gave a series of the London Lectures in Contemporary Christianity (founded by John Stott) on 'Greens, Gaia and God'. His Gifford Lectures were published as *God's Book of Works* (T&T Clark 2003). He edited the collections of essays *The Care of Creation: Focusing concern and action* (IVP 2000) and *Environmental Stewardship* (T&T Clark 2006). Later books included *Ecology and the Environment: The mechanism, marring, and maintenance of nature* (Templeton 2011) and *Environmental Attitudes through Time* (Cambridge 2018). He contributed to many educational initiatives for Christians on natural history and the environment, and for broad audiences on theology and science. Along with John Stott, he was a founding member of A Rocha's Council of Reference, and from the 1960s called Christians to care for creation within their normal life of discipleship to a loving Creator. He served on the General Synod of the Church of England.

Dr Caroline Berry, Sam's life partner for sixty years, notes that 'the work Sam put into the current book was to help our understanding of a friend, rather than an analytical study'. This family friendship spanned decades. In 1974, Sam asked John Stott if he and his family could borrow the Hookses, John's farmhouse on a cliff in south Wales, to stay for a week while Sam pursued some of his genetic studies on local mouse populations in that region. John replied that Dick Lucas (who had preached at the Berrys' wedding) and he were having a writing week there then, but the Berrys were welcome to come as there was enough space for all. Caroline recalls being concerned how the presence of three young children might disturb their writing, only to find that John's Christlikeness was evident in how he received them all with grace and a friendly welcome. John enjoyed having the children there, gave them a few chores, and always asked after them following that time together. After that, John and Sam exchanged ideas periodically, with Sam filling in scientific insights on many creation-related topics about which John was curious. They met regularly at A Rocha meetings, and Sam and Caroline were involved from the beginning with the London Institute of Contemporary Christianity (LICC), which John Stott founded in 1982. Sam and John often exchanged letters on multiple topics of common interest as well. In 1995, it was Sam Berry who assembled the extensive submission nominating John Stott for the Templeton Prize (Dudley-Smith 2001 p. 419). In John's later years, the Berrys enjoyed visiting him at the College of St Barnabas as well.

Laura S. Meitzner Yoder, PhD, serves as John Stott Endowed Chair and Director of Human Needs and Global Resources, and Professor of Environmental Studies, at Wheaton College, Illinois, in the USA. The edited volume *Living Radical Discipleship* (Langham 2021) reflects her current work with global scholar-practitioners in integral mission. Living in London as an A-level and post-university student shaped her commitments to engaging environmental matters within the global church. She joined her British host family's active involvement at All Souls Langham Place (including a discipleship group that met in the Weymouth Street vicarage basement, where John Stott sometimes came downstairs to visit near the end of the evening); an Au Sable Institute internship with Professor Sir Ghillean Prance at the Royal Botanic Gardens, Kew, honed her global ecological interests. For many years she has lived, learned and advocated with marginalized smallholder farmers and forest dwellers, especially in Latin America and Asia. Her current research and writing focus on human–environment interactions in rural South-East Asia and the enduring legacies of colonial land policy worldwide. She is a founding board member of Tearfund USA;

on the boards of ECHO Inc. and Nazareth Project International; and advisory boards of the Bethany Land Institute (Uganda), and the Center for Reconciliation, Duke Divinity School. Through Mennonite Central Committee, she taught with state universities in Aceh and West Papua, Indonesia, and is active in a local Mennonite congregation.

Foreword

I grew up familiar with John Stott's love for the Bible and his writings on the cross. As a keen evangelical and a theology student at university, I read several of Stott's best-known books, including *The Cross of Christ* and *Issues Facing Christians Today*, but I knew little of his love for the wider natural world. It amazed me to learn that he had such a powerful message concerning caring for God's world, holistic mission and simple living. I wondered, how did the church miss his messages on these things that clearly mattered so much to him?

I knew that Stott was an avid birdwatcher and was on the original board for A Rocha (alongside my father), but I also didn't realize, until seeing this collection, how integral the wider natural world was to him. As I read, I considered how my interest in and passion for caring for the environment has developed through my own observations and reading, and was not aware of a direct connection with John Stott. Now I see that some people who have influenced me were themselves very influenced by Stott, and I have a new appreciation for how my own work stands on his amazing shoulders. It has been really interesting to discover just how much and how early he was preaching and writing on the issues that I care so passionately about: John Stott was talking about Christian care for God's world before I was born! I found the timeline of his involvement on this quite fascinating.

It is clear to me that two particular sources lie behind Stott's love of the wider natural world and his environmental interest: his time spent in the natural world and his love of the Scriptures. First, it was his time outdoors in the natural world that opened his eyes to environmental concerns, through birdwatching and living at the Hookses and learning more about God's world from his scientist friends. We become who we are because of our experiences. It seems that even if we don't set out to become interested in the wider natural world or see it as a Christian concern, there is something about spending time outside that leads this naturally to grow within us, that forms and shapes us as particular people. Accompanying that, of course, was Stott's total love of and immersion in the Scriptures: his immersion in the natural world fully accompanied his immersion in the scriptural world.

Stott's interest in and care of the world doesn't come so much from an awareness of the problems that the world is facing, as from his rootedness in the Scriptures. And so, he gives us a great example (that, sadly, isn't widely replicated) of how it should be impossible to be thoroughly rooted in the Scriptures, as a follower of Jesus, and not to care about the wider natural world. What we see in John Stott is how a deep immersion in Scripture should lead inevitably to caring for the world that God has made. If it doesn't, then we're not reading our Bibles correctly; we're reading them with the wrong pair of glasses, a pair that restricts our vision only to people and that stops us seeing how and where the whole of God's creation fits into the biblical narrative. John Stott set a wonderful example of this.

Another aspect that flows naturally from Stott spending time in the natural world and from him being utterly rooted and immersed in the Scriptures is his emphasis on simplicity and simple living, which, again, wasn't something that I knew much about in relation to him until I read his final book, *The Radical Disciple*. I knew it was often said that he lived very simply and generously, but I did not realize that came from a thorough understanding of the way we live and the impact our lives have on other people and on the wider natural world, on God's world. Being a follower of Jesus – being people who care for *who* God has made and *what* God has made – should lead us inevitably to live in a simpler way than most of us do. It should make us want to live in a way that is careful and respectful, that doesn't consume an unfair amount of the world's resources, that thinks about our neighbours living both next door to us and thousands of miles away; our neighbour who shares a garden with us or lives in the rainforest.

John Stott shows us that simple living should be the default for the Christian life rather than an abnormality. This calls us to ask ourselves, 'How do I live in relationship to what God has made – both the human part and the wider non-human part? Am I living in ways that take care of other people and take care of nature or am I living in ways that are destructive of them?' That link with simple living really is key: it challenges us and was important for Stott. Alongside simplicity, as we seek to live this way of life, an accompanying strand is calling governments and businesses to account for their policies and practices that harm other people and God's world. As we seek to put into practice what we learn from Stott, this is an area that is vital for us to engage in actively.

These writings issue a compelling invitation to church leaders to follow Stott's example in his thorough integration of the rest of God's wider whole creation into his church life. With firm grounding in the whole of Scripture, Stott did not keep creation care in a box to be pulled out for one annual service or limited to one particular sermon: it's about wearing those wide-angle glasses so God's world is there as we read the Scriptures and as we write our sermons and preach on the Scriptures and think about all of our church life. Stott demonstrated that considering the wider natural world is an integral part of church life and discipleship, rather than something separate.

I want to mention, too, that I had the joy of knowing Sam Berry. My first contact with him was a time that we shared a platform together at an event in my early adult life as I was beginning to speak around issues of the Christian faith and environmental care, and just starting to become known in this area. As I remember that event, I want to commend Sam for being so encouraging towards me, for inviting me to speak alongside him (a minnow next to a giant!) and supporting me in my work as my ministry and calling was emerging. His support meant a great deal, and I always felt that he believed in me, which added strength to my work.

In closing, I have one recommendation: *read this book outside!* And follow Jesus' exhortation and Stott's example, observing the birds and the lilies of the field. Read it outside, and pause between sections or chapters to reflect and to see what and who is around you. Allow God's creation to speak to you while you're reading these wonderful words from John Stott. Then, as you get up from having read it, use his words to strengthen your resolve to take action – for God's sake. We know now, even more than Stott did, just what a desperate state our world is in and the terrible destruction that we have wrought on it, and we need to act. We cannot read his words, as we cannot read the Scriptures, and fail to take action. All of this must be done out of love for our Creator God.

Ruth Valerio
Global Advocacy and Influencing Director, Tearfund
Canon Theologian at Rochester Cathedral

Foreword

The heavens declare the glory of God;
the skies proclaim the work of his hands
(Psalm 19:1)

The psalmist joyfully introduces his celebration of God's revelation through creation, yet we cannot help but ask: 'Is this true? Is this currently so?' With skies thick with exhaust, with acid rain, with the ozone layer depleted and with bird life disappearing, are the heavens really declaring God's glory today? Or are they, rather, a testament to the abuse and callous indifference of humanity?

I live in Central America, where the picture is far from joyful. The Northern Triangle – Guatemala, Honduras and El Salvador – particularly is a microcosm of the devastating impact of human beings on global ecological conditions. Though these countries are among those that contribute least to the greenhouse gas emissions that are heating the planet, they are among the most vulnerable to the effects of climate change. Added to poverty and violence, intense drought is forcing thousands of people to pack up their meagre belongings and form yet another migrant caravan of climate refugees who are fleeing north in search of sustenance. In these very same countries, evangelical and Pentecostal churches have been growing, as has the percentage of self-titled Christians.

Why, we ask, does a collection of writings such as those contained in this volume matter to the church worldwide? Well, John Stott was a Bible expositor who was recognized and appreciated around the world. His preaching and teaching, along with his prolific writing, continue to offer followers of Christ from Korea to Argentina solid Biblical grounding and a sense of the breadth of the Good News. His personal engagement with people earned him the endearing title

'Uncle John', or 'tío Juan' as my family knew him. His simple lifestyle sets an inspiring example of Christian integrity to all who come to know of it.

This book invites readers into an area of biblical teaching and Christian living that is too often neglected in much of the teaching, preaching and practice of evangelical circles around the world. To be fair, there are individuals and movements outside the North Atlantic who recognize creation care as a form of worship of our Creator and are teaching and living in light of that recognition. Among them are people such as Ken Gnanakan and Kuki (Lalbiakhlui) Rokhum in India, Juliana Morillo in Colombia, Benita Simon in Guatemala, Andrew Shepherd in New Zealand, Sara Kaweesa in Uganda and Andrew Leake in Argentina, to name a few. The influential work of Roman Catholic theologian Leonardo Boff must also be mentioned, along with the deeply insightful papal encyclical 'Laudato Si''. Local expressions of global Christian organizations, such as A Rocha, Tearfund, World Renew, World Vision and Lausanne, engage in conservation, environmental education, advocacy, reducing vulnerability and addressing climate change in different ways. Among Micah Global members, a network of grassroots non-profits around the world, several include creation care as a core dimension of their work.

Outside of these, however – and this takes us back to our question regarding the value of this collection – efforts are few and isolated, voices are disregarded and the battle to inject concern for creation into the lifeblood of the church is often lonely and discouraging. In many parts of the world, activists and advocates are silenced – even killed. Far too many Christians consider concern for the planet to be an ideological rather than a gospel issue. Blinded by this presupposition, they set ecological concerns aside and discredit those who raise them. Within this setting, the words of a respected biblical expositor who faithfully exegetes Scripture and demonstrates how care for our common home is a core dimension of our human vocation do two things. First, John Stott's words encourage followers of Jesus to forge forwards, acknowledging that we are not alone in our struggle against indifference and irresponsible action as waters rise, deserts grow, species disappear and more and more people are forced to migrate because of climate change. Second, his words and lived example offer these very Christians solid biblical and theological grounding for our commitment, helping us tie together and demonstrate to others, including many sceptics, how our faith and our involvement in creation care are indivisible and a necessary outworking of the good news of God's good creation.

I look forward to the day when the growing numbers of self-identified evangelicals around the world repent this sin of omission, recognize that care for our common home is not optional for followers of Jesus and join other people of good will in loving ecological action. I look forward to the day when citizens, and especially Christians, of the places most responsible for the changing climate that is so drastically affecting millions of vulnerable people, will acknowledge their responsibility in the global scene and take radical steps to mend their ways, out of love for God and neighbour. Meanwhile, I trust churches, educational institutions and publishers in the so-called First World will highlight and expand the reach of voices and experiences of creation care springing up locally outside their borders. I have no doubt that this volume, with its rich contribution, will water those seeds while we await the day when the heavens will more freely and cleanly declare God's glory.

Ruth Padilla DeBorst
Comunidad de Estudios Teológicos Interdisciplinarios (CETI)
International Fellowship for Mission as Transformation (INFEMIT)

Preface

This volume began in August 2013 when, after Sam Berry preached one evening on 'The Bible and the environment' in his local church, a congregant asked him for the best source to read John Stott's views about the environment. Sam named a few sources he knew. The following day, he wrote to Peter Harris of A Rocha, asking Peter's thoughts on whether or not it would be worth 'bringing together "Stott on the environment" into a single volume? It could be a powerful witness, as well as being a highly appropriate memorial to John.'

With affirmation from Peter and also from Chris Wright of the Langham Partnership, Sam drafted a list of materials to include in a collection of John Stott's various dispersed writings and sermons on environmental topics, as well as materials by others who knew how this commitment grew and was expressed in Stott's life and ministry. From the outset, Sam chose to include Lausanne-related context in the collection, as he perceived how Stott's environmental teaching was grounded in his missiology and resonated with his ministry's wider themes – that is, 'that creation care is a part of eschewing dualism and responding to the Great Commandment and the Great Commission as improperly separated' (Sam Berry, email to Chris Wright, 8 August 2013).

Peter Harris noted Stott's biblical grounding from the outset: 'When I first met John in the late 1970s, he was already thinking deeply about how the care of creation (what he termed "environmental concerns" in those days) integrated with discipleship and mission. By the time A Rocha celebrated its tenth anniversary in 1993, he was even ahead of our own thinking in his understanding that in Psalms 104 and 111 and elsewhere, "the works of the Lord" were sometimes to be understood as what God does in creation, and sometimes what he does in salvation. So John saw creation as the subject of our study, worship, and witness' (Peter Harris, email to Laura Yoder, 15 April 2021).

Sam, Peter, Chris, Dave Bookless of A Rocha, and Lowell Bliss of Eden Vigil, continued in conversation about the project, though sometimes it lay dormant due to busy schedules. In October 2016, Sam Berry devoted new attention to the manuscript, initiating much correspondence throughout 2017 – clarifying connections, gathering excerpts, transcribing materials and adding his annotations, which gave a narrative thread to the development of John's thoughts on the scriptural foundations for Christian care of the environment. Stott's literary executors gave advice and encouragement as Sam collected and selected materials. He worked steadily on the compilation until a debilitating stroke in late August 2017. Sam passed away on 29 March 2018. The manuscript he left included excerpts of Stott's work spanning 1958 to 2010 and selections from several other authors, interspersed with Sam's narrative thread and commentary, which comprised just over 10 per cent of the text.

This book entered my life during a conversation with Ed Brown of the Lausanne/WEA Creation Care Network in June 2018. Ed knew of Sam Berry's unfinished manuscript, and he suggested that I might be able to advance the project. Taking this on suited my current role, so Ed introduced me to Julia Cameron, who in turn introduced me to Sam's widow, Caroline Berry. Caroline and I met briefly at St Pancras Station when I was in London ten days later, and she gave me a memory stick containing the draft manuscript and associated materials from Sam's computer to carry forward as much as possible. During our conversation, Caroline mentioned that one thing always impressed her about John Stott (the Berrys had known him personally for several decades): he was unusual in that he was a prominent public figure who was not afraid to change his mind. She also said that the church would benefit from having more leaders who exhibited this quality. Her comment framed the book's text for me as a journey of learning, of coming to see things differently from the received categories and divisions we inherit from our upbringing, education, contexts and social circles.

This volume's contents closely reflect Sam Berry's original selections and structure for this project as he proposed it in August 2013 and eventually compiled into his final August 2017 manuscript. Sam initially gave it the title *Stott on the Environment/Creation Care* in August 2013, but then changed it to another provisional title using the term Stott sometimes applied to his bird-related biblical reflections: *John Stott, Orni-theologian.* Sam Berry noted that this collection would be usefully extended by additional dialogue between this text and an outline of natural theology as developed by N. T. Wright (2008, 2013, 2014) or James Barr (1993), but that did not appear in the manuscript he left.

Although I never met Sam Berry in person, it has been a rich experience to get to know him through this work.

Laura S. Meitzner Yoder

Note

The extracts collected together in this volume have been updated but reproduced faithfully as in the original sources. As such, they reflect the language used and society at the time, so with any wording that may jar with modern usage, please note the publication dates and keep reading!

An outcome of this approach, however, is that we can trace the developments in Stott's thought and changes that occurred over time, which is fascinating.

Acknowledgments

This project was completed during the year the COVID-19 pandemic began, 2020–2021, which provided a pause from some normal activities and so enabled me to give sustained attention to these texts, but also presented particular challenges, such as obtaining original copies required for text editing when libraries were closed or offering only limited services. Sincere thanks are therefore due to Peter Harris, Chris Wright, Dave Bookless, Ed Brown, Julia Cameron, Caroline Berry, Lowell Bliss and John Wyatt for providing hard-to-find materials and timely responses to countless enquiries in the course of several years and particularly during 2020 to 2021.

I am deeply grateful that Ruth Valerio, Ruth Padilla DeBorst and all other early readers, even during the difficult time of the pandemic, still made time to prepare their contributions to this volume.

The members of the leadership and editorial teams at IVP (UK) proved to be the champions that this project needed to carry it over the publication finish line – thanks to each one of you! Special appreciation goes to Tom Creedy, Caleb Woodbridge, Allie Douglas, Samantha Snedden, Michelle Clark and Glenn Cauchi for your patient and careful expert assistance.

HNGR colleagues – Jamie Huff, Mandy Kellums Baraka, Corrie Johnson, Kristen Page, George Kalantzis and Camille Frey – brought much encouragement and joy to this journey.

Finally, it is certain that this project could never have been completed in time for Stott's centennial year without the immense support and tireless, painstaking work and close companionship of five individuals: my indefatigable *JSOCC* partners Nina Mantalaba and Laura Atkinson for critical practical assistance alongside moral support on so many facets of this project, as well as Jeff Yoder, Micah Yoder and Joni Weatherley. Thank you for believing that it was possible, and for making that so!

Introduction

Is the health of birds, plants, soil, watersheds, forests, air and the Earth's atmosphere too worldly or mundane to merit the attention of faithful disciples? For John Stott, active care for the Earth and all its inhabitants is not a special domain for some believers with an interest in nature; it is integral to the normal life of Christian discipleship. Creation care matters because 'God intends . . . our care of the creation to reflect our love for the Creator' (Stott 2010b, p. 59).

In multiple senses, this volume is the story of a journey. Drawing on Stott's writings from 1958 to 2010, we see the development of his thought, theologically and in relation to the natural world. It illustrates the life journey of a renowned global church leader growing into and traversing a field marked by controversy and neglect in the church and society. It also points us towards an ongoing journey of growing in hope, listening better to the Word and to the world, as God leads us to new awareness of how to love God and neighbour. The story intertwines relationships and reorientating experiences, a tale of learning and growing in conviction alongside new knowledge, and into new ways of living out worshipful lives of faithful and loving obedience. Our guide is R. J. (Sam) Berry, who walked alongside John Stott for many decades on matters of faith, science and creation care; his commentary narrates the development of Stott's knowledge and convictions over time, theologically and in relation to the natural world.

This book invites us to think, and to grow roots of new understanding, alongside Stott and others on the subject of creation care. As we follow Stott's journey towards a deepening commitment to learning about God's world and humanity's place in nature, we see a coming together of multiple influences on his life. His journey into engaging integral mission with the global church paralleled his

1

growing commitment to creation care as an essential part of Christian discipleship. Stott identified a pivotal point for him that occurred during middle age, from reading the Bible and through developing personal relationships with church leaders in the Majority World.

John Stott experienced a growing into awareness and concern: awe and wonder at how the created world reflects and gives glory to God, seeing how our overconsumption obscures and harms God's creative work, and understanding how our environmental degradation causes suffering among vulnerable people in God's world today. Degradation affects landscapes and wild inhabitants, and it also threatens the lives and livelihoods of the people God created and loves. With these principles, Stott came to embrace and to model a gospel witness that engages the world, even when this is not mainstream, and thought controversial. Sermons and writings on environmental concerns as an inseparable part of missional life and identity reflect Stott's strong aversion to dualism, a conviction that also increasingly shaped his missiology.

This work shows us hopeful ways forwards on several fronts. It shows a way for contemporary Christians to engage with the world we inhabit – not to ignore the needs and troubles and harm, but to be involved directly from a faith grounding that moves us to action. It provides a pastoral orientation, inviting reflection on what we notice and how we live. We see how Stott's engagement in mission and evangelism mirrored his commitment to a life of simplicity; there is no getting round the importance of everyday witness in the life of faith. John Stott reminds us, with his life's testimony, of the embodiment of Christian commitment. He closed his address on 'Radical discipleship' to InterVarsity's 2003 Urbana Student Missions Conference (Stott 2003c), delivered on Stott's behalf by Joshua Wathanga, with this emphasis: 'I sometimes wonder if anything is more essential to evangelism than the Christlikeness of the evangelist. As [John] Poulton wrote, "The most effective preaching or evangelism comes from those who embody the things they are saying. They *are* their message. Christians need to look like what they are talking about. What communicates now is basically personal authenticity."'

We can anticipate a new vibrancy as Christians worldwide develop a theology of creation, more deeply learning, caring and acting on the connections between ecological degradation and injustice. It is abundantly clear that environmental injustice on local and global scales, often linked to discrimination that does not recognize others as God's image-bearers, exhibits our failure to love our neighbours across space and time (Rokhum 2021). There remains much scope for Christians to accompany and to advocate alongside communities harmed by pollution, overconsumption and waste, pursuing restoration of God's creation and seeking wholeness for both perpetrators and those who suffer from environmental injustice. While this book highlights Stott's writing connected to his understanding of creation care, Lowell Bliss has wondered what else we could learn by applying the whole corpus of Stott's work, and the theological reflection it inspires, to the challenge of environmental loss on God's Earth.

Where might this journey take us? There is a long road ahead, and we can learn from and be inspired by the commitments of diverse perspectives on creation care from the church worldwide. Make some time to absorb Norman Wirzba's contributions on food and creatureliness (2015, 2019). I am grateful for Sandy Richter's (2020) significant commitment to making her lucid teaching on creation care accessible via an array of curricula and new media. Dave Bookless (2008) and Justo González (2015) have the gift of asking good questions that invite believers into conversations on creation. Jocabed Solano Miselis (2016) and Randy Woodley (2012) communicate Indigenous understandings of our Creator God and subsequent implications for humanity's being in relation to all of creation. Isaac (2015), Khua Hnin Thang (2014) and the authors in Yeo and Green (2021) prompt us to connect biblical understandings of land to current political and ecological ramifications. Warners and Heun (2019) provide a thought-provoking resource that queries the dominant stewardship paradigm which has long dominated evangelical creation care. Contributors to Reed and Ngaruiya (2019) address creation relationally from multiple African perspectives. Ken Gnanakan (1999, 2014), who encouraged me in the early stages of completing this book and passed away the week its text was finalized, demonstrated a long commitment to creative education and community action on environmental health from his home in India.

As you read this book – perhaps following Ruth Valerio's invitation regarding *where* to read it – I would like you to consider some questions that these texts surfaced for me.

- What are the influences – scriptural, cultural, familial and experiential – that have shaped my own interaction with the wider natural world in which I dwell, both right where I live and on others who live far away?
- How would I describe my own journey in coming to know God more through close attention to and growing knowledge of creation?
- How do I hope to see a joyful awareness of God as Creator and habits of creation care integrated into my life of everyday discipleship?

May our lives and lifestyles bear witness that the earth is the Lord's! Through these writings, may we come to radiate hope ever more brightly, actively caring for what God has made and owns as we demonstrate our loving obedience to the Creator-Redeemer-Sustainer of all things.

Laura S. Meitzner Yoder

1

John Stott's journey

Living to reflect love
for our Creator

When John Stott died in 2011 at the age of ninety, a service of thanks-giving for his life filled St Paul's Cathedral, with archbishops and the Bishop of London present. It was said of Stott that, along-side William Temple, he was 'the most influential clergyman in the Church of England' in the twentieth century (*The Times* 2011). His reputation was even greater outside the UK. Billy Graham wrote:

> Few people have influenced my life and ministry more than my good friend John Stott. His dedication to Jesus Christ, his commitment to the authority of the Bible, and his passion for world evangelization were a great encouragement to me. His commitment to social justice and his profound compassion for the poor and oppressed of the world challenged us to think more deeply about these important dimensions of our faith. (Graham 2012)

In the 2005 *TIME* magazine citation that included Stott on its annual list of the 100 most influential people in the world, Billy Graham noted that John Stott 'represents a touchstone of authentic biblical scholarship that . . . has scarcely been paralleled since the days of the 16th-century European Reformers.' His work was 'a significant factor in the explosive growth of Christianity' worldwide, given his intentional personal investment in training and resourcing church leaders in Asia, Africa and Latin America from the early 1960s and throughout his life's ministry (Graham 2005). Despite his heritage of class privilege and a significant public profile, Stott embraced a simple lifestyle as part of his life of faith (Stott 2010b; Labberton 2021). Notably, Billy Graham's short 2005 commendation mentioned that Stott's own royalties funded much international ministry, and that the 'modesty of his lifestyle is evidenced in the simplicity of his living quarters, limited to a two-room flat in London . . . and a renovated farm on the Welsh coast, where he has written his books' longhand, in rustic conditions. A *New York Times* commentator suggested that if evangelicals had a pope, it would have been Stott (Brooks 2004).

In his *A History of the Church of England 1945–1980*, Paul Welsby wrote:

> In the pre-war and immediately post-war years many evangelicals had been more concerned with preserving their own purity of doctrine than with attempting to co-operate with others in evangelism and the ecumenical movement and were too parochially orientated to take any influential part in the higher councils of the Church . . . During the nineteen-fifties, however, a gradual change took place and this was largely due to the status and influence of one man. John Stott was a person of wide vision and deep understanding, and very persuasive. A gifted expositor of the Bible, a prolific writer and an evangelist, he was also a statesman who possessed the ability to understand other points of view.
> (Welsby 1984, pp. 212–213)

Stott made major contributions to biblical understanding, particularly the theology of the atonement, together with the nature of mission and social ethics. He was also a highly effective evangelist. In 1952, only two years after becoming Rector of All Souls Church Langham Place, in the heart of London's West End, he led a mission to his alma mater, Cambridge; it was the first of what would become more than forty university missions and it ushered in a new style of thoughtful evangelism. It was reported that 'he was biblical, scholarly though not academic, firm but not caustic, more evidently a man with love for people than some of the older preachers' (Barclay and Horn 2002, p. 238). Crowds attended and many professed faith. His addresses formed the basis of his book *Basic Christianity*, published in 1958, which by 2010 had sold more than 2.5 million copies and had been translated into more than fifty languages (Stanley 2013, p. 122). He wrote around fifty books. Two compilations of his writings have been published (Dudley-Smith 1995b; Keswick Classics 2008); he has been the subject of five biographies (Catherwood 1984; Dudley-Smith 1999, 2001; Steer 2009; Cameron 2012; Chapman 2012); a bibliography (Dudley-Smith 1995a); and two books of reminiscences (Cameron 2020; Wright 2011). Many of his books have been reprinted often; two of them (*Men with a Message* and *Christian Mission in the Modern World*) have been republished with extensive commentaries.

Stott's reputation was built on the basis of disciplined Bible study and careful expository preaching. It could well be said of him, as Charles Spurgeon wrote of John Bunyan, 'Prick him anywhere – his blood is Bibline, the very essence of the Bible flows from him.' His ministry has been described as both apostolic and Abrahamic (Wright 2020, p. 31). Apostolic because 'it faithfully reflected the passion and priorities of the biblical apostles: evangelism and teaching'; and Abrahamic because of his commitment to reaching out to the nations through the number of international evangelical bodies with which he had close association – the Lausanne Movement, World Evangelical Alliance, International Fellowship of Evangelical Students, Scripture Union, A Rocha, Tearfund – together with his passion for the truth of a gospel that he believed had not been grasped until its radical demands, as well as its gracious promises, had been grasped and lived out by 'integrated Christians'.

Christopher Catherwood, his first biographer, writing in 1984, described him as 'above all a preacher', albeit with 'the aim to relate God's unchanging Word to our ever-changing world . . . earthing of the Word in the World is not something optional' (Catherwood 1984, p. 31). Stott himself wrote that 'the Christian preacher is neither a speculator who invents new doctrines which please him, nor an editor who excises old doctrines which displease him, but a steward, God's steward, dispensing faithfully to God's household the truths committed to him in the Scriptures, nothing more, nothing less, and nothing else' (Catherwood 1984, p. 37). Catherwood is careful to emphasize Stott's concern for social issues and his insistence on 'balanced Christianity' but, to him, Stott was first and foremost a preacher and expositor. Near the end of his life, Stott declared that he would like to be remembered as 'an ordinary Christian who has struggled to understand, expound, relate and apply the word of God' (Cameron 2020, p. 5).

Notwithstanding, and despite his formidable intellect and personal asceticism, Stott was a 'people person'. He had an enviable ability to remember people he had met and had a quick rapport with all ages, without in any way lessening or compromising any of his beliefs or his submission to Jesus as his master and Saviour. This did not reduce at all his acknowledging and teaching the authority of God's revelation in Scripture.

Accepting the danger of oversimplifying, it is possible to identify five interconnected, consistent and progressive themes that characterized Stott's life and became ever clearer to him as his ministry developed and matured.

- He was immersed in and subordinated to God's word as set out in the Scriptures.
- He insisted that God's workings can – and should – be seen in both creation and redemption.
- He abominated the dualistic separation of body and spirit; his emphasis was on the necessity of 'double listening' – to both ancient word and modern world.
- He believed that it was illegitimate to separate the 'Great Commandment' ('To love one's neighbour as oneself') from the 'Great Commission' ('Go and make disciples'): the two should be seen as complementary.
- He was prepared to change his mind if he believed his interpretation of Scripture was wrong. He changed his attitude to pacifism, creationism, abortion and, most importantly in the present context, to God's mandate for creation care.

These elements of Stott's life can be seen clearly in his last book *The Radical Disciple*, published the year before he died, and which reasonably can be taken to be his considered testament to the Church. In it, Stott presented a challenge:

> That we who claim to be disciples of the Lord Jesus will not provoke him to say again, 'Why do you call me Lord, Lord, and do not do what I say?' (Luke 6:46) ... Our common way of avoiding radical discipleship is to be selective; choosing those areas in which commitment suits us, and staying away from those areas in which it will be costly. But because Jesus is Lord, we have no right to pick and choose the areas in which we will submit to his authority.
> (Stott 2010b, pp. 14–16)

The Radical Disciple lists eight characteristics of Christian discipleship that Stott considered essential but neglected. Seven of them were shown by Stott in his own life: non-conformity, Christlikeness, maturity, simplicity, balanced judgment, involvement in community and death, in the sense of death and life in Christ. Death for Stott, as he approached his own physical death, was not merely the termination of life but also the gateway to life. He quoted Paul: 'For to me, to live is Christ and to die is gain' (Philippians 1:21, NIV 2011). Taken together, these characteristics show the need to define what Christlikeness might mean in terms of personal commitment: happily accepting the authority of Scripture but with a critical attitude rather than as wooden literalism; and seeking a brutally honest and balanced maturity in one's discipleship, even if this involves dissenting from traditional interpretations. They may be regarded as manifestations of the five themes noted above, modelled by Stott himself.

All of these seven characteristics could be regarded as traditional and behavioural – perhaps religious, in a wide sense – but Stott's eighth quality seems to be entirely different. He included the care of creation as a necessary mark of a radical disciple. On the face of it, this seems eccentric, even startling. Most Christians will probably agree that care of creation is commendable and should be encouraged but would be unlikely to rate it as a required discipline for all believers. For some evangelicals in particular, earth tends to be regarded as little more than a theatre for salvation, a preparation for eternal life elsewhere. Why did Stott include 'creation care' in his marks of radical discipleship?

We can certainly rule out any pragmatic motive on Stott's part. He was certainly aware of the damage that we are doing to the environment. In his chapter on creation care in *The Radical Disciple*, he discusses four ingredients of our current ecological crisis: the problems caused by a constantly increasing human population; the damage to and depletion of the world's resources, both non-renewable and renewable; the growing problem of waste; and the insidious effects of climate change. He notes the involvement of the global community in international conferences and the need for 'sustainable development', but his focus is firmly on the need for theological commitment rather than institutional response or personal commitment. His approach is unapologetically biblical. It begins with creation involving the nature of humankind being in God's image, continues with human disobedience ('the fall') and concludes with God's restoring work in repairing the broken relationships we have with God, one another and the creation itself. Our role – part of our God-given mission – is to cooperate with God as stewards. Stott's approach turns the common approach to caring for the environment on its head: it begins with God, not human misdemeanours. Creation care matters because 'God intends . . . our care of the creation to reflect our love for the Creator' (Stott 2010b, p. 59).

Stott's commitment and advocacy of creation and its care need to be examined because it comes from an evangelical 'giant' and biblical scholar arguing for its importance, and because it is contrary to its generally being neglected by religious believers and disregarded by Bible expositors. This book is an attempt to remedy this by collecting and commenting on Stott's writings on ecology and, importantly, examining how his concern for creation care developed and led to him accepting that it is not simply an option for a few dedicated 'greens' but, rather, an integral part of the mission of the Church and a challenge for all Christians. His writings on the subject are scattered and bringing them together could involve a fair amount of repetition (for example, Psalm 104 was important in Stott's thought and he expounded it in a number of contexts), so it has seemed appropriate to employ some (hopefully judicious) editing to minimize this.

Stott's environmental concern arose firmly and squarely out of a faithfulness to Scripture. He did not expound a detailed theology of creation or creation care. Nonetheless, he laid a firm foundation for a systematic theology of the environment, and he seems to have expected that others might build on the basis he laid. Indeed, in *The Radical Disciple* he explicitly hands on such a task to Chris Wright, his chosen successor to maintain and nurture the Langham Partnership founded by Stott. In the chapter on creation care, Stott asks, 'What can the radical disciple do to care for the environment?' He then specifically commissions Chris Wright to answer his question, and prompts the reply he wants with a quotation from Wright's magisterial *The Mission of God*:

> In the past, Christians have instinctively been concerned about great and urgent issues in every generation . . . These have included the evils of disease, ignorance, slavery, and many other forms of brutality and exploitation . . . It seems quite inexplicable to me that there are some Christians who claim to love and worship God, to be disciples of Jesus and yet have no concern for the earth that bears his stamp of ownership. They do not care about the abuse of the earth, and indeed by their wasteful and overconsumptive lifestyles they contribute to it.
> (Wright 2006, pp. 413–414)

In the light of this, it seems both legitimate and useful to extend Stott's own writings with Wright's further development, and also to add supplementary offerings from others: Dave Bookless on the Bible and biodiversity and Jonathan Moo on the global extension of the work. Stott's own journey (is 'pilgrimage' too strong a word?) is set out in the timeline below.

Timeline for John Stott's journey in creation care

1921 John Stott born 27 April 1921, in London. Introduced to natural history by his father.

1938 Opened the door to Christ.

1940 Entered Trinity College, Cambridge. Befriended by zoologist Oliver Barclay, who went on to become General Secretary of UCCF. The two used to cycle out to birdwatch – and talk theology as well as ornithology.

1950 Appointed Rector of All Souls Langham Place, in London's West End.

1952 Took a university mission at Cambridge and introduced a new style of thoughtful evangelism.

1954 Bought 'The Hookses' on the Pembrokeshire cliffs, on the coast of south-west Wales, and periodically retreated there.

1966 *The Canticles and Selected Psalms* published, including expositions of Psalms 19, 103, 104 (reprinted, in part, as *Favorite Psalms*, in 1988).

1966 Gave Bible studies on the 'Great Commission' at the World Congress on Evangelism in Berlin and, in view of the Johannine version, began to doubt if the Great Commission was solely about evangelism.

1967 National Evangelical Anglican Congress in Keele, marking a fresh look at evangelicalism. One immediate reaction was that close friend Norman Anderson was provoked to write *Into the World: The needs and limits of Christian involvement* (1968).

1968 Attended the World Council of Churches Assembly in Uppsala. Stott was impressed by the social concerns of the WCC, but worried by the lack of spiritual urgency.

1970 *Whose World?* by Oliver Barclay emphasized God as sustainer as well as redeemer.

1972 Research Scientists' Christian Fellowship Conference on the 'Abuse of the Environment' was organized by Oliver Barclay.

1974 International Congress on World Evangelization in Lausanne, at which the Lausanne Covenant was drafted, which states *inter alia*, 'We affirm that evangelism and social concern are both part of our Christian duty.'

1975 Reflected on the nature and extent of mission in *Christian Mission in the Modern World*.

1975 Established the London Lectures in Contemporary Christianity to 'encourage biblical thinking on contemporary issues'.

1977 All Souls Langham Place sermon on 'God and the environment', largely an exposition of Psalm 104.

1980 Co-convened, with Ron Sider, the International Consultation on Simple Lifestyle.

1982 Established the London Institute of Contemporary Christianity (LICC).

1983 Member of the International Council of Reference for the newly founded A Rocha, established as an organization for 'Christians in Conservation'.

1984 *Issues Facing Christians Today* published, with chapter 'Our human environment' (became 'Caring for creation' in later editions).

1985 Organized joint conference of LICC and Christian Ecology Group on 'People, technology and the environment', chaired by Rowland Moss (author of *The Earth in Our Hands*, 1982) and which involved Sam Berry (author of *Ecology and Ethics*, 1972) and Ron Elsdon (author of *Bent World*, 1981).

1989 Gave 'The biblical imperative' keynote at the conference 'Caring for God's world', organized by A Rocha and Christian Impact, in Reading.

1990 Study Pack *Green Issues* produced by LICC, with succinct paper by Stott on 'the biblical imperative for conservation'.

1992 *The Contemporary Christian: An urgent plea for double listening* published as a companion volume to *Issues Facing Christians Today*.

1993 Delivered 'The works of the Lord' address at the tenth anniversary of the A Rocha Trust in London.

1994 Endorsed the 'Evangelical declaration on the care of creation', drafted by the Theological Commission of the World Evangelical Fellowship as a response to the WCC consultation on 'Justice, peace and the integrity of creation'. Wrote the foreword to *The Care of Creation* (2000), produced as a commentary on the declaration.

1999 *The Birds Our Teachers* published.

2003 Scheduled to give plenary address and 'Caring for creation' seminar at InterVarsity's Urbana Student Missions Conference in Illinois, USA, but was unable to travel due to ill health.

2004 BBC Radio 4 Sunday worship 'Let the little birds be your theologians', broadcast from the Hookses, Pembrokeshire, Wales.

2006 *The Mission of God* published by Chris Wright, with chapter 'Mission and God's Earth', building on Stott's work.

2009 Audio greetings sent in advance of the Cape Town Congress opened by noting the challenging 'spectre of global warming, which adds new urgency to our evangelism'.

2010 Third Lausanne Congress in Cape Town, South Africa, issued the Cape Town Commitment, which stated *inter alia* that 'creation care is a gospel issue within the Lordship of Christ'.

2010 *The Radical Disciple* published, with 'creation care' as one of the marks of Christian discipleship.

2011 Died 27 July 2011, in Lingfield, Surrey.

2012 Lausanne Creation Care Network issued the 'Jamaica call to action' and produced *Creation Care and the Gospel* (2016).

The case for our role in creation care, as argued by Stott in *The Radical Disciple*, is:

> The Bible tells us that in creation God established for human beings three fundamental relationships: first to himself, for he made them in his own image; second to each other, for the human race was plural from the beginning; and third, to the good earth and its creatures over which he set them.
>
> Moreover, all three relationships were skewed by the fall. Adam and Eve were banished from the presence of the Lord

God in the garden, they blamed each other for what had happened, and the good earth was cursed on account of their disobedience.

It stands to reason therefore that God's plan of restoration includes not only our reconciliation to God and to each other, but in some way the liberation of the groaning creation as well. We can certainly affirm that one day there will be a new heaven and a new earth, for this is an essential part of our hope for the perfect future that awaits us at the end of time (e.g., 2 Peter 3:13; Revelation 21:1). But meanwhile the whole creation is groaning, experiencing the birth pains of the new creation (Romans 8:18–23). How much of the earth's ultimate destiny can be experienced now is a matter for debate. But we can surely say that just as our understanding of the final destiny of our resurrection bodies should affect how we think of and treat the bodies we have at present, so our knowledge of the new heaven and earth should affect and increase the respect with which we treat it now.
(Stott 2010b, pp. 49–50)

It is against the background of this wholesome biblical teaching that we need now to confront the current ecological crisis.
(Stott 2010b, pp. 54)

2
Early explorations

Psalms and first sermon on creation care

Stott's understanding of the environment certainly developed and matured from the straightforward exegesis of Bible texts to include what he called the cultural mandate. It reflects a response involving his obedience to God's word, his refusal to separate God's working in creation from that in redemption, and his willingness to rethink his interpretations if appropriate.

Stott's approach can be seen in one of the earliest pieces he wrote that relates to the natural world. It is an exposition of Psalms 103 and 104 from his 1966 book, *The Canticles and Selected Psalms* (slightly revised and shortened in *Favorite Psalms*, 1988a). He called Psalm 104 ('The works of God in nature') a meditation on the creation story in Genesis and an early expression of the study of ecology. It seems to have had a special place in the development of what Stott later called 'orni-theology'. He regarded Psalm 104 as necessarily linked with Psalm 103 ('The benefits of God's grace').

Psalm 104: The works of God in nature

Psalms 103 and 104 form a perfect pair and illustrate the balance of the Bible. Both begin and end with the words *Praise the Lord, O my soul*. Psalm 103 goes on to tell of the goodness of God in salvation, Psalm 104 of the greatness of God in creation (verse 1). Psalm 103 depicts God as the father with His children, Psalm 104 as the Creator with His creatures.

Psalm 103 catalogues His *benefits* (verse 2), Psalm 104 His *works* (verses 13, 24, 31).

The author evidently has in mind the narrative of Genesis 1 and draws his inspiration from it. He follows approximately the same order, beginning with light and ending with human beings. He describes with great poetic beauty how God made the heavens and the earth (verses 1–9), and provides drink, food and shelter for all birds and beasts (verses 10–23). After a further meditation on God's many varied works in both creating and preserving 'all creatures great and small' (verses 24–30), he concludes with a prayer that God's glory may endure, a resolve to worship God throughout his life, and a desire that sinners who spoil God's world shall be no more (verses 31–35).

It is important to notice the form which the psalmist's 'gusto for nature', as C. S. Lewis (1958, p. 85) called it, took. He does not praise nature for its own sake; 'there are no nature lyrics in the psalms. Nature is referred to only to the extent that it points to him who made everything' (Ringgren 1962, p. 36). This emphasis is preserved in Sir Robert Grant's fine (if free) paraphrase, 'O Worship the King' (1833).

God's creation of heaven and earth (verses 1–9)

Most of the verbs in this paragraph should probably be put in the past tense and understood to refer to the creation of the heavens (verses 1–4) and the earth (verses 5–9). We should beware of taking these verses literally. The author writes as a poet, not as a scientist. We are not intended to picture God riding on a chariot of clouds or building the earth like a house on actual, material foundations. All this is imagery.

What the passage does teach us is that God is the creator of the universe, and that He has revealed Himself in it. In His essential being He is invisible, but He makes Himself known in the visible order which He has made. The light is His garment, the heavens are His tent, the sky His chambers, and the clouds His chariot, while He makes the winds His messengers and fire and flame His servants (verses 2–4). 'In comparing the light to a robe,' comments the reformer John Calvin, 'he signifies that, though God is invisible, yet his glory is manifest.'

Similarly, the earth is described as having been established upon firm foundations and then covered with the deep. This is the primeval chaos, when 'the earth was formless and empty' and 'darkness was over the surface of the deep' (Genesis 1:2). Then the separation of earth from sea is dramatically portrayed (as in Genesis 1:9, 10): the waters *flowed over the mountains, they went down into the valleys, to the place you assigned for them* (verse 8).

God's provision for birds and beasts (verses 10–23)

In this part of the psalm the verbs are mostly in the present tense, and remind us that Christians are not deists. The nineteenth-century deists believed that God had wound up the universe and set it in motion like a gigantic clockwork toy. The Bible teaches, however, that God is a living God, ceaselessly active in the control and the care of what He has made. He makes provision for the *beasts of the field* and *the birds of the air* (verses 11, 12). 'Ecology' would be a term too grandiosely scientific to apply to this paragraph; yet this is what the author is depicting. He is fascinated by God's marvellous adaptation of the earth's resources to the needs of living creatures, and vice versa.

Thus, the streams which flow through the valleys provide drink for the animals (verses 10, 11), while God's rain waters the mountains (verse 13) and the trees (verse 16). Similarly, humans and beasts are supplied with food from the earth, including wine, oil and bread (verses 14, 15). Even carnivorous lions are said to seek their food from God (verse 21).

Living creatures require more than food and drink, however; they need shelter also, to protect them from the fury of the elements and in their breeding season. So birds, which *sing among the branches* (verse 12), also *make their nests in them* (verse 17). Storks build *in the pine trees* (verse 17), while *the high mountains* are a refuge *for the wild goats* and *the crags for the coneys* (verse 18; this is also translated badger and rabbit; it is evidently a hyrax). Further safety is provided by the cover of darkness, when *all the beasts of the forest prowl*. Then, when *the sun rises ... they steal away ... and lie down in their dens*; whereas human beings, by contrast, work by day and sleep at night (verses 19–23).

God's creation and preservation of all creatures (verses 24–30)

The psalmist interrupts his descriptions with an outburst of praise (verse 24). Both earth and sea teem with His creatures, *living things both large and small* (verse 25). The sea is also the place of ships and the playground of Leviathan (verse 26). The latter is evidently a great sea creature, which some scholars think 'is the whale, some the porpoise; in Job 41 it is probably the crocodile'. Whatever Leviathan is, God is represented in the Talmud as playing with it.

Further, if God has made all creatures in His wisdom, He also cares for them in His faithfulness. They *all look to you* (verse 27). They depend upon Him for their food and breath. Not that they are inactive in feeding themselves, for they have to *gather up* their food; but God *gives* it. This truth is further enforced by striking anthropomorphisms, which speak of God's *hand* and *face* (verses 28, 29). Just as we have seen a child at the zoo or in the farmyard, offering food to some animal on the palm of an outstretched hand, so God opens His hand, that His creatures may be *satisfied with good things*. But when He turns away from them and hides His face, *they are terrified*. When further, He takes away their breath, *they die and return to the dust*. When, on the other hand, He sends His Spirit (or 'breath'), they are not only created in the first place, but continuously renewed.

Food and life are the basic needs of every creature, and here their presence is attributed to the open hand and quickening breath of God, their absence to His hidden face. To modern ears it all sounds very naive. Can we believe such things in this age of science and technology? We have already noted that the descriptive passages are figurative, whether in the use of poetic or of anthropomorphic imagery.

But the truth behind the figures stands. God the Creator is lord of His creation. He has not abdicated His throne. He rules what He has made. No Christian can have a mechanistic view of nature. The universe is not a machine which operates by inflexible laws, nor has God made laws to which He is himself now a slave. The very term 'natural laws' is only a convenient expression for the observed consistency of God's working. He is living and active in His universe, and we depend upon Him for our 'life and breath and everything else' (Acts 17:25). It is right to thank Him not only for our creation, but for our preservation as well.

In conclusion, the psalmist expresses the fervent wish that God's glory (seen in His works) may always endure, and that God may continue to rejoice in His works, as He did when they left His hand at the beginning (verse 31; compare Genesis 1:31), lest He should look upon the earth with judgment instead of favor (verse 32). The psalmist determines himself to spend his whole life praising God and hopes that this psalm, his meditation upon the works of God, may please Him (verses 33, 34). Yet he recognises that there are *sinners* and *wicked* people who do not give to God, their creator and preserver, the glory that is due to His name (verse 35). The God in whose hand their breath is, they have not honored (Daniel 5:23). His earnest desire is that such sinners should no longer be permitted to deface God's good world (Stott 1998a, pp. 98–101).

Psalm 103: The Benefits of God's Grace

Psalm 103 is, undoubtedly, one of the best-loved psalms, just as Henry Francis Lyte's free paraphrase, 'Praise my Soul, the King of heaven' (1834), is one of the most popular hymns in the English language. We have here the authentic utterance of a redeemed child of God, who piles up words to express his gratitude to the God of grace. His praise expands in three concentric circles. First, he addresses himself and seeks to arouse himself to the proper worship of God: *Praise the LORD, O my soul* (verses 1–5). Next, he recalls the mercy of God to all the people of His covenant (verses 6–18). Finally, he summons the whole of creation to join in the chorus of praise (verses 19–22).

God's benefits to me (verses 1–5)

The first five verses of the psalm are very personal, as the author confronts himself with his duty and exhorts his own sluggish soul to worship. He desires, not only to praise God's *holy name* (verse 1), acknowledging the holiness or unique 'otherness' of His being, but to remember *all his benefits*. Indeed, he is determined that his worship of God shall be as total as are God's blessings to him: *all my inmost being* in response to *all his benefits*. These benefits have been given to both body and soul, for God both *forgives all my sins* and *heals all my diseases* (verse 3). Further, he redeems my life *from the pit* (verse 4), that is, the grave or Sheol. Not content with saving the psalmist from sin, disease and death, God lavishes positive blessings upon him as well. He *crowns* him (verse 4), that is, He makes His child a king (compare Psalm 8:5).

God also satisfies him *with good things* (verse 5), so that our *youth is renewed like the eagle's*. Maybe this alludes to an ancient fable that the eagle soars periodically so near to the sun that it drops scorched into the sea and emerges miraculously rejuvenated, or to the bird's annual molt and 'eclipse' after the breeding season, until the plumage is renewed the following spring. Here, as in Isaiah 40:31, the eagle is used as a symbol of youth and strength.

These, then, are God's personal benefits to the psalmist. Delivered from sin, sickness, and death, he feels himself as privileged as a king and as vigorous as an eagle.

God's mercy to His people (verses 6–18)

The psalmist now changes from the singular to the plural, from the particular benefits which he has himself received to God's general grace to all the people of His covenant. Whenever they have been *oppressed* he has displayed on their behalf both *righteousness and justice* (verse 6). The most signal revelation of this was to Moses and to the children of Israel under Moses' leadership (verse 7). Such just dealing with His people was an expression of His grace.

Indeed, what the psalmist goes on to write is a kind of meditation on that glorious revelation of God's name to Moses: 'The Lord, the Lord, the compassionate and gracious God, slow to anger, abounding in love and faithfulness' (Exodus 34:6). After quoting these words (verse 8), our author proceeds to enforce them by two negative statements, three illustrations and a striking contrast.

The two negatives indicate that God sets limits to his own righteous wrath against sin. The first is a time limit, that He *will not always accuse*. The second is a restraint upon the expression of His anger that, instead of that just judgment, *he does not treat us as our sins deserve* (verses 9, 10). Then follow three positive illustrations of God's grace. His steadfast love is as high as heaven, His forgiveness removes our sins as far away as infinity, and His pity is as tender as a father's love for his children, because He knows our human frailty (verses 11–14).

The mention of human weakness leads to the final underlining of the mercy of God, which, as in Psalm 90, takes the form of a contrast between human transience and the eternity of God's love. Humankind flourishes like grass, and perishes like grass too when the hot desert wind blows upon it; but toward those who reverence God, keep His covenant and remember His commandments, His *love* and *righteousness* endure for ever and enrich their posterity (verses 15–18). This assurance of God's unfailing love to successive generations has brought comfort to many mourners as they have stood round the grave and watched a coffin lowered to its final resting place.

God's dominion over all creation (verses 19–22)

In the last paragraph the psalmist turns from the love of the Lord for His covenant people to His sovereignty over all His creation. He has *established his throne in heaven* and from there *rules over all* (verse 19). Thus convinced of God's universal kingdom, the author summons the whole created order to praise him. First, he addresses the mighty *angels*, called also God's *hosts* and *servants*, whose characteristic activity is to *do his will* (verses 20, 21). Next he turns to the lower orders of God's creation and calls on *all his works everywhere* to worship Him. Finally, he comes back to himself and concludes the psalm as he began it, with the personal exhortation: *Praise the Lord, O my soul* (verse 22).

(Stott 1988a, pp. 95–97)

On 14 August 1977, Stott preached on 'God and the environment', developing and applying his exegesis of Psalm 104 in *The Canticles and Selected Psalms*. It seems to have been his first explicit pronouncement on creation care. It was preached in his home church, All Souls Langham Place, in a series on the Psalms under the general title 'All human life is here', a title borrowed from the *News of the World*, a Sunday newspaper that used to advertise itself under that slogan. Stott expounded Psalm 104 in a very similar way to how he did in *The Canticles and Selected Psalms*, but he went on to apply his understanding to encourage a respectful attitude to the environment and to urge nature study as a necessary preliminary to nurturing such an attitude.

All human life is in the Psalms. Psalm 104 is about 'God and the environment'. Man has always been conscious of his natural environment. He can't help being a human being, and being conscious of nature and the environment in which we live, we know that we are part of the created natural order ourselves. And in addition to that, God has given man dominion over the earth and over the beasts and the birds and the fish and the rest, so man is part of nature and yet he has dominion over nature, and man has always known this.

And yet it is only in recent years that the environmental issue has come to the forefront of the public mind. We have become aware of the enormously accelerated population growth – on the one hand, some one thousand million people in 1800, two thousand million people in 1900, four thousand million by 1980, and seven thousand million people by AD 2000. And the public have become suddenly aware of this threat to our very existence, by the population explosion on the one hand, and on the other the dependence of man on his living environment.

Barbara Ward, one of the best-known contemporary economists, herself a Christian, a Roman Catholic Christian, has spoken in her book, *Only One Earth,* of the most majestic unity of our planet: in other words, everything depends upon everything else. She writes of the dynamic equilibrium of biological forces held in position by checks and balances of the most delicate sort. She writes elsewhere of the eggshell delicacy of the agents that can be upset.

Now all of us know that, even more threatening to human survival than the appalling stockpile of nuclear weapons, is the pollution of the air and of the sea and of the earth. We may be thankful in this country that in 1970, the Department of the Environment [now the Department for Environment, Food and Rural Affairs] was formed, with its chief a member of the Cabinet, and with a responsibility, in addition to housing and public works and the like, a responsibility to fight pollution or join in the worldwide fight against pollution.

I don't hesitate to say that Christians ought to be far more environmentally conscious than we have often been. Biblical Christians who think biblically, who have a biblical understanding about God and the universe, and about man and the environment. We ought to know more, and we ought to be giving a lead in these things instead of other people taking the initiatives. Well, Psalm 104 is on this docket. It seems to deal with nature much in the same order in which the Creation is recorded as having taken place in Genesis 1. It may well be a conscious kind of meditation on Genesis 1 . . . I would like to try to develop with you this morning what I believe comes right out of the psalm, and that is the two stages of the psalmist's thought: he begins with God's creation of the environment in verses 1–9, and then goes on to the wonderful divine preservation of living creatures in relation to their environment from verse 10 onwards.

Firstly, then, God created the natural environment. The opening verses (1–9) affirm in beautiful poetic imagery that God created and now controls the universe. In verses 2–4 and then 5–9, the light is God's garments; the sky is His tent; the waters are the foundation of His palace. He makes the clouds His chariot; He rides upon the wings of the wind; He appoints the wind and the fire to be his messengers. In verse 5, he set the earth upon a firm foundation; he wrapped the sea round it like a cloak; he supervised the lengthy geological process by which the contours of the mountains and the valleys came to be . . .

Now this paragraph should caution us against a misuse of the Bible, as if it claimed to be giving an account of the origin of things in scientific terms. It never claims to do that. Of course, what is here affirmed, we believe – or ought to believe – is true: namely that all nature is God's creation and under God's control. But this truth, this biblical truth is the revealed truth of God; is not expressed in scientific terms, it is expressed in poetic terms. For example, in verse 5, we are told that the earth is like a building upon foundations. Now, from that verse of the Bible, it is quite gratuitous to argue, as some Old Testament scholars do argue today, that the ancients believed in a literal three-decker universe, as a kind of building in three storeys with the sky above and the earth beneath and Hades under the earth. I say it is gratuitous to say that the ancients believed that literally. Oh, they spoke of it poetically, but they were not speaking in scientific or literal terms, and it's gratuitous to argue that they did any more than that they believed that the light is literally clothing which God puts on, or that the clouds are a chariot, or that the winds have wings. It is all poetic imagery and we must not press into scientific language what is deliberately couched in poetic terms.

So dear friends, we who are biblical Christians, beware of biblical literalism. Beware of the wooden, unimaginative literalism beyond what the authors of Scripture themselves intended. It's a warning for all of us from Scripture itself.

Now we move from that first point, God's creation of the environment, to, secondly, the main purpose, I think, of the psalm, which is God's adaptation of the environment for the benefit of living creatures. For, in this next paragraph, the dominant tense of the Hebrew verbs moves from the past to the present, and so from the creation at the beginning to the continuing preservation and control of nature today. And it is not fanciful, I think, to discern six gifts of God to living creatures, a six-fold provision in the environment for living creatures.

First, God provides living creatures with drink. We can't survive without it. Verse 10 [RSV]: Thou makest springs gush forth in the valleys; they flow between the hills; they give drink to every beast. The wild asses quench their thirst, the birds too, living in the trees, and in the context, of course, the implication is they need to drink as well. They sing among the branches. From thy lofty abode, thou waterest the mountains. The earth is satisfied with the fruit of thy works.

So you see, earth, beasts, and birds all drink from God's own water supply. Every Palestinian knew that very well. He lived in a country in which the water supply from the heavens was indispensable to agriculture. He waited anxiously for the former rains in the autumn without which he couldn't plough; he waited anxiously for the latter rains in the spring without which, if he reaped, the corn would never have grown into its fullness and been ripe for the reaping. And what is true of living creatures is true of human beings. Thirst is a most painful experience. I understand, I think I'm right – about sixty per cent of the constitution of the human body is water. We need water. God gives drink to His creatures. Jesus said He sends rain upon the just and on the unjust, and it's His gift.

Secondly, God makes provision for His living creatures in terms of food. Verse 14 [RSV]: Thou didst cause the grass to grow for the cattle, plants for man to cultivate, that he may bring forth food from the earth, and in particular (verse 15) wine to make men happy, oil to make them cheerful – the shining face seems to be a metaphor of cheerfulness – and bread to make them strong, food.

Thirdly, shelter. Verses 16–18: the Lord's trees are well watered. Notice, by the way, to whom they belong. Next time you cut one down, you might just remember whose trees you're cutting down, and make sure that you have authority to do so, because they don't belong to you, they're His. The trees of the Lord are well watered. So are the cedars of Lebanon that he planted. He plants them, He waters them, they belong to Him. Moreover, the trees supply nesting sites for many birds, and the treetops, as the psalmist who, as a good observer, knew very well, are excellent nesting sites for storks. The white storks that fly north through the Palestinian corridor from their wintering grounds in Africa fan out from Palestine, both east to Asia and west to Europe, and they still build their nests on the tops of either trees or buildings.

And the high mountains are a good habitat for wild goats, and the rocks for badgers. The Hebrew word, translated in the Authorized Version as 'coney' means neither a rabbit nor a badger, but a hyrax. A hyrax is a shy rock-dwelling mammal that is vegetarian, and whose nearest living relation I understand is the elephant. It has a tiny couple of tusks, and is a very beautiful furry creature, the hyrax. And it was an unclean animal, ritually speaking. The Jews were not allowed to eat it because it didn't part the hoof, but, although it was ritually unclean, who gives it a habitat in which to breed? God does. He supplies refuges for the hyrax. So you see, there is shelter, especially for breeding, for all the creatures of God.

The fourth provision I'm going to call 'rhythm' – the rhythm of life. For we come in verse 19 to the sun and the moon, which know their times and mark the seasons. So, when the sun goes down and it gets dark, it is a signal for many wild animals to creep forth out of their lairs and to go hunting. The lions roar after their prey and seek their meat from God. Notice the uninhibited way in which Scripture acknowledges the fact of predation. And then, when the sun sets again, the animals slink back into their dens, but man gets up. He goes to work in the daytime, until the evening when he goes to bed and the animals get up, and the rhythmic cycle begins again. Thus all living creatures adapt themselves to the sun and the moon and the motions of the heavenly bodies, and enjoy the rhythm that God intends of activity and rest, and activity and rest again.

Drink, food, shelter, rhythm. And the fifth [provision] is sport. In verse 24, the psalmist breaks off to express his wonder at the diversity of creation, of all God's works, of the wisdom with which He's made them all. Verse 24: the earth is full of your creatures. Verse 25: the sea is full of them also. It teems with innumerable creatures, and the ships ply their trade in the sea, and Leviathan, a word which is often translated as a crocodile, but here obviously is a general word for monsters of the deep of different kinds. God has formed them to sport in the sea. Did you ever know that God was concerned about Leviathan's sport? That He made provision for Leviathan to enjoy playtime in the ocean? The sea is depicted as a divinely supplied playground for all its creatures.

Jewish tradition, from the Talmud onwards, translated the Hebrew not 'Leviathan to play in it', but you created 'Leviathan to play with you', or for 'you to play with it'. And some of the Christian versions follow that early Jewish tradition. The New English Bible translates it, 'Leviathan whom you have made your plaything.' It's not impossible that that is the correct translation, and God is then represented as taking time off in order to enjoy, to join in the sport, and to play with his own creatures. Why shouldn't He? He made them. He rejoices in His works. He plays with them. He finds pleasure in them.

God makes provision then for drink, food, shelter, rhythm, sport, and most important of all, sixthly, breath and life itself. In verses 27–30, we find the total dependence of all living creatures upon their creator. These all (verse 27) 'look to you to give them their food in due season' [RSV] and they look to you not only for food but for life. The psalmist goes on and makes a couple of contrasts: when you give them food they gather it. You make provision, but they have to feed themselves. Like a child opens its hand and feeds its pet or an animal in the zoo, so when God opens his hand they are filled with good, but when he hides his face, turning away from them, they are dismayed. The other contrast is that when he takes away their breath, they die, but when, on the other hand, he sends his spirit or sends his breath, they are created. But by the same divine breath the face of the ground and all living creatures are constantly renewed.

Here then, you see, is a six-fold divine provision out of the environment and its resources to all the living creatures that God has made: drink, food, shelter, rhythm, sport, and breath itself.

Now this is one of the earliest studies in the whole of human literature of what today we call ecology. Ecology is defined as the branch of biology which deals with the mutual relations between organisms and their environment. God invented ecology and the relationships of living things to their environment. Maybe ecology is too grandiose a word to use of this psalm, because as I said earlier, it is not a scientific study. Nevertheless, the theme is clear: the relation between living things and the resources of the environment, and how God has made provisions in the one for the other. He makes the springs gush in the valleys in order that there may be drink for animals. He causes the grass to grow in order that man may bring food out of the earth. He plants trees for the birds to build their nests in, while mountains are for the goats and rocks are for the hyrax. He makes the sun and moon and the motions of the heavenly bodies and the rotation of the earth in order that there may be rhythm in the life of men and animals.

So how do we conclude from this study of God and the environment? I want to ask what ought the Christian's attitude to nature to be? . . . to animals and to the whole of the created universe? Well, let's avoid extremes. One extreme is idolatrous nature worship. You know, the worship of the ancient world – the Canaanites, the Babylonians, the Egyptians, and the rest – it was all idolatrous nature worship. The Egyptians worshiped the sun. The Bible says that's ludicrous. God made the sun. Worship the creator of the sun, not the sun itself. And many of these ancient peoples created or manufactured their little images and their idols of beasts and birds and the rest. But let's beware of the more subtle idolatry of today: of the romantics who idealize nature, or of the sentimentalists who give a devotion to pets, whether animals or cats or the budgerigar, a devotion which is due to God alone. Beware of idolatrous nature worship.

But then, there is the opposite extreme to avoid – wanton destruction. Scripture authorizes us to cultivate the soil, to domesticate animals, but the dominion that we have been given is not the same as domination, still less as destruction. And that is so whether we are thinking of the wholesale spoliation of rivers, lakes, and forests. I believe that this is a reliable statistic, that fourteen acres of woodland are deforested in the world every minute, fourteen acres a minute, not least for all the paper we consume. So this is true, whether we are thinking of the wholesale destruction of the environment or whether we are thinking of the crass swatting of a butterfly, or for that matter the picking of a flower not to enjoy its beauty, which I would want to defend as legitimate, but for no better reason than we like to destroy the things that God has created. How dare we? We ought to be good stewards of God's creations.

So let us avoid the two extremes: of nature worship on the one hand, which is idolatry, or wanton nature destruction on the other hand, which is blasphemy, because nature is God's creation.

And instead, and I finish with this thought, but a few more moments, we need a thoughtful wondering praise of God the Creator. God is said in this psalm to rejoice in his works, so his people ought to rejoice in them also. And I don't hesitate to say that every Christian ought to be interested in natural history, doesn't matter what branch of natural history you take up, but many of us have a good doctrine of salvation and a bad doctrine of creation. Some of us don't have a doctrine of creation at all. We're not interested in the works of the Lord, but we ought to be. And we ought, moreover, to study nature in order to be able to praise God for His works. Over the [entrance to the] Cavendish Laboratory in Cambridge University is inscribed the words of Psalm 111 verse 2: 'the works of the Lord are great, studied by all those who take pleasure in them.' We ought to take pleasure in them, we ought to study them, because only then can we worship the God who has created them.

That leaves me, you see, to end on this note, that study is a necessary preliminary to worship. We can't worship God adequately if we don't study His works in order to worship Him who has created them. There is a popular evangelical ditty today, which is a mindless repetitive crooning of the world 'hallelujah'. And those who go in for it croon it repetitively. I've given up counting, I forget if it's 12 or 20 times. I don't hesitate to say that that is an unbiblical, a totally unbiblical understanding of worship. Hallelujah means 'praise the Lord'. You can't just sing 'praise the Lord, hallelujah', unless you are defining what you are praising Him for. And Scripture never exhorts us to praise God without giving us reasons for our worship. And I think the psalm before us today [Psalm 104], together with its predecessor Psalm 103, is a wonderful example of this biblical truth, because Psalm 103 celebrates the goodness of God in salvation, Psalm 104 the greatness of God in creation. Psalm 103 says God is gracious. Psalm 104 says God is great. In Psalm 103 he is depicted as the Father with His children, in Psalm 104 as the creator with His creatures. Both psalms begin and end with the word 'hallelujah'. They begin and end with the injunction, 'praise the Lord, oh my soul', so both of them are hallelujah psalms, but each, if I may put it like this, is a hallelujah sandwich, because in between the beginning and the end hallelujah there is a great bulging sandwich of reasons why we sing hallelujah. It's a rehearsal of what God has done. Psalm 103 is all of His benefits in salvation that we are not to forget. Psalm 104 is all His works of creation at which we are constantly to wonder.

So let us study the works of God in creation as well as in salvation. Let us recognize that the environment is the creation of God, that He has provided resources in the environment for all living creatures. Let us acknowledge our own dependence upon Him, so that we look to him for life and breath. When He opens His hand, we are filled with good; when He hides His face, we are troubled; when He takes away our breath, we die; when He sends His spirit, we are renewed. We depend upon Him every moment of the day, and then and only then can we worship Him with our understanding. Let us be quiet as we sit for a moment in prayer and worship. Let us praise Him for our creation, the creation of the whole natural environment and all the intricate creatures that he has made, the beauty, the wonder, the diversity, the delicacy, the skill. Praise God for creation.

> Our Father, we pray that we may think Christianly about creation, we may study it, wonder at it, acknowledge our dependence on you, rejoice in the beauty and intricacy of what you have made, and praise you with our understanding as the Creator. We ask it for the glory of your great name. Amen.

(Stott 1977b)

Although Stott returns to Psalm 104 on a number of occasions when he is speaking about the environment, in no way does he limit himself to it as the only (or chief) grounds for our attitude to the natural word. He points out that the Bible repeatedly speaks of the wonders of creation and of our proper response to it. For example, in the words of Psalm 148:7–12 [NIV]:

Praise the LORD from the earth,
    you great sea creatures and all ocean depths,
lightning and hail, snow and clouds,
    stormy winds that do his bidding,
you mountains and all hills,
    fruit trees and all cedars,
wild animals and all cattle,
    small creatures and flying birds,
kings of the earth and all nations,
    you princes and all rulers on earth,
young men and women,
    old men and children.

Stott did not select Psalm 148 in his 1988 book *Favorite Psalms*, but he included it in his earlier book, *The Canticles and Selected Psalms* (1966), albeit he expounds through the canticle *Benedicite, Omnia Opera*, which he describes as a poetic elaboration of the psalm.

A Summons to Universal Praise

This canticle is taken from 'The Song of the Three Holy Children', a book of the Apocrypha. In the Septuagint 'The Song' is inserted between verses 23 and 24 of Daniel Chapter 3, so that it immediately follows the words: 'And these three men, Shadrach, Meshach, and Abednego, fell down bound into the midst of the burning fiery furnace' [KJV 1966] . . .

The setting which the *Benedicite* is given in 'The Song of the Three Holy Children' is of course entirely fictitious. It was probably composed by some pious Jew in the third century B.C.

It was used in Jewish worship before Christ and in Christian worship at least by the fourth century A.D. . . .

It is noteworthy that, whereas the *Te Deum* is an indicative, whose first verb is *laudamus, we praise*, this canticle is throughout an imperative: *Benedicite! O bless ye!* In other words, the *Te Deum* is a statement that we who sing it, in company with earth and heaven and the whole Church, do in fact praise God; the *Benedicite* is a summons to all God's works, animate and inanimate, to do so. Each is addressed personally. It is as if the worshipping congregation is not willing that any of God's works should be dumb. We turn from one to the other, exhorting them to bless the Lord, until the chorus of worship is universal, and continues to *praise him and magnify him for ever*.

The first verse supplies the key to our understanding of the whole. It is all the *works of the Lord* who are summoned to praise him. His *works* comprise everything that he has made, and the canticle proceeds to list them. Here, then, is the creation worshipping its creator, recognising that it owes the beginning and the continuing of its existence to him. It is an earthly echo of the heavenly anthem, 'Worthy art thou, our Lord and God, to receive glory and honour and power, for thou didst create all things, and by thy will they existed and were created' (Revelation 4:11, RSV). If it be objected that birds, beasts and fish cannot worship God, still less inanimate things like the sun, the moon and stars, we can only reply that the Scripture does not hesitate to use this language. 'Bless the Lord, all his works, in all places of his dominion.' 'All thy works shall give thanks to thee, O Lord . . .' (Psalm 103:22; 145:10, RSV). Indeed, there is no doubt that the *Benedicite* is a poetical elaboration of Psalm 148, which has the same three divisions. First comes the command 'praise the Lord from the *heavens*', then 'praise the Lord from the *earth*', and finally 'the people of *Israel*' are specifically named as those whom God has brought 'near to him'. So we may say that, although the *Benedicite* is quite apocryphal in the setting it has been given, it is thoroughly biblical in its thought and language.

The heavens (vv. 2–17)

The angels are mentioned first. This is appropriate, for they are ceaselessly praising God. Perhaps all the *powers of the Lord* (v. 5) should be linked with them, as other created, spiritual beings who are not necessarily included within the category of *angels*. From these celestial inhabitants, we turn to the heavens themselves, and *the waters . . . above the firmament* (vv. 3, 4), mentioned in Genesis 1:6–8, and to the *sun and moon* and *stars of heaven* (vv. 6, 7). Next comes the weather. It ill becomes us to grumble about it if we believe, as the Bible teaches, that 'fire and hail, snow and frost, stormy wind' are all engaged in 'fulfilling his command' (Psalm 148:8). Thus, the winds here are termed the *winds of God* (v. 9). All this is consistent with the scriptural phraseology, figurative yet true, that the wind is God's 'breath', the thunder his 'voice' and the lightning his 'fire'. This control of God over nature embraces all things, including the extremes of *fire and heat* (v. 10) on the one hand (even in the burning fiery furnace!), and *frost and cold, ice and snow* (vv. 13, 14) on the other. In order to enforce this truth, the contrasted *winter and summer, nights and days, light and darkness* (vv. 11, 15, 16) are called to bless God together, in fulfilment of God's covenant with Noah after the Flood that 'while the earth remains, seedtime and harvest, cold and heat, summer and winter, day and night, shall not cease' (Genesis 8:22).

The earth (vv. 18–26)

Turning from the *heavens* to the *earth*, it is the *mountains and hills* (v. 19) which are first addressed, followed by all the *green things upon the earth*, every form of plant life, which God 'causes to grow' (Psalm 104:14; cf. Genesis 1:11, 12). After earth and vegetation comes water, *wells* (v. 21) or 'fountains' (AV), *seas and floods* (v. 22), the latter meaning 'rivers' (AV). Next we reach the animal creation – the fish of the sea (v. 23), the birds of the air (v. 24) and beasts both wild and domesticated (v. 25). We have been made familiar with this threefold classification in Genesis 1:28 and Psalm 8:7, 8, although the addition of reptiles as a separate category makes it fourfold in Genesis 9:2 and James 3:7. Finally, as in Genesis and throughout the Bible, comes man, the crown and climax of all the creative activity of God: *O ye children of men, bless ye the Lord!* (v. 26).

Israel (vv. 27–32)

'Man' as such is not the end-product of God's 'works', however, for man fell through disobedience and was soon giving to God a homage less than the rest of creation. So the real climax of God's work, according to the Scriptures, is not 'man' but 'redeemed man', man regenerated and renewed according to the image of the second Adam, Jesus Christ, the 'man from heaven' (1 Corinthians 15:45, 48). This 'new man' is also one of God's works, numbered among the *works of the Lord* (v. 1) which are summoned to bless him; for God's works are 'manifold' (Psalm 104:24) and are works of grace as well as of nature. They include his 'new creation' in Christ Jesus (cf. 2 Corinthians 5:17; Ephesians 2:10), and when the new creation worships its creator, what we hear is the redeemed adoring their redeemer. And the redeemed are *Israel* (v. 27), not 'Israel after the flesh' but 'the Israel of God' (Galatians 6:16), the new Israel, 'the true circumcision' (Philippians 3:3), namely, the Christian Church incorporating all believers whether Jew or Gentile. In the Old Testament some were specially set apart to be his *priests* (v. 28) and *servants* (v. 29), ministering to him in the worship of the tabernacle and temple, but now the whole Church is a royal and holy priesthood, engaged in the priestly service of offering him the spiritual sacrifices of our worship, praise and thanksgiving (1 Peter 2:5, 9). Others who are praising God are the blessed dead, the *spirits and souls of the righteous* (v. 30), who see his face and worship him (Revelation 22:3, 4). But we cannot wait till after death to begin to worship God. The living people of God praise him too. They are beautifully described as the *holy and humble men of heart* (v. 31). We cannot allow that this expression is meant to denote a minority in the Church of God, for, however far we may fall short of this standard, holiness and humility are indispensable marks of the followers of him who called himself 'meek and lowly in heart' (Matthew 11:29). And notice that, with them as with him, it is not merely in word and deed but in *heart* that this holiness and humility are to exist. (Stott 1966, pp. 30–34)

In *The Canticles and Selected Psalms* (1966) Stott expounded the meaning and relevance of 49 out of the 150 Psalms. Besides Psalms 103, 104 and 148 (expanded as the *Benedicite*), two others of his chosen thirty-seven are particularly relevant to a proper understanding of the natural world – Psalms 8 and 19, which were also adapted for inclusion in *Favorite Psalms* (1988a).

Psalm 8 firmly fixes humankind in relation and subordinate to the Creator of all things.

Psalm 8: What is a Human Being?

'This short, exquisite lyric,' as it was called by C. S. Lewis, begins and ends with the refrain: *O Lord, our Lord, how majestic is your name in all the earth.* Here is a recognition of the majesty of God's name, or nature, which His works reveal in both earth and heaven. The enemies of God, blinded by their proud rebellion, do not see His glory; but they are confounded by *children and infants.* Jesus quoted these words when the children acclaimed Him in the Temple with their hosannas, while the chief priests and scribes indignantly objected (Matthew 21:15, 16). God is still glorified in the simple faith of children and in the childlike humility of Christian believers (see Matthew 11:25, 26; 1 Corinthians 1:26–29).

What particularly evokes the wondering worship of the psalmist is God's condescension toward human beings (verses 3, 4) and the position of dominion which He has granted to them on earth (verses 5–8). Seen in relation to each other, these two truths enable us to have a balanced judgment of humankind and to give a proper answer to the psalmist's rhetorical question, *What is man?* (verse 4), that is, What does it mean to be a human being?

The littleness of human beings (verses 3, 4)

The question was prompted by a consideration of the night sky. If David was the author of this psalm, there can be little doubt that he was referring to the experience of his youth. In his shepherd days, tending his father's flock in the hills near Bethlehem, he often slept under the stars. Lying on his back, he would survey the fathomless immensity above him, seeking to penetrate the clear depths of the eastern sky. He recognised that the heavens, with the moon and the stars, were the work of God's fingers (verse 3), and as he contemplated their greatness and mystery, he cried out: *What is man that you are mindful of him, and the son of man that you care for him?* (verse 4). [NIV 1984]

If that was David's reaction, nearly three thousand years ago, how much more should it be ours who live in days of astrophysics and the conquest of space? As we consider the orbiting planets of our solar system, so infinitesimally small in comparison with countless galaxies millions of light years distant, it may seem to us incredible that the great God of the universe should take any note of us at all, let alone *care for* us. Yet He does; and Jesus assured us that even the hairs of our head are all numbered.

The greatness of human beings (verses 5–8)

The psalmist moves from the littleness of a human being, in comparison with the vastness of the universe, to the greatness which God has given him on earth: *You made him a little lower than the heavenly beings and crowned him with glory and honor. You made him ruler over the works of your hands* (verses 5, 6) [NIV 1984].

Our position of only slight inferiority to the heavenly beings, or even to God Himself, is supremely seen in our *rule*. God has invested human beings with royal sovereignty, crowning us with glory and honor (verse 5) and delegating to us the control of His works. It is even stated that God has put *everything . . . under his* (man's) *feet.*

The psalmist is referring primarily to the animal creation – beasts both domesticated and wild, *the birds of the air, and the fish of the sea*, and all other creatures inhabiting the depths of the ocean (verses 7, 8). This is not poetic fiction. As the universe yields more and more of its secrets to scientific research, so our dominion increases. Yet even now humankind is not, in fact, lord of creation, with *everything* under our feet, as is recognised in the three New Testament quotations of these verses.

According to Hebrews 2:5 and the following verses: '. . . at present we do not see everything subject to him.' It is immediately added, however: 'But we see Jesus, who was made a little lower than the angels, now crowned with glory and honour.' Humankind has sinned and fallen, and consequently has lost some of the dominion which God had given us; but in Jesus, the second Adam, this dominion has been restored. It is in Him rather than in us that humankind's dominion is exhibited. By His death He even destroyed the devil and delivered his slaves (verses 14, 15). He has now been 'crowned', and exalted to God's right hand.

Although the Psalm's description of humankind's dominion is true rather of the man Christ Jesus than of us, it applies to us also if we have come by faith to share in His exaltation. The apostle Paul wrote that the exceeding greatness of God's power, which exalted Jesus and 'put everything under his feet,' is available to us who believe (Ephesians 1:19–22). Indeed, we have experienced it, for it has raised us from the death of sin, exalted us with Christ and made us sit with Him in the heavenly places, where we are partakers of his victory and dominion (Ephesians 2:5, 6).

Even this is not the end. Although Christ is exalted far above all rule and authority, and all things are potentially under His

feet, not all His enemies have yet conceded their defeat or surrendered to Him. Only when He appears in glory and the dead rise, will He destroy 'all dominion, authority and power. For he must reign until he has put all his enemies under his feet. The last enemy to be destroyed is death. For He "has put everything under his feet"' (1 Corinthians 15:24–26).
(Stott 1988a, pp. 10–13)

Psalm 19 links God's revelation through the natural world with his revelation of himself through the written word, the 'two books of God' as they have been called. The psalmist reminds his reader that 'the heavens declare God's handiwork', a verse recalled by Paul in Romans 10:18 in his argument that there is no excuse for the claim that some had never heard the word of God, since God's 'voice has sounded all over the world'. Stott describes how this is expressed in Psalm 19:1.

Psalm 19: The Self-Revelation of God

According to C. S. Lewis (1958, p. 63), this is 'the greatest poem in the Psalter and one of the greatest lyrics in the world.' From the Christian point of view it contains the clearest summary of the doctrine of revelation to be found in the Old Testament, namely that God has made Himself known to all humankind as Creator (verses 1–6), to Israel as Lawgiver (verses 7–10), and to the individual as Redeemer (verses 11–14).

General revelation (verses 1–6)

Human beings cannot plead ignorance of God, since He never ceases to give a revelation of Himself, which is called 'general' because it is made to all people everywhere. As the apostle Paul put it, he has not 'left himself without testimony' (Acts 14:17; compare Acts 17:22–28 and Romans 1:20).

This witness is in nature, especially here *the heavens*, which *declare the glory of God* because they are *the work of his hands* (verse 1). Even more today, through the cosmology of modern astrophysics, the heavens, 'their vastness, splendor, order and mystery' as one commentator puts it, reveal God's glory and greatness.

God's witness to Himself through the heavens has three characteristics. First, it is continuous. *Day after day . . . night after night* (verse 2) the testimony is given without intermission. Secondly, it is abundant. The verb in verse 2 is expressive: *they* (the heavens) *pour forth speech*. Thirdly it is universal. Although *there is no speech or language* (verse 3), yet by sight rather than sound their message penetrates to the end of the world (verse 4). Paul even applies this last verse to the worldwide spread of the gospel (Romans 10:18).

Of this universal witness to God by the heavens, the sun is a particular example. In dramatic imagery, which is not of course intended to be taken literally, the psalmist likens the sunrise to the emergence of a bridegroom from his chamber, and its daily course across the sky to the running of an athlete, so that *nothing is hidden from its heat* (verse 6).

Special revelation (verses 7–10)

Abruptly and without warning the subject changes from God's general and natural revelation through creation to His special and supernatural revelation through *torah*, 'the law', which refers not merely to the law of Moses but to all Old Testament Scripture. The transition, though abrupt, is not arbitrary. The heavens and the law both make God known. Further, C. S. Lewis may be right to detect a link in the reference to the all-pervasive heat of the sun, so that 'the searching and cleansing sun becomes an image of the searching and cleansing law' (1958, p. 81; cf. pp. 63, 64). With the change of subject comes a significant change in the divine name. The One who reveals Himself in nature to all people is *God,* Hebrew *El* (verse 1), the God of creation; but it is the LORD Yahweh (seven times in the second half of the psalm), the God of the covenant, who has revealed Himself through His law to His covenant people Israel. It is a revelation not now of His glory but of His will, and its excellencies are set forth in perfect Hebrew parallelism (verses 7–9).

The symmetry of these verses is so precise that each begins with a different aspect of God's will, and goes on to describe both what it is and what it does. Thus, *the law,* or divine instruction, is *perfect,* bearing witness to God's nature expressed in His will, and consists of particular *statutes, precepts,* and *commands.* Its perfection is seen in the fact that its injunctions are *trustworthy, right, radiant, pure, sure and altogether righteous.* It is also called *the fear of the LORD* (verse 9) because the great end of all revelation is to inspire a humble and reverent worship of God. This disclosure of God's will is said to be *pure.*

But the psalmist does not merely contemplate the law of the Lord as it is in itself; he also unfolds its beneficial effects, *reviving the soul,* rejoicing the heart and, above all, *making wise* (verse 7) and *giving light* (verse 8) to those who are humble enough, or (as our Lord was later to teach) childlike enough, to receive it. The inherent qualities and health-giving results of God's law make it *more precious than gold . . . sweeter . . . than honey from the comb* (verse 10) [NIV 1984].

It may be surprising to us that the writer did not find God's law a burden to him; we may feel with C. S. Lewis that his reference to its sweetness is at first sight 'very mysterious', even 'utterly bewildering' (1958, pp. 54, 55). The explanation is not just that its commandments were right, nor that its promises were sure, but that it was the revelation of God, the special means which He had chosen to make Himself known to His people Israel.

Personal revelation (verses 11–14)

With verse 11 the psalmist for the first time mentions himself. He has been describing how *all the earth* (verse 4) may apprehend God's glory from nature, and how *the simple* (verse 7) may derive wisdom from God's law. But he concludes his psalm by disclosing his personal spiritual aspirations as God's *servant* (verses 11, 13).

He has himself found wholesome warning in God's law and knows that conformity to it brings great reward (verse 11). He seems to have discovered in his own experience the dual purpose of the divine law, namely to reveal sin (Romans 3:20) and to promote holiness. This leads him both to pray for cleansing from the *hidden faults* (verse 12) which he has committed, and for deliverance from *wilful sins* (verse 13) which he longs to avoid, so that he is not mastered by them but is kept *innocent of great transgression*. The psalmist is not referring here to any one particularly grievous sin, or even the blasphemy against the Holy Spirit (as poor John Bunyan thought), but to all deliberate wrongdoing, sins committed 'defiantly' (Numbers 15:30, 31).

The psalm ends with a prayer which is frequently echoed by Christian ministers before they preach. In it the writer goes beyond his plea for deliverance, to a positive and very personal desire that all his words, and even his thoughts, shall be *pleasing* in the sight of God, whom he now declares to be both his *Rock* ('strength') and his *Redeemer*. Redemption is in itself negative deliverance from sin; it needs to be completed by a life that is pleasing to God (see Titus 2:14).

(Stott 1988a, pp. 21–25)

3

Fall and redemption

Dualism, science and mandate to 'watch birds!'

The Bible repeatedly affirms that creation is God's work. He declared it to be 'good', 'very good', but there is much amiss with it – the result of human action (or inaction). Stott fully recognized this and the need to recognize the reality of sin. In *Basic Christianity* he wrote:

> Sin is not a convenient invention of parsons to keep them in their job; it is a fact of human experience. The history of the last hundred years or so has convinced many people that the problem of evil is located in man himself, not merely in his society. In the nineteenth century a liberal optimism flourished. It was then widely believed that human nature was fundamentally good, that evil was largely caused by ignorance and bad housing, and that education and social reform would enable men to live together in happiness and goodwill. But this illusion has been shattered by the hard facts of history. Educational opportunities have spread rapidly in the western world, and many welfare states have been created. Yet the atrocities which accompanied both world wars, the subsequent international conflicts, the continuance of political oppression and racial discrimination, and the general increase of violence and crime have forced thoughtful people to acknowledge the existence in every man of a hard core of selfishness.
>
> Much that we take for granted in a 'civilized' society is based upon the assumption of human sin. Nearly all legislation has

grown up because human beings cannot be trusted to settle their own disputes with justice and without self-interest. A promise is not enough; we need a contract. Doors are not enough; we have to lock and bolt them. The payment of fares is not enough; tickets have to be issued, inspected and collected. Law and order are not enough; we need the police to enforce them. All this is due to man's sin. We cannot trust each other. We need protection against one another. It is a terrible indictment of human nature.
(Stott 1974a, pp. 61–62)

This takes us back to Stott's 'last word' to the church in the creation care chapter of *The Radical Disciple*, where he affirms:

The three 'fundamental relationships' established in creation by God: 'first to himself, for he made them in his own image; second to each other, for the human race was plural from the beginning; and third, to the good earth and its creatures over which he set them'.
(Stott 2010b, pp. 49–50)

But, he says:

all three relationships were skewed by the fall. Adam and Eve were banished from the presence of the Lord God in the garden, they blamed each other for what had happened, and the good earth was cursed on account of their disobedience.
(Stott 2010b, p. 50)

The interpretation of these events as described in Genesis 3 is much debated (see, for example, Cavanaugh and Smith, 2017). The 'fall story' is often treated as mere fable on the grounds that it conflicts with our knowledge of human ancestry and is not explicitly referred to in the Old Testament (although the effects of the broken relationships described in Genesis 3 are mentioned time and time again). It would be worse than foolish to deny the 'skewing' of the threefold relationships. In the New Testament they are explicitly dealt with in Romans 8:18–27. This is a key passage for any Christian understanding of the environment and the most extensive treatment of the fall in the New Testament. It comes at the end of Paul's proclamation of the nature of salvation in chapters 5 – 8 of the epistle. Stott expounded it in depth in a 1994 commentary on Romans ([1994] 2020). He lays out our relation to a fallen creation and the hope of a future glory in the world that is to come.

The glory of God's children (8:18–27)

. . . [T]he sufferings and the glory concern both God's creation and God's children. Paul now writes from a cosmic perspective. The sufferings and glory of the old creation (the material order) and of the new (the people of God) are integrally related to each other. Both creations are suffering and groaning now; both are going to be set free together. As nature shared in the curse (Genesis 3:17ff.), and now shares in the pain, so it will also share in the glory. Hence *the creation waits in eager expectation for the children of God to be revealed* (19) [NIV 1984]. The word for 'eager expectation' is *apokaradokia*, which is derived from *kara*, the head. It means 'to wait with the head raised, and the eye fixed on that point of the horizon from which the expected object is to come' (Godet 1969, p. 313). It depicts somebody standing 'on tiptoe' (JBP) or 'stretching the neck, craning forward' (Cranfield 1975, vol. 1, p. 410) in order to be able to see. And what the creation is looking for is the revelation of God's children, that is, the disclosure of their identity on the one hand and their investiture with glory on the other. This will be the signal for the renewal of the whole creation.

But what is meant by the creation (*hē ktisis*), an expression which occurs four times in verses 19–22, once in each verse? Paul's focus is on the earth, as the stage on which the drama of fall and redemption is being played.

a The sufferings and glory of God's creation (8:20–22)

Paul personifies 'the creation', much as we often personify 'nature'. Such personifications are quite common in the Old Testament. For example, the heavens, earth and sea, with all their contents, the fields, trees of the forest, rivers and mountains are all summoned to rejoice and to sing to the Lord (Psalms 96:11ff.; 98:7ff.).

The apostle now makes three statements about the creation, which relate respectively to its past, future and present.

First, *the creation was subjected to frustration* (20a). This reference to the past must surely be to the judgment of God, which fell on the natural order following Adam's disobedience. The ground was cursed because of him (Genesis 3:17ff.; cf. Revelation 22:3: 'No longer will there be any curse.'). In consequence, it would 'produce thorns and thistles', so that Adam and his descendants would extract food from it only by 'painful toil' and sweat, until death claimed them and they returned to the dust from which they had been taken. Paul does not refer to these details. Instead, he sums up the result of God's curse by the one word *mataiotēs*, *frustration*. It means 'emptiness, futility, purposelessness, transitoriness' (BAGD). The basic idea is emptiness, whether of purpose or of result. It is the word chosen by the translators of the Greek Septuagint for 'Meaningless! Meaningless! . . . Utterly meaningless!' (Ecclesiastes 1:2) It expresses the existential absurdity of a life lived 'under the sun', imprisoned in time and space, with no ultimate reference point to either God or eternity.

The apostle adds that the creation's subjection to frustration was *not by its own choice, but by the will of the one who subjected it, in hope* (20b). These last two words are enough to prove that the person in mind, whose will subjected the creation to futility, was neither Satan nor Adam, as a few commentators have suggested. Only God, being both Judge and Saviour, held any hope for the world he cursed.

Second, *the creation itself will be liberated* (21a). The word 'hope' is the pivot on which Paul turns from the past to the future of creation. Its subjection to frustration will not last for ever, God has promised. One day it will experience a new beginning, which Paul terms a 'liberation', with both a negative and a positive aspect.

Negatively, creation will be *liberated from its bondage to decay* (21b). *Phthora* (decay) seems to indicate not only that the universe is running down (as we would say), but that nature is also enslaved, locked into an unending cycle, so that conception, birth and growth are relentlessly followed by decline, decay, death and decomposition. In addition, there may be a passing reference to predation and pain, especially the latter which is mentioned in the next verse. So futility, bondage, decay and pain are the words the apostle uses to indicate that creation is out of joint because it is under judgment. It still works, for the mechanisms of nature are fine-tuned and delicately balanced. And much of it is breathtakingly beautiful, revealing the Creator's hand. But it is also in bondage to disintegration and frustration. In the end, however, it will be 'freed from the shackles of mortality' (REB).

Positively, creation will be *liberated . . . into the freedom and glory of the children of* God (21c). These nouns correspond to those of the previous clause, for nature will be brought out of bondage into freedom, out of decay into glory; that is, out of corruption into incorruption. Indeed, God's creation will share in the glory of God's children, which is itself the glory of Christ (see 17–18).

This expectation that nature itself will be renewed is integral to the Old Testament prophetic vision of the messianic age, especially in the Psalms and Isaiah. Vivid images are used to express Israel's faith that the earth and the heavens will be changed like clothing (Psalm 102:25ff.); that God 'will create new heavens and a new earth', including a new Jerusalem (Isaiah 65:14ff.; cf. 66:22); that the desert will blossom like the crocus, and so display the glory of the Lord (Isaiah 35:1ff.;

cf. 32:15ff.); that wild and domestic animals will co-exist in peace, and that even the most ferocious and poisonous creatures 'will neither harm nor destroy' throughout God's new world (Isaiah 11:6ff.; cf. 65:25).

The New Testament writers do not take up the details of this poetic imagery. But Jesus himself spoke of the 'new birth' (*palingenesia*) of the world at his coming (Matthew 19:28, 'the renewal of all things', NIV); Peter of the 'restoration' (*apokatastasis*) of all things (Acts 3:19, 21); Paul here of the liberation, and elsewhere of the reconciliation, of all things (Ephesians 1:10; Colossians 1:20); and John of the new heaven and earth, in which God will dwell with his people, and from which all separation, sorrow, pain and death will have been eliminated (Revelation 21; 22; cf. 2 Peter 3:13; Hebrews 12:26f.). It would not be wise for us to speculate, let alone be dogmatic, about how the biblical and the scientific accounts of reality correspond or harmonize, either in the present or in the future. The general promise of the renovation and transformation of nature is plain, including the eradication of all harmful elements and their replacement by righteousness, peace, harmony, joy and security. But we should be cautious in pressing the details. The future glory is beyond our imagination. What we do know is that God's material creation will be redeemed and glorified, because God's children will be redeemed and glorified.

Third, *the whole creation has been groaning . . . right up to the present time* (22). So far the apostle has told us that the creation 'was subjected to frustration' in the past (20) and 'will be liberated' in the future (21). Now he adds that meanwhile, in the present, even while it is eagerly awaiting the final revelation (19), the creation is *groaning* in pain. Its groans are not meaningless, however, or symptoms of despair. On the contrary, they are like *the pains of childbirth*, for they provide assurance of the coming emergence of a new order. In Jewish apocalyptic literature Israel's current sufferings were frequently called 'the woes of the Messiah' or 'the birthpangs of the messianic age'.

That is, they were seen as the painful introduction to, indeed the herald of, the victorious arrival of the Messiah. Jesus himself used the same expression in his own teaching about the end times. He spoke of false teachers, wars, famines and earthquakes as 'the beginning of birth-pains', that is, preliminary signs of his coming (Matthew 24:8; Mark 13:8; cf. John 16:20ff.).

Verse 22 actually brings together the past, present and future. For not only is the creation groaning now, but it is groaning 'right up to the present time'. And since its groans are labour pains, they look forward to the coming new order. Although we must be careful not to impose modern scientific categories on Paul, we must hold on to his combination of present sufferings and future glory. Each verse expresses it. The creation's subjection to frustration was *in hope* (20). The bondage to decay will give place to freedom and glory (21). The pains of labour will be followed by the joys of birth (22). There is therefore going to be both continuity and discontinuity in the regeneration of the world, as in the resurrection of the body. The universe is not going to be destroyed, but rather liberated, transformed and suffused with the glory of God.

b The sufferings and glory of God's children (8:23–27)

Verses 22–23 draw an important parallel between God's creation and God's children. Verse 22 speaks of the whole creation groaning; verse 23 begins: *Not only so, but we ourselves . . . groan inwardly.* Even we, who are no longer in Adam but in Christ, we who no longer live according to the flesh but *have the firstfruits of the Spirit*, we in whom God's new creation has already begun (cf. 2 Corinthians 5:17), even we continue to groan inside ourselves *as we wait eagerly for our adoption to sonship, the redemption of our bodies* (23). This is our Christian dilemma. Caught in the tension between what God has established (by giving us his Spirit) and what he will accomplish (in our final adoption and redemption), we groan with discomfort and longing. The indwelling Spirit gives us joy (e.g. Galatians 5:22; 1 Thessalonians 1:6), and the coming glory gives us hope (e.g. 5:2), but the interim suspense gives us pain.

Paul now highlights different aspects of our half-saved condition by five affirmations.

First, *we . . . have the firstfruits of the Spirit* (23a). *Aparchē*, the firstfruits, was both the beginning of the harvest and the guarantee that the full harvest would follow in due time. Perhaps Paul had in mind that the Feast of Weeks, which celebrated the reaping of the firstfruits, was the very festival (called in Greek 'Pentecost') on which the Spirit had been given. Replacing this agricultural metaphor with a commercial one, Paul also described the gift of the Spirit as God's *arrabōn*, the 'first instalment, deposit, down payment, pledge' (BAGD), which guaranteed the future completion of the purchase (see 2 Corinthians 1:22; 5:5; Ephesians 1:14). Although we have not yet received our final adoption or redemption, we have already received the Spirit as both foretaste and promise of these blessings.

Second, *we . . . groan inwardly* (23b). The connection between the Spirit's indwelling and our groaning should not surprise us. For the very presence of the Spirit (being only the firstfruits) is a constant reminder of the incompleteness of our salvation, as we share with the creation in the frustration, the bondage to decay and the pain. So one reason for our groaning is our physical frailty and mortality. Paul expresses this elsewhere: 'Meanwhile we groan, longing to be clothed instead with our heavenly dwelling [meaning probably our resurrection body] . . . For while we are in this tent [our temporary, flimsy, material body], we groan and are burdened' (2 Corinthians 5:2, 4). But it is not only our fragile body (*sōma*) which makes us groan; it is also our fallen nature (*sarx*), which hinders us from behaving as we should, and would altogether prevent us from it, were it not for the indwelling Spirit (7:17, 20). We long, therefore, for our *sarx* to be destroyed and for our *sōma* to be transformed. Our groans express both present pain and future longing. Some Christians, however, grin too much (they seem to have no place in their theology for pain) and groan too little.

Third, *we wait eagerly for our adoption to sonship, the redemption of our bodies* (23c). Just as the groaning creation waits eagerly for God's children to be revealed (19), so we groaning Christians wait eagerly for our adoption, even our bodily redemption. We have, of course, already been adopted by God (15), and the Spirit assures us that we are his children (16). Yet there is an even deeper and richer child–Father relationship to come when we are fully 'revealed' as his children (19) and 'conformed to the image of his Son' (29). Again, we have already been redeemed (cf. Ephesians 1:7; Colossians 1:14; cf. Romans 3:24; 1 Corinthians 1:30), but not yet our bodies. Already our spirits are alive (10), but one day the Spirit will also give life to our bodies (11). More than that, our bodies will be changed by Christ to be 'like his glorious body' (Philippians 3:21; cf. 1 Corinthians 15:35ff.). 'Bondage to decay' will be replaced by 'freedom and glory' (21).

Fourth, *in this hope we were saved* (24a). *We were saved* (*esōthēmen*) is an aorist tense. It bears witness to our decisive past liberation from the guilt and bondage of our sins, and from the just judgment of God upon them (cf. Ephesians 2:8). Yet we remain only half saved. For we have not yet been saved from the outpouring of God's wrath in the day of judgment (5:9), nor have the final traces of sin in our human personality been eradicated. Not yet has our *sarx* been obliterated; not yet has our *sōma* been redeemed. So we were saved *in . . . hope* of our total liberation (24a), as the creation was subjected to frustration 'in hope' of being set free from it (20). This double hope looks to the future and to things which, being future, are so far unseen. For *hope that is seen*, having been realized in our experience, *is no hope at all. Who hopes for what they already have?* (24b). *Instead, we hope for what we do not yet have* (25a) (cf. Hebrews 11:1).

Fifth, *we wait for it patiently* (25b), that is, for the fulfilment of our hope. For we are confident in God's promises that the firstfruits will be followed by the harvest, bondage by freedom, decay by incorruption, and labour pains by the birth of the new world. This whole section is a notable example of what it means to be living 'in between times', between present difficulty and future destiny, between the already and the not yet, between sufferings and glory. *In this hope we were saved* brings them together. And in this tension the correct Christian posture is that of waiting, waiting *eagerly* (23; cf. 19) with keen expectation, and waiting patiently (25), steadfast in the endurance of our trials (*hypomonē*). The same verb occurs in both verses (*apekdechomai*, 23 and 25, as also in 19), and includes in itself the note of 'eagerness', whereas 'patience' or 'perseverance' is added to it in verse 25. The combination is significant. We are to wait neither so eagerly that we lose our patience, nor so patiently that we lose our expectation, but eagerly and patiently together . . .

In this life of expectancy Paul now brings us another encouragement. It again concerns the ministry of the Holy Spirit . . . *In the same way*, Paul begins (26), probably meaning that as our Christian hope sustains us, so does the Holy Spirit. In general, *the Spirit helps us in our weakness* (26a), that is, in the ambiguity and frailty of our 'already–not yet' existence. In particular, he helps our frailty in prayer. In this sphere our weakness is our ignorance: *We do not know what we ought to pray for* (26b). But he knows what we do not know. In consequence, *the Spirit himself intercedes for us* (26c).
(Stott [1994] 2020, pp. 231–239)

Stott expressed the implications of all this in rather unexpected ways in two books he wrote near the end of his life and which complement each other: *The Birds Our Teachers* ([1999] 2007) and *People My Teachers* (2002), both illustrated by his own photographs and both showing his abhorrence of dualism and compartmentalized thinking, which he regarded as an effect of the fall.

People My Teachers describes seventeen people who had influenced Stott in one way or another. Some were traditional saints – Paul the apostle, Thomas Becket, David the patron saint of Wales; some were pioneering missionaries – Temple Gairdner of Egypt, Hudson Taylor of China, Allen Gardiner of South America; others were modern Christian heroes – Richard Wurmbrand in Romania, Lily O'Hanlon and Hilda Steele in Nepal, Festo Kivengere in Uganda, Paul White in Tanzania and Australia. Three were more unlikely, associated with places memorable to Stott himself: Ernest Shackleton in the Antarctic, John Franklin in the Arctic and, perhaps most unexpected, Charles Darwin.

The entry of Charles Darwin into Stott's canon is perhaps surprising. For many Christians, Darwin is much maligned for the assumption that his ideas contradict the early chapters of Genesis. Indeed, this belief is likely to be one of the reasons why the church has failed to develop a strong doctrine of creation; it suggests a fear that atheistic science might sully a proper understanding of God's creative activity (Berry 2013). The result is, as Stott insisted on a number of occasions, Christians have a much weaker doctrine of creation than of redemption. Stott deplored this imbalance, seeing it as producing a dangerous dualism between spirit and matter and one that is countermanded throughout the Scriptures. In the Noahic covenant (Genesis 9:8-17), God explicitly includes 'all creatures' alongside Noah and his family. Indeed, there is a strong case that God first covenanted with creation itself when he established order in it, long before humans appeared on the scene (Jeremiah 33:25: 'These are the words of the Lord: If there were no covenant for day and night, and if I had not established a fixed order in heaven and earth, then I could spurn the descendants of Jacob and of my servant David'). He renewed his covenant repeatedly through history – with Abraham, Jacob, Moses, David, culminating with Jesus the Christ. The God of Creation and the God of Redemption are one and the same (Revelation 4:6–11). Stott condemned dualism as a consequence of the fall. In an article in *Christianity Today*, he wrote:

What we are (our self or personal identity) is partly the result of the Creation (the image of God), and partly the result of the Fall (the image defaced). The self we are to deny, disown, and crucify is our fallen self, everything within us that is incompatible with Jesus Christ (hence Christ's command, 'let him deny himself and follow me'). The self we are to affirm and value is our created self, everything within us that is compatible with Jesus Christ (hence his statement that 'if we lose ourselves by self-denial we shall find ourselves') ... So, then, whatever we are by creation, we must affirm: our rationality, our sense of moral obligation, our masculinity and femininity, our aesthetic appreciation and artistic creativity, our stewardship of the fruitful earth, our hunger for love and community, our sense of the transcendent mystery of God, and our inbuilt urge to fall down and worship him. All this is part of our created humanness. True, it has all been tainted and twisted by sin. Yet Christ came to redeem and not destroy it. So we must affirm it. But whatever we are by the Fall, we must deny or repudiate: our irrationality ... our pollution and spoliation of the environment ... and our idolatrous refusal to worship God ... Christ came not to redeem this, but to destroy it. So we must deny it. (Stott 1984)

Stott saw the widespread unease and suspicion of science by Christians as an effect of dualism. In his chapter on Darwin in *People My Teachers*, he describes what he calls 'an important correspondence between theology and science' (2002, p. 109). He sets out the proper roles of science and Scripture in the context of the extraordinary creatures of the Galapagos Islands.

Visiting the Galapagos

Let no man ... think or maintain that a man can search too far or be too well studied in the book of God's Word or in the book of God's works, divinity or philosophy; but rather let men endeavour an endless progress or proficiency in both.

These words come from the pen of Francis Bacon, the seventeenth-century English philosopher and statesman. They conclude his book *The Advancement of Learning* (1605). But Charles Darwin found them there and put them on the flyleaf of his book *The Origin of Species* (1859).

It is an intriguing concept that God has written not one book, but two. The book of God's Word we call 'Scripture', and the book of God's Works 'Nature'. Both are divine revelations, the disclosure of God's glory in nature and of his grace in Scripture. Moreover, he invites us to study both, so that nature study and Bible study should go hand in hand. And as we engage in these studies, we find ourselves, in the famous words of the German astronomer Johannes Kepler, 'thinking God's thoughts after him'.

In consequence, there is an important correspondence between theology and science. Theology is the human attempt to understand and synthesize what God has revealed in Scripture, while science is the human attempt to understand and systematize what God has revealed in nature.

There should, therefore, be no conflict between the two, since all truth is God's truth, whether it is biblical or scientific. Indeed, the creation – evolution debate, especially when it involved a headlong confrontation, has been largely unnecessary, and remains confused and confusing today. The reason for this is that it has been, and still is, conducted in 'conditions of low visibility'. That is to say, the participants have tended to plunge into combat without first pausing to define their terms. When people affirm that creation and evolution are incompatible with each other, what do they mean by 'creation'? And what do they mean by 'evolution'?

First, it must not be assumed that 'creation' can only mean a literal, six-day programme. That understanding of creation is certainly incompatible with evolution, if only because each has a totally different time-span. No. All Christians believe in creation, including those who do not subscribe to young earth creationism. One might even go so far as to say that one cannot be a Christian and not believe in creation. The apostles' creed, which is the universal faith of the church, begins with the dogmatic assertion 'I believe in God, the Father Almighty, Creator of heaven and earth'.

Secondly, it must not be supposed that 'evolution' can only mean a blind and purely random process in which God has been eliminated from his universe and replaced by 'Chance'. This understanding of evolution is indeed incompatible with creation, inasmuch as chance and purpose exclude one another. Those Christians who believe in evolution, however, mean that the huge variety of animal and vegetable forms can best be accounted for not by the independent creation of each, but by a gradual process of 'descent with modification', whether or not Darwin's 'natural selection' is the best explanation of its mechanism . . .

There are also many Christians who consider that any form of evolution contradicts, or is contradicted by, the early chapters of Genesis. We would be wise to remember, however, that the Bible is essentially a book of salvation, not of science. It has been given to us in order to unfold the way of salvation through Christ, which we could not know otherwise, and not to reveal scientific truths which human beings could themselves discover by the empirical method. I do not mean by this that the biblical and the scientific accounts of things are necessarily incompatible, but rather that they are complementary. Their purposes are different. Science addresses itself to 'how' things function; Scripture is preoccupied with 'why' questions.

What, then, does Genesis 1 teach about origins? Six lessons stand out: (1) that God created everything out of an original nothing; (2) that his creation proceeded in progressive stages; (3) that the means of his creation was his will (Revelation 4:11), expressed in his Word; (4) that man, male and female, bearing God's image, is the crown of creation; (5) that everything God made was good, and (6) that what he created he continues to sustain.

Darwin himself does not seem to have renounced his belief in creation when he developed his belief in evolution. In this respect I am glad to have read his *Autobiography* [consisting of recollections and letters compiled and edited by his son Francis]. In it he expresses 'the impossibility of conceiving that this grand and wondrous universe, with our conscious selves, arose through chance, seems to me the chief argument for the existence of God'. He also considered 'that the theory of evolution is quite compatible with the belief in a God'. At the same time he confesses to fluctuations in his faith (Barlow, *op.cit.*, p. 93). It is obvious that throughout his life he was caught in a dilemma between belief and unbelief. Colin Russell (1985, p. 154) quotes him [in a letter to his friend Joseph Hooker, the Director of Kew Gardens]: '*I am conscious that I am in an utterly hopeless muddle. I can-not think that the world as we see it, is the result of chance' and yet I cannot look at each separate thing as the result of design.*

Charles Darwin was born in 1809, went up to Edinburgh as a medical student, and transferred to Cambridge to train for the pastoral ministry of the Church of England. But he spent much of his time hunting and shooting, and collecting plants and beetles. Graduating in 1831, aged twenty-two, he was invited by Captain Robert FitzRoy to sail round the world with him on HMS *Beagle* as the ship's naturalist. In the end the voyage lasted five years, and changed his life.
(Stott 2002, pp. 108–112)

A particularly memorable time for Darwin was the month he spent on and around the Galapagos, an archipelago of volcanic islands some 600 miles off the west coast of Ecuador. Stott wrote of this time:

I read his account of this visit with the greatest interest [Darwin, 1839], for in 1977 my Argentinian friend Dr René Padilla and I spent a week visiting some of the very islands he visited . . . Our next destination was Española or Hood island, the most south-easterly of the archipelago. The cliff ledges were occupied by Masked Boobies (Gannets), dazzling white except for black edges to their wings and tail and their black facial mask. Further inland we came to a colony of Waved Albatrosses. Española is their only breeding ground in the world, and there are said to be 12,000 pairs on the island. A dozen or so pairs, with newly hatched chicks were very accessible . . .

On several islands we became acquainted with the two species of iguana confined to the Galapagos. The marine iguana is black with red back markings. It inhabits rocky sea beaches, and walks on the sea bed feeding on seaweed and algae. The land iguana, however, is yellowish-orange beneath and brownish-red above, with a livid yellow head and front feet. It lives in burrows, is also a herbivore, specializing in cactus plants. Both iguanas grow up to three feet in length and look like primitive dragons with sharp dorsal combs. Darwin called them 'hideous-looking creatures', while Captain FitzRoy went further and declared that 'few animals are uglier'. But I find this a rather harsh judgment. Grotesque, perhaps, and even fearsome, but very docile, and skilled in clambering over the rocks.

On Santa Cruz island a primary schoolboy called Mario was appointed our guide in looking for giant tortoises ('*galapagos*') which gave the archipelago its name . . . 'These huge reptiles', Darwin wrote, 'seemed to my fancy like some antediluvian animals'. Herman Melville, author of *Moby Dick*, was more eloquent in his comments; 'they seemed newly crawled forth from beneath the foundations of the world . . . Such worshipful venerableness of aspect!' Darwin was fascinated by the variations between them. Each island seemed to have its own endemic subspecies, and they differed from one another in the pattern of their carapace, in some physical features, and in their feeding habits.

Darwin observed a similar diversity in the finches. 'A most singular group of finches', he called them, 'related to each other in the structure of their beaks, short tails, form of body and plumage'. 'Darwin's Finches' they are now called, and there are thirteen species of them.

So the Galapagos is a living laboratory of mini-evolution . . . Yet the whole area is extremely vulnerable. For centuries the islands had been devastated by looting sailors. Next domestic animals (dogs, goats and pigs) were introduced, became wild, and are doing much damage. Then in 2000 local fishermen, whose lobster quota was reduced, staged a violent protest; and in 2001 a tanker spilled 200,000 gallons of oil. Meanwhile the tourist trade continues to grow and to threaten the endemic wildlife and its habitat. Every possible effort needs to be taken to protect this unique archipelago.
(Stott 2002, pp. 112–114)

Stott's fascination with the wildlife of the Galapagos was typical of his enthusiasm for the places he visited. He was a dedicated and unapologetic birdwatcher. In the introduction to his book *The Birds Our Teachers*, the companion book to *People My Teachers*, he wrote:

It was Jesus Christ himself in the Sermon on the Mount who told us to be birdwatchers! 'Behold the fowls of the air' is how the King James' Version renders his command (Matthew 6:26). Translated into basic English, however, his instruction becomes 'watch birds!' So we have the highest possible authority for this activity.
(Stott [1999] 2007, p. 9)

In his book *Christian Counter-Culture* (1978, republished as *The Message of the Sermon on the Mount* 1984; revised, with additions, 2020), Stott expounded Matthew 6:25–30:

I tell you, do not worry about your life, what you will eat or drink; or about your body, what you will wear. Is not life more than food, and the body more than clothes? Look at the birds

of the air; they do not sow or reap or store away in barns, and yet your heavenly Father feeds them. Are you not much more valuable than they? Can any one of you by worrying add a single hour to your life? And why do you worry about clothes? See how the flowers of the field grow. They do not labour or spin. Yet I tell you that not even Solomon in all his splendour was dressed like one of these. If that is how God clothes the grass of the field, which is here today and tomorrow is thrown into the fire, will he not much more clothe you – you of little faith.
[NIV 2011]

Our human experience is this: God created and now sustains our life; he also created and now sustains our body. This is a fact of everyday experience. We neither made ourselves, nor keep ourselves alive. Now our 'life' (for which God is responsible) is obviously more important than the food and drink which nourish it. Similarly our 'body' (for which God is also responsible) is more important than the clothing which covers and warms it. Well then, if God already takes care of the greater (our life and body), can we not trust him to take care of the lesser (our food and clothing)? . . .

Next, Jesus turns to the sub-human world and argues the other way round. He uses birds as an illustration of God's supply of food (26) and flowers to illustrate his supply of clothing (28–30). In both cases he tells us to 'look at' or 'consider' them, that is, to think about the facts of God's providential care in their case. Some readers may know that I happen myself to have been since boyhood an enthusiastic birdwatcher. I know, of course, that birdwatching is regarded by some as a rather eccentric pastime; they view the likes of me with quizzical and patronizing amusement. But I claim biblical – indeed dominical – warrant for this activity. 'Consider the fowls of the air,' said Jesus according to the AV, and this in basic English could be translated 'watch birds'! Indeed, I am quite serious, for the Greek verb in his command (*emblepsate eis*) means 'fix your eyes on, so as to take a good look at'. If we do take an interest in birds and flowers (and we should surely, like our Master, be gratefully aware of the natural world around us), then we will know that although birds *neither sow nor reap*, yet our *heavenly Father feeds them*, and that although *the lilies of the field* (anemones, poppies, irises and gladioli have all been suggested as alternatives to lilies, although the reference may be to all the beautiful spring flowers of Galilee) . . . *neither toil nor spin*, yet our heavenly Father *clothes* them, indeed more gorgeously than *Solomon in all his glory*. This being so, can we not trust him to feed and clothe us who are of much more value than birds and flowers? Why, he even clothes the common grass *which today is alive and tomorrow is thrown into the oven!* (Stott [1978] 1984, 2020, pp. 163–164)

Birdwatching was a life-long passion for Stott. What began as a hobby developed in his later decades into a major concern for the care of creation. Indeed, it formed a significant element in his desire and charge for the whole future of the church, as set out in *The Radical Disciple* (2010b). We can seek transcendence or significance independently of Christ's work and calling, but our answers will be incomplete. This was Stott's thesis in his book *Why I Am a Christian* (2003a). His repeated message is that our understanding of ourselves as made in his image and redeemed by him is only possible if we respond as he wants us to. Creation care is not merely a worthy activity; it is a response to Christ's work and calling of us. It is an expression of our worship. In a foreword to *The Care of Creation*, Stott wrote:

It is a noble calling to cooperate with God for the fulfilment of his purposes, to transform the created order for the pleasure and profit of all. In this way our work is to be an expression of our worship, since our care of the creation will reflect our love for the Creator . . . We human beings find our humanness not only in relation to the Earth, which we are to transform, but in relation to God, whom we are to worship; not only in relation

to the creation, but especially in relation to the Creator. God intends our work to be an expression of our worship, and our care of the creation to reflect our love for the Creator. Only then, whatever we do, in word or deed, shall we be able to do it to the glory of God (1 Corinthians 10:31).
(Stott in Berry 2000, pp. 8–9)

These are strong words and worth pondering. They are Stott's thought-out and rational opinion. He repeated the conclusion, 'God intends . . . our care of the creation to reflect our love for the Creator' at the end of the creation care chapter in *The Radical Disciple* (Stott 2010b, p. 59). We cannot ignore it as mere rhetoric or a preacher's hyperbole. It represented a hard-won and rational position. This should not be taken to imply that creation care itself is contentious. It is true that there are a few Christians who fervently believe that degrading creation is to be encouraged because it might accelerate the return of the Lord Jesus, but they are a small minority (see Oreske and Conway 2010; Rawles 2012; Wilkinson 2012; Northcott 2014). Most Christians would accept that it is entirely proper to treat God's world responsibly, even though they might not regard creation care as a high priority and certainly not one of the key markers of discipleship. Perhaps the most common attitude is that it is a legitimate and laudable but optional involvement for 'green' enthusiasts. Evangelicals in particular, with their emphasis on the primacy of individual conversion and holy living, are wont to regard creation care as much less important than (say) missionary endeavour or corporate worship. Stott rejected this as a weak assumption.

Is it possible to interpret the inclusion of creation care in Stott's desiderata for a mature ('radical') disciple as simply an idiosyncratic aberration, perhaps an attempt to justify his personal passion for watching birds, or is he pointing believers to something much more basic? Put crudely: is the widespread lack of concern for creation a failure of theological understanding or is it little more than a red herring for Christian discipleship?

Stott took both creation and sin seriously. That is almost a trite statement. We would not expect anything different from a Bible scholar and Christian believer of Stott's calibre and honesty, but we need to probe further to understand – and learn from – the link he made between creation care and 'our love for the Creator'. The start to answering this question must be to search the Scriptures. This might seem obvious, but it is salutary to remember that Jesus repeatedly rebuked his hearers for not knowing the Scriptures (Matthew 22:29; Mark 12:10, 24; Luke 24:25), even though his hearers would certainly have known the Hebrew Bible well. Is the widespread lack of interest in creation care a case of deafness, of 'open ears, but hearing nothing' (Isaiah 42:20; Jeremiah 6:10; Matthew 13:15)?

4

Missional developments

New learning from the
Word and the world

Despite his immersion in the Scriptures from his schooldays, it was only in the 1960s, when Stott was in his forties, that he found himself having to reflect afresh on the Scriptures and their implications. He had been a dedicated birdwatcher for many years and was well-acquainted with the natural world, but the priority mandate for creation care was a message that only seems to have dawned on Stott himself at this time. He was characteristically honest about his rethink. It began in 1960; he wrote to his former curate, John Lefroy, that he was quite happy to be 'a despised evangelical' so long as he could resolve his own doubts. He had been greatly helped by reading *Supreme Authority* (1953) by the South African Norval Geldenhuys, which examined and propounded the supreme authority of Jesus and the authority given by Jesus to his apostles (Steer 2009, p. 120). On top of his inner searchings, he was involved in three major conferences in three years – 1966, 1967, 1968 – all of which challenged him in various ways, and then a major event in 1974 that had reverberations which continue around the world to this day. The theological development of integral mission during this time, as expressed by Stott's Latin American colleagues René Padilla (2010), Samuel Escobar and others, happened in close tandem with Stott's own deepening understanding of creation care as an integral part of Christian discipleship.

The first gathering was the 1966 World Congress on Evangelism in Berlin, where Stott gave three Bible studies on the 'Great Commission' ('Go to all nations and make disciples', Matthew 28:19).

It marked his emergence as a global figure. Notwithstanding, he commented years later that, in retrospect, he was relieved that his addresses were not widely published, since:

> I now consider that I was unbalanced to assert that the risen Lord's commission was entirely evangelistic, not social . . . I later argued that at least the Johannine version of the Commission (with its words 'as the Father sent me, so I send you') implies in us as in Christ a ministry of compassionate service that is wider than evangelism.
> (Stott quoted in Dudley-Smith 2001, p. 123)

In other words, in 1966 'he had believed and taught that the Great Commission was solely a command to preach and teach and make disciples, not a command to heal and to take social responsibility' (Dudley-Smith 2001, p. 127). Interviewed over twenty years later by the American magazine *World Christian* in 1989, he described the reasons for his change of mind:

> But gradually, and I don't think it was through anybody's particular influence but through my own reflection on the New Testament, I came to see that this view was very narrow and unbiblical. In the early 1960s, I began to travel in the Third World, and I saw poverty in Latin America, Africa, and Asia as I had not seen it before. It became clear to me that it was utterly impossible to take that old view. Since then I have come to a much more holistic position.
> (Stott quoted in Dudley-Smith 2001, p. 127)

The year after the Berlin Congress, Stott served as Chairman of a very different and entirely British assembly, the first National Evangelical Anglican Congress in Keele. Stott's expectations for it were high. He saw it as an opportunity for evangelicals to move away from the partisanship, isolationism, defensiveness, obstructionism and ghetto mentality that had characterized them for most of the twentieth century (Atherstone 2011, p. 177). His experiences and the actual challenges he faced at Keele were different, however, and they undoubtedly forced Stott to re-examine his own assumptions about what needed to be communicated and how the communication could be done.

The plan for Keele was the traditional pattern for a conference of this nature, with a series of keynote addresses delivered by eminent scholars followed by a limited amount of discussion and implied assent from those present. It was assumed that these words of wisdom would then be circulated to parishes for further study. Stott accepted that this would amount to little more than an exercise in public relations (Atherstone 2011, p. 178). This intention was not to come to pass. In November 1966, a few months before the conference, a group of thirty-year-olds at an Eclectic Society conference (an organization established by Stott in 1955 for fellowship and mutual support among young evangelical clergy, following the pattern of an earlier Eclectics Society founded in 1783 by ex-slave trader John Newton and John Venn of the early Church Missionary Society) objected that the conference might merely repeat platitudinous generalities. They prevailed on the organizing committee to change the planned procedure and pre-circulate the invited papers and so allow their digestion by the conference attendees, giving time for discussion at the meeting itself. Stott resisted this but was forced to yield. The programme changed from respectful acquiescent silence to critical participation, and led to an agreed statement that could be truly accepted as a general consensus.

The only non-clergy member of the original group of keynote speakers was a distinguished lawyer, Sir Norman Anderson. He had been given the topic of 'Christian worldliness'. The following year, he expanded his congress text into a book – *Into the World: The needs and limits of Christian involvement* (Anderson 1968). In the foreword, he recalled the statement issued at the end of the congress affirming:

We believe that our evangelical doctrines have important ethical implications. But we confess to our shame that we have not thought sufficiently or radically about the problems of our

society. We are therefore resolved to give ourselves to more study of these crucial issues.
(Anderson 1968, p. 8)

Reflecting on this years later in his autobiography, Anderson wrote:

Since then, thank God, others . . . have written on this topic more fully and radically, and there has been a palpable change in evangelical thinking. Instead of shrinking from anything labelled 'the social gospel', we have come to see that the basic Evangel of spiritual salvation by faith alone is given its proper place only when we recognize the implications which that gospel should always have had in the field of social, racial and economic justice.
(Anderson 1985, p. 214)

Stott was obviously beginning to reconsider his earlier expositions at Berlin. At Keele he tried and failed to stem criticisms of traditional ways of doing things.

He was even more seriously challenged by his experience at the third conference he was involved in, the World Council of Churches Assembly in Uppsala in 1968. There, the lessons he had begun to learn in Berlin and Keele were reinforced. He wrote of Uppsala:

The Assembly has given its earnest attention to the hunger, poverty and injustices of the contemporary world. Rightly so. I have myself been moved by it. But I did not find a similar compassion for the spiritual hunger of man . . . The Lord Jesus Christ wept over the impenitent city which had rejected him; I do not see this Assembly weeping any similar tears.
(Stott quoted in Dudley-Smith 2001, p. 126)

Stott reflected on the lessons he had learnt in a major book, *Christian Mission in the Modern World*, which had implications far beyond his own evangelical constituency. He described how his thinking had changed since the Berlin Congress:

Today, however, I would express myself differently. It is not just that the commission includes a duty to teach converts everything Jesus had previously commanded (Matthew 28:20), and that social responsibility is among the things which Jesus commanded. I now see more clearly that not only the consequences of the commission but the actual commission itself must be understood to include social as well as evangelistic responsibility, unless we are to be guilty of distorting the words of Jesus.

The crucial form in which the Great Commission has been handed down to us (though it is the most neglected because it is the most costly) is the Johannine. Jesus had anticipated it in his prayer in the upper room when he said to the Father: 'As thou didst send me into the world, so I have sent them into the world' (John 17:18 [RSV]). Now, probably in the same upper room but after his death and resurrection, he turned his prayer-statement into a commission and said: 'As the Father has sent me, even so I send you' (John 20:21 [RSV]). In both these sentences Jesus did more than draw a vague parallel between his mission and ours. Deliberately and precisely he made his mission the *model* of ours, saying '*as* the Father sent me, *so* I send you.' Therefore our understanding of the church's mission must be deduced from our understanding of the Son's. (Stott [1975] 2016 (updated and expanded by Wright), p. 23)

Then, in 1974, Stott partnered with Billy Graham at an International Congress on World Evangelization at Lausanne in Switzerland. About half the speakers were from the 'developing world', many of them critical of an evangelism shaped as much by culture as by biblical understanding. Stott gave an opening address on the nature of biblical evangelism. He built on his earlier thinking and was blunt:

Is it not in a servant role that we can find the right synthesis of evangelism and social action? For both should be authentic expressions of the service we are sent into the world to give . . . Here then are two instructions, 'love your neighbor' and 'go and make disciples.' What is the relation between the two? Some of us behave as if we thought them identical, so that if we have shared the Gospel with somebody, we consider we have completed our responsibility to love him. But no. The Great Commission neither explains, nor exhausts, nor supersedes the Great Commandment. What it does is to add to the command of neighbor-love and neighbor-service a new and urgent Christian dimension. If we truly love our neighbor we shall without doubt tell him the Good News of Jesus. But equally if we truly love our neighbor we shall not stop there . . . Love does not need to justify itself. It just expresses itself in service wherever it sees need.

(Stott 1974b)

Guided by Stott as Chairman of a drafting committee, the Congress accepted a Covenant making it clear that 'the results of evangelism include . . . responsible service in the world':

For the results of evangelism include . . . *responsible service in the world* (for conversion means nothing if it does not result in a change from self-centered living to sacrificial service, Mark 10:43–45).

(Stott 1975)

In 1975, Stott expanded his own understanding in *Christian Mission in the Modern World*:

All Christians everywhere, whatever their cultural background or theological persuasion, must think at some time or other about the relation between the church and the world. What is a Christian's responsibility toward non-Christian relatives, friends and neighbors, and indeed to the whole non-Christian community?

In reply to these questions most Christians would make some use of the term *mission*. One can hardly discuss church–world relations and omit the concept of 'mission'. But there would be a wide divergence in our understanding of what our 'mission' is, of what part 'evangelism' plays in mission, and of what part 'dialogue' plays in evangelism. I fear further that we would diverge from one another not only in our understanding of the *nature* of mission, evangelism and dialogue, but also in our understanding of the *goal* of all three . . .

In recent years, relations between ecumenical and evangelical Christians (if I may use these terms as a convenient shorthand, for I recognize that they are by no means mutually exclusive) have hardened into something like a confrontation. I have no wish to worsen this situation. However, I do believe that some current ecumenical thinking is mistaken. But then, candidly, I believe some of our traditional evangelical formulations are mistaken also. Many ecumenical Christians do not seem to have begun to learn to live under the authority of Scripture. We evangelicals think we have – and there is no doubt we sincerely want to – but at some times we are very selective in our submission, and at others the traditions of the evangelical elders seem to owe more to culture than to Scripture. My chief concern, therefore, is to bring both ecumenical and evangelical thinking to the same independent and objective test, namely, that of the biblical revelation.

. . . Before attempting a biblical definition [of mission] it may be helpful to take a look at the contemporary polarization.

Two extreme views

The older or traditional view has been to equate mission and evangelism, missionaries and evangelists, missions and evangelistic programs. In its extreme form this older view of mission as consisting exclusively of evangelism also concentrated on verbal proclamation. The missionary was often caricatured as standing under a palm tree, wearing a pith helmet and declaiming the gospel to a group of ill-clad 'natives' sitting respectfully around him on the ground. Thus the traditional image of the missionary was of the preacher, and a rather paternalistic kind of preacher at that. Such an emphasis on the priority of evangelistic preaching sometimes left little room for any other kind of work to be counted as 'real mission', including even schools and hospitals. Most adherents of the traditional view of mission, however, would regard education and medical work as perfectly proper, and indeed as very useful adjuncts to evangelistic work, often out of Christian compassion for the ignorant and the sick, though sometimes as being unashamedly 'platforms' or 'springboards' for evangelism – hospitals and schools providing in their patients and pupils a conveniently captive audience for the gospel. In either case the mission itself was understood in terms of evangelism.

This traditional view is far from being dead and buried. Sometimes it goes along with a very negative view of the world of culture and society. The world is like a building on fire, it may be said, and a Christian's only duty is to mount a rescue operation before it is too late. Jesus Christ is coming at any moment; there is no point in tampering with the structures of society, for society is doomed and about to be destroyed. Besides, any attempt to improve society is bound to be unproductive since unrenewed people cannot build a new world. A person's only hope lies in being born again. Only then might society conceivably be reborn. But it is too late now even for that.

Such world-denying pessimism is a strange phenomenon in those who say they believe in God. But then their image of God is only partially shaped by the biblical revelation. He is not the Creator who in the beginning gave humanity a 'cultural mandate' to subdue and rule the earth, who has instituted governing authorities as his 'ministers' to order society and maintain justice, and who, as the Lausanne Covenant [paragraph 5] puts it, because he is 'both the Creator and the Judge of all people', is concerned for 'justice and reconciliation throughout human society'.

At the opposite extreme to this unbiblical concept of mission as consisting of evangelism alone there is the viewpoint that has been advocated in the ecumenical movement since the 1960s. This is the view that God is at work in the historical process, that the purpose of God's mission, of the *missio Dei,* is the establishment of *shalom* (Hebrew for 'peace') in the sense of social harmony, and that this *shalom* (which is identical with the kingdom of God) is exemplified in such areas as the battle against racism, the humanization of industrial relations, the overcoming of class divisions, community development, and the quest for an ethic of honesty and integrity in business and other professions.

Moreover, in working toward this goal God uses people both inside and outside the church. The church's particular role in the mission of God is to point out where God is at work in world history, to discover what God is doing, to catch up with it and to get involved in it ourselves. For God's primary relationship is to the world, it was argued, so that the true sequence is to be found no longer in the formula 'God-church-world' but in the formula 'God-world-church'. This being so, it is the world that should set the agenda for the church. Churches must take the world seriously and seek to serve according to its contemporary sociological needs.

What are we to say about such identification of the mission of God with social renewal? A fourfold critique may be made.

First, the God who is Lord of history is also the Judge of history. It is naive to hail all revolutionary movements as signs of divine renewal. After the revolution the new status quo sometimes enshrines more injustice and oppression than the one it has displaced.

Second, the biblical categories of *shalom,* the new humanity and the kingdom of God are not to be identified with social renewal. It is true that in the Old Testament *shalom* (peace) often indicates political and material well-being. But can it be maintained, as serious biblical exegesis, that the New Testament authors present Jesus Christ as winning this kind of peace and as bestowing it on society as a whole? To assume that all Old Testament prophecies are fulfilled in literal and material terms is to make the very mistake that Jesus' contemporaries made when they tried to take him by force and make him a king (John 6:15 [RSV]). The New Testament understanding of Old Testament prophecy is that its fulfillment *transcends* the categories in which the promises were given. So according to the apostles the peace that Jesus preaches and gives is something deeper and richer, namely, reconciliation and fellowship with God and with each other (for example, Ephesians 2:13–22 [RSV]). Moreover, he does not bestow it on all people but on those who belong to him, to his redeemed community. So *shalom* is the blessing the Messiah brings to his people. The new creation and the new humanity are to be seen in those who are in Christ (2 Corinthians 5:17 [RSV]); and the kingdom has to be received like a little child (Mark 10:15 [RSV]). Certainly it is our Christian duty to commend by argument and example the righteous standards of the kingdom to those who have not themselves received or entered it. In this way we see the righteousness of the kingdom, as it were, 'spilling over' into segments of the world and thus to some extent blurring the frontiers between the two. Nevertheless the kingdom remains distinct from godless society, and actual entry into it depends on spiritual rebirth.

Third, the word *mission* cannot properly be used to cover everything God is doing in the world. In providence and common grace he is indeed active in all people and all societies, whether they acknowledge him or not. But this is not his 'mission'. 'Mission' concerns his redeemed people, and what he sends *them* into the world to do.

Fourth, such preoccupation with social change sometimes leaves little or no room for evangelistic concern. Of course we must give earnest attention to the hunger, poverty and injustices of the world. But we cannot then fail to have comparable concern or compassion for people's spiritual hunger, or fail to care about the millions who are perishing without Christ. The Lord Jesus Christ sent his church to preach the good news and make disciples, and we must not become so absorbed with legitimate social goals and activity that we fail to obey that command.

A biblical synthesis?

From the traditional view of mission as exclusively evangelistic and the current ecumenical view of it as the establishment of *shalom*, we ask whether there is a better way, a more balanced and more biblical way of defining the mission of the church, and of expressing the relationship between the evangelistic and social responsibilities of the people of God.

The need for such a balanced relationship was recognized within the ecumenical movement itself. At the Uppsala Assembly of the World Council of Churches in 1968, its recently retired secretary general, Dr W. A. Visser 't Hooft, made the following fine statement in an opening address:

> I believe that, with regard to the great tension between the vertical interpretation of the Gospel as essentially concerned with God's saving action in the life of individuals, and the horizontal interpretation of it as mainly concerned with human relationships in the world, we must get out of that rather primitive oscillating movement of going from one extreme to the other, which is not worthy of a movement which by its nature seeks to embrace the truth of the Gospel in its fulness. A Christianity which has lost its vertical dimension has lost its salt and is not only insipid in itself, but useless for the world. But a Christianity which would use the vertical preoccupation as a means to escape from its responsibility for and in the common life of man is a denial of the incarnation, of God's love for the world manifested in Christ. (Visser 't Hooft 1968, pp. 317–318)

Sadly, the issue was not clarified at that conference and remained a divisive issue among ecumenicals and evangelicals alike. The old polarization continues.

All of us should be able to agree that mission arises primarily out of the nature not of the church but of God himself. The living God of the Bible is the sending God. Some have even applied the word *centrifugal*, normally used of the church reaching out in mission, to God himself. It is a dramatic figure of speech. Yet it is only another way of saying that God is love, always reaching out after others in self-giving service.

So God sent forth Abraham, commanding him to go from his country and kindred into the great unknown, and promising to bless him and to bless the world through him if he obeyed (Genesis 12:1–3 [RSV]). Next he sent Joseph into Egypt, overruling even his brothers' cruelty, in order to preserve a godly remnant on earth during the famine (Genesis 45:4–8 [RSV]). Then he sent Moses to his oppressed people in Egypt, with good news of liberation, saying to him, 'Come, I will send you to Pharaoh that you may bring forth my people . . . out of Egypt' (Exodus 3:10, [RSV]). After the exodus and the settlement he sent a continuous succession of prophets with words of warning and of promise to his people. As he said through Jeremiah, 'From the day that your fathers came out of the land of Egypt to this day, I have persistently sent all my servants the prophets to them, day after day; yet they did not listen to me' (Jeremiah 7:25, 26; compare 2 Chronicles 36:15–16 [RSV]). After the Babylonian captivity he graciously sent them back to the land, and sent more messengers with them and to them to help them rebuild the temple, the city and the national life. Then at last 'when the time had fully come, God sent forth his Son'; and after that the Father and the Son sent forth the Spirit on the day of Pentecost (Galatians 4:4–6; compare John 14:26; 15:26; 16:7; Acts 2:33 [RSV]).

All this is the essential biblical background to any understanding of mission. The primal mission is God's, for it is God who sent his prophets, his Son, his Spirit. Of these missions the mission of the Son is central, for it was the culmination of the ministry of the prophets, and it embraced within itself as its climax the sending of the Spirit. And now the Son sends as he himself was sent. Already during his public ministry Jesus sent out first the apostles and then the seventy as a kind of extension of his own preaching, teaching and healing ministry. Then after his death and resurrection he widened the scope of the mission to include all who call him Lord and call themselves his disciples. For others were present with the Twelve when the Great Commission was given (see, for example, Luke 24:33 [RSV]). We cannot restrict its application to the apostles alone.

The Great Commission

This brings us to a consideration of the terms of the Great Commission. What was it that the Lord Jesus commissioned his people to do? There can be no doubt that most versions of it (for he seems to have repeated it in several forms on several occasions) place the emphasis on evangelism. 'Go into all the world and preach the gospel to the whole creation' is the familiar command of the 'longer ending' of Mark's Gospel, which seems to have been added by some later hand after Mark's original conclusion was lost (Mark 16:15, [RSV]). 'Go . . . and make disciples of all nations, baptizing them . . . and teaching them' is the Matthean form (Matthew 28:19, 20 [RSV]), while Luke records at the end of his Gospel Christ's word 'that repentance and forgiveness of sins should be preached in his name to all nations' and at the beginning of the Acts that his people would receive power to become his witnesses to the end of the earth (Luke 24:47; Acts 1:8 [RSV]). The cumulative emphasis seems clear. It is placed on preaching, witnessing and making disciples, and many deduce from this that the mission of the church, according to the specification of the risen Lord, is exclusively a preaching, converting and teaching mission. Indeed, I confess that I myself argued this at the World Congress on Evangelism in Berlin in 1966, when attempting to expound the three major versions of the Great Commission.

Today, however, I would express myself differently. It is not just that the Commission includes a duty to teach baptized disciples everything Jesus had previously commanded (Matthew 28:20 [RSV]), and that social responsibility is among the things that Jesus commanded. I now see more clearly that not only the consequences of the Commission but the actual Commission itself must be understood to include social as well as evangelistic responsibility, unless we are to be guilty of distorting the words of Jesus.

The crucial form in which the Great Commission has been handed down to us (though it is the most neglected because it is the most costly) is the Johannine. Jesus had anticipated it in his prayer in the upper room when he said to the Father, 'As thou didst send me into the world, so I have sent them into the world' (John 17:18 [RSV]). Now, probably in the same upper room but after his death and resurrection, he turned his prayer-statement into a commission and said, 'As the Father has sent me, even so I send you' (John 20:21 [RSV]). In both these sentences Jesus did more than draw a vague parallel between his mission and ours. Deliberately and precisely he made his mission the *model* of ours, saying '*as* the Father sent me, *so* I send you'. Therefore our understanding of the church's mission must be deduced from our understanding of the Son's. Why and how did the Father send the Son?

Of course the major purpose of the Son's coming into the world was unique. Perhaps it is partly for this reason that Christians have been hesitant to think of their mission as in any sense comparable to his. For the Father sent the Son to be the Saviour of the world, and to that end to atone for our sins and to bring us eternal life (1 John 4:9, 10, 14 [RSV]). Indeed, he himself said he had come 'to seek and to save the lost' (Luke 19:10 [RSV]). We cannot copy him in these things. We are not saviors. Nevertheless, all this is still an inadequate statement of why he came.

It is better to begin with something more general and say that he came to serve. His contemporaries were familiar with

Daniel's apocalyptic vision of the Son of Man receiving domin-ion and being served by all peoples (Daniel 7:14 [RSV]). But Jesus knew he had to serve before he would be served, and to endure suffering before he would receive dominion. So he fused two apparently incompatible Old Testament images, Daniel's Son of Man and Isaiah's Suffering Servant, and said, 'The Son of man . . . came not to be served but to serve, and to give his life as a ransom for many' (Mark 10:45 [RSV]). The ransoming sin-offering was a sacrifice that he alone could offer, but this was to be the climax of a life of service, and we too may serve. 'I am among you,' he said on another occasion, 'as one who serves' (Luke 22:27 [RSV]). So he gave himself in selfless service for others, and his service took a wide variety of forms according to people's needs. Certainly he preached, pro-claiming the good news of the kingdom of God and teaching about the coming and the nature of the kingdom, how to enter it and how it would spread. But he served in deed as well as in word, and it would be impossible in the ministry of Jesus to separate his works from his words. He fed hungry mouths and washed dirty feet; he healed the sick, comforted the sad and even restored the dead to life.

Now he sends us, he says, as the Father had sent him. Therefore our mission, like his, is to be one of service. He emptied himself of status and took the form of a servant, and his humble mind is to be in us (Philippians 2:5–8 [RSV]). He supplies us with the perfect model of service, and sends his church into the world to be a servant church. Is it not essential for us to recover this biblical emphasis? In many of our Chris-tian attitudes and enterprises we have tended (especially those of us who live in Europe and North America) to be bosses rather than servants. Yet it seems that it is in our servant role that we can find the right synthesis of evangelism and social action. For both should be for us, as they undoubtedly were for Christ, authentic expressions of the love that serves.

Then there is another aspect of the mission of the Son that is to be paralleled in the mission of the church, namely, that in order to serve he was sent *into the world*. He did not touch down like a visitor from outer space, or arrive like an alien bringing his own alien culture with him. He took to himself our humanity, our flesh and blood, our culture. He actually became one of us and experienced our frailty, our suffering and our temptations. He even bore our sin and died our death. And now he sends us 'into the world', to identify with others as he identified with us (though without losing our Christian identity), to become vulnerable as he did. It is surely one of the most characteristic failures of us Christians, not least of us who are called evangelical Christians, that we seldom seem to take seriously this principle of the incarnation. It comes more natural to us to shout the gospel at people from a distance than to involve ourselves deeply in their lives, to think ourselves into their culture and their problems, and to feel with them in their pains. Yet this implication of our Lord's example is inescapable. As the Lausanne Covenant [paragraph 6] put it, 'We affirm that Christ sends his redeemed people into the world as the Father sent him, and that this calls for a similar deep and costly penetration of the world.'

The relation between evangelism and social action

What, then, should be the relation between evangelism and social action within our total Christian responsibility? If we grant that we have no liberty either to concentrate on evangelism to the exclusion of social concern or to make social activism a substitute for evangelism, we still need to define the relation between the two. Three main ways of doing this have been attempted.

First, some regard social action as *a means to evangelism*. In this case evangelism and the winning of converts are the primary ends in view, but social action is a useful preliminary, an effective means to these ends. In its most blatant form this makes social work (whether food, medicine or education) the sugar on the pill, the bait on the hook, while in its best form it gives to the gospel a credibility it would otherwise lack. In either case the smell of hypocrisy hangs around our philanthropy. A frankly ulterior motive impels us to engage in it. And the result of making our social program the means to another end is that we breed so-called rice Christians. This is inevitable if we ourselves have been 'rice evangelists'. They caught the deception from us. No wonder Gandhi said in 1931, 'I hold that proselytizing under the cloak of humanitarian work is, to say the least, unhealthy. . . why should I change my religion because a doctor who professes Christianity as his religion has cured me of some disease?'

A second way of relating evangelism and social action is better. It regards social action not as a means to evangelism but as *a manifestation of evangelism*, or at least of the gospel that is being proclaimed. In this case philanthropy is not attached to evangelism rather artificially from the outside, but grows out of it as its natural expression. One might almost say that social action becomes the 'sacrament' of evangelism, for it makes the message significantly visible. Actions of love and compassion themselves 'preach' the gospel message they flow from. We should not hesitate to agree with this, so far as it goes, for there is a strong precedent for it in the ministry of Jesus. His words and deeds belonged to each other, the words interpreting the deeds and the deeds embodying the words. He did not only announce the good news of the kingdom; he performed visible 'signs of the kingdom'. If people would not believe his words, he said, then let them believe him 'for the sake of the works themselves' (John 14:11 [RSV]).

Nevertheless, this second view still leaves me uneasy. For it makes service a subdivision of evangelism, an aspect of the proclamation. I do not deny that good works of love did have an evidential value when performed by Jesus and do have an evidential value when performed by us (compare Matthew 5:16 [RSV]). But I cannot bring myself to accept that this is their only or even major justification. If it is, then still, and rather self-consciously at that, they are only a means to an end. If good works are visible preaching, then they are expecting a return; but if good works are visible loving, then they are 'expecting nothing in return' (Luke 6:35 [RSV]).

This brings me to the third way of stating the relation between evangelism and social action, which I believe to be the truly Christian one, namely, that social action is *a partner of evangelism*. As partners the two belong to each other and yet are independent of each other. Each stands on its own feet in its own right alongside the other. Neither is a means to the other, or even a manifestation of the other. For each is an end in itself. Both are expressions of unfeigned love. Evangelism and compassionate service belong together in the mission of God.

The apostle John has helped me to grasp this by these words from his first letter: 'If any one has the world's goods and sees his brother in need, yet closes his heart against him, how does God's love abide in him? Little children, let us not love in word or speech but in deed and in truth' (1 John 3:17–18, [RSV]). Here love in action springs from a twofold situation, first 'seeing' a brother in need and secondly 'having' the wherewithal to meet the need. If I do not relate what I 'have' to what I 'see', I cannot claim to be indwelt by the love of God. Further, this principle applies whatever the nature of the seen need. I may see spiritual need (sin, guilt, lostness) and have the gospel knowledge to meet it. Or the need I see may be disease or ignorance or bad housing, and I may have the medical, educational or social expertise to relieve it. To see need and to possess the remedy compels love to act, and whether the action will be evangelistic or social, or indeed political, depends on what we 'see' and what we 'have'.

This does not mean that words and works, evangelism and social action, are such inseparable partners that all of us must engage in both all the time. Situations vary, and so do Christian callings. As for situations, there will be times when a person's eternal destiny is the most urgent consideration, for we must not forget that people without Christ are perishing. But there will certainly be other times when a person's material need is so pressing that he would not be able to hear the gospel if we shared it with him. The man who fell among robbers needed above all else at that moment oil and bandages for his wounds, not evangelistic tracts in his pockets! As the saying goes, 'a hungry man has no ears.' If our enemy is hungry, our biblical mandate is not to evangelize him but to feed him (Romans 12:20 [RSV]). Then too there is a diversity of Christian callings, and every Christian should be faithful to her own calling. The doctor must not neglect the practice of medicine for evangelism, and neither should the evangelist be distracted from the ministry of the word by the ministry of tables, as the apostles quickly discovered (Acts 6 [RSV]).

The Great Commandment

Let me return now to the Great Commission. I have tried to argue that its Johannine form, according to which the church's mission is to be modeled on the Son's, implies that we are sent into the world to serve, and that the humble service we are to render will include for us as it did for Christ both words and works, a concern for the hunger and the sickness of both body and soul, in other words, both evangelistic and social activity. But supposing someone remains convinced that the Great Commission relates exclusively to evangelism, what then?

I venture to say that sometimes, perhaps because it was the last instruction Jesus gave us before returning to the Father, we give the Great Commission too prominent a place in our Christian thinking. Please do not misunderstand me. I firmly believe that the whole church is under obligation to obey its Lord's commission to take the gospel to all nations. But I am also concerned that we should not regard this as the only instruction that Jesus left us. He also quoted Leviticus 19:18 [RSV], 'you shall love your neighbour as yourself', called it 'the second and great commandment' (second in importance only to the supreme command to love God with all our being), and elaborated it in the Sermon on the Mount. There he insisted that in God's vocabulary our neighbor includes our enemy, and that to love means to 'do good', that is, to give ourselves actively and constructively to serve our neighbor's welfare.

Here then are two instructions of Jesus – a great commandment, 'love your neighbor', and a great commission, 'go and make disciples.' What is the relation between the two? Some of us behave as if we thought them identical, so that if we share the gospel with somebody, we consider we have completed our responsibility to love him or her. But no. The Great Commission neither explains, nor exhausts, nor supersedes the Great Commandment. What it does is to add to the requirement of neighbor-love and neighbor-service a new and urgent Christian dimension. If we truly love our neighbor, we shall without doubt share with him or her the good news of Jesus. How can we possibly claim to love our neighbor if we know the gospel but keep it from them? Equally, however, if we truly love our neighbor we shall not stop with evangelism. Our neighbor is neither a bodiless soul that we should love only their soul, nor a soulless body that we should care for its welfare alone, nor even a body-soul isolated from society. God created the human person, who is my neighbor, as a body-soul-in-community. Therefore, if we love our neighbor as God made him or her, we must inevitably be concerned for their total welfare, the good of their soul, their body and their community. Moreover, it is this vision of the human person as a social being, as well as a psychosomatic being, that obliges us to add a *political* dimension to our social concern. Humanitarian activity cares for the casualties of a sick society. We should be concerned with preventive medicine or community health as well, which means the quest for better social structures in which peace, dignity, freedom and justice are secured for all. And there is no reason why, in pursuing this quest, we should not join hands with all people of good will, even if they are not Christians.

To sum up, we are sent into the world, like Jesus, to serve. For this is the natural expression of our love for our neighbors. We love. We go. We serve. And in this we have (or should have) no ulterior motive. True, the gospel lacks visibility if we merely preach it, and lacks credibility if we who preach it are interested only in souls and have no concern about the welfare of people's bodies, situations and communities. Yet the reason for our acceptance of social responsibility is not primarily in order to give the gospel either a visibility or a credibility it would otherwise lack, but rather simple, uncomplicated compassion. Love has no need to justify itself. It merely expresses itself in service wherever it sees need.

Mission, then, is not a word for everything the church does. 'The church is mission' sounds fine, but it's an overstatement. For the church is a worshipping as well as a serving community, and although worship and service belong together they are not to be confused. Neither, as we have seen, does 'mission' cover everything God does in the world. For God the Creator is constantly active in his world in providence, in common grace and in judgment, quite apart from the purposes for which he has sent his Son, his Spirit and his church into the world. 'Mission' describes rather everything the church is sent into the world to do. 'Mission' embraces the church's double vocation of service to be 'the salt of the earth' and 'the light of the world'. For Christ *sends* his people into the earth to be its salt, and *sends* his people into the world to be its light (Matthew 5:13–16 [RSV]).

Practical implications

In conclusion, it may be helpful to consider what the realistic outworkings of this understanding of mission are likely to be. Evangelical Christians are now repenting of the former pietism that ended to keep us insulated from the secular world, and are accepting that we have a social as well as an evangelistic responsibility. But what will this mean in practice? I would like to explore two areas: Christian vocation and the local church.

I begin with vocation, by which I mean a Christian's life's work. We've often given the impression that if a young Christian is really keen for Christ he or she will undoubtedly become a foreign missionary, that if they are not quite as keen as that they will stay at home and become a pastor, that if they lack the dedication to be a pastor, they will no doubt serve as a doctor or a teacher, while those who end up in social work or the media or (worst of all) in politics are not far removed from serious backsliding!

It seems to me urgent to gain a truer perspective in this matter of vocation. Jesus Christ calls all his disciples to 'ministry', that is, to service. He himself is the Servant par excellence, and he calls us to be servants too. This much then is certain: if we are Christians, we must spend our lives in the service of God and others. The only difference between us lies in the nature of the service we are called to render. Some are indeed called to be missionaries, evangelists or pastors, and others to the great professions of law, education, medicine and the social sciences. But others are called to commerce, to industry and farming, to accountancy and banking, to local government or parliament, and to the mass media, to home-making and family building. In all these spheres, and many others besides, it is possible for Christians to interpret their life's work Christianly, and to see it neither as a necessary evil (necessary, that is, for survival), nor even as a useful place in which to evangelize or make money for evangelism, but as their Christian vocation, as the way Christ has called them to spend their lives in his service. Further, a part of their calling will be to seek to maintain Christ's standards of justice, righteousness, honesty, human dignity and compassion in a society that no longer accepts them.

. . . Can we now liberate ourselves from the human-made bondage (for that is what it is) of supposing that every really keen Christian will devote all their spare time to some 'soul-winning' enterprise? Surely the biblical doctrine of the body of Christ, with different members gifted to fulfil different functions, should be enough to give us this larger freedom?

... If we can accept this broader concept of mission as Christian service in the world comprising both evangelism and social action – a concept that is laid on us by the model of our Savior's mission in the world – then Christians could under God make a far greater impact on society, an impact commensurate with our numerical strength and with the radical demands of the commission of Christ.
(Stott [1975] 2016 (updated and expanded by Wright), pp. 15–33)

Christian Mission in the Modern World was repeatedly reprinted and then, in 2016 was reissued with extended reflections by Chris Wright, who refers in passing in the extract below to two follow-ups of the original Lausanne Conference – in Manila in 1989 and Cape Town in 2010. These major gatherings, from Lausanne to Cape Town, framed the time span of Stott's leadership and ministry within the global church. It was in this context of working regularly and steadily alongside church leaders worldwide that his understanding and exposition of mission took shape over time.

Reflections on mission

The theology and practice of mission was close to John Stott's heart, from the earliest days following his conversion as a schoolboy to the closing days of his ninetieth year on earth. [His 1975 book *Christian Mission in the Modern World*] ... emerged in the immediate aftermath of the First Lausanne Congress on World Evangelization in 1974, in which he played such a significant role as the architect of its defining document, the Lausanne Covenant. And in the closing months of his life, when his eyesight had completely failed, he insisted that the

Cape Town Commitment, the statement of the Third Lausanne Congress in 2010, should be read to him, section by section over a period of several days. He rejoiced in it, endorsed it and was greatly encouraged by the continuing commitment of evangelicals globally to world mission as understood in all its wholeness and fullness in those great documents.

. . .

Our mission flows from the mission of God

When Stott seeks to move beyond the polarized extremes of seeing mission as either exclusively evangelism or almost wholly sociopolitical action, toward what he calls 'a better way, a more balanced and more biblical way of defining the mission of the church,' he rightly emphasizes a God-centred under-standing of what mission is. 'All of us should be able to agree,' he hopes, 'that mission arises primarily out of the nature not of the church but of God himself. The living God of the Bible is the sending God.' This, of course, is a move that is character-istic of Stott's habitual turn of thought. Whatever the problem or issue that he was seeking to address, he would ask, 'What does the Bible say?' and 'How does this connect with what we know from the biblical revelation about the character, purposes and actions of God, especially as revealed in Christ?' John Stott had a Bible-saturated, God-centered, Christ-focused world-view. Those were the spectacles he put on before settling his gaze on any issue.

. . .

All this is the essential biblical background to any under-standing of mission.

. . .

So 'the mission of God' has come to refer not merely to the God who sent and sends, but to the God who has an overarching purpose for his whole creation and is constantly 'on mission' to accomplish it. When God sent people, in the Old or New Testament, it was in relation to this ultimate, universal purpose – at whatever specific point in the history of its outworking they happened to be at that point.

. . .

Mission, then, is fundamentally the activity of God, driving this whole story forward and bringing it to its glorious conclusion. For this reason, when the Cape Town Commitment comes to define the mission to which we are committed, it begins by presenting a summary of the mission of God himself – in a paragraph full of biblical echoes.

We are committed to world mission, because it is central to our understanding of God, the Bible, the Church, human history and the ultimate future. The whole Bible reveals the mission of God to bring all things in heaven and earth into unity under Christ, reconciling them through the blood of his cross. In fulfilling his mission, God will transform the creation broken by sin and evil into the new creation in which there is no more sin or curse. God will fulfil his promise to Abraham to bless all nations on the earth, through the gospel of Jesus, the Messiah, the seed of Abraham. God will transform the fractured world of nations that are scattered under the judgment of God into the new humanity that will be redeemed by the blood of Christ from every tribe, nation, tongue and language, and will be gathered to worship our God and Saviour. God will destroy the reign of death, corruption and violence when Christ returns to establish his eternal reign of life, justice and peace. Then God, Immanuel, will dwell with us, and the kingdom of the world will become the kingdom of our Lord and of his Christ and he shall reign for ever and ever. [Genesis 1–12; Ephesians 1:9–10; Colossians 1:20; Revelation 21–22 [RSV]] (Lausanne Congress on World Evangelization, Third (2010) The Cape Town Commitment, I.10)

This has enabled a broader understanding of *our* mission, since it is wholly derived from God's mission. Once we grasp the comprehensiveness of God's great plan and purpose for all people and all creation, then there must be some analogous comprehensiveness to the way in which we are called by God to participate with him in that mission. *Not*, of course, in the sense that we do all that God does. God is God, and we (thank God) are not. We do not rule the world or save the world. As Stott puts it, 'we cannot copy him in these things. We are not saviors.' Rather, in the sense that when God calls us and sends us out to participate with God in fulfilling God's own great purpose for creation and humanity, he calls us into a very big agenda indeed. Or as Stott puts it [elsewhere]: 'The word *mission* . . . is properly a comprehensive word, embracing everything that God sends his people into the world to do.' And that 'everything' is indeed broad and inclusive, if we take account of what the whole Bible shows us concerning what God requires of his whole people in their engagement with the world around them.

. . .

The impetus for a greater awareness of the centrality of mission, not only in biblical studies but in the whole theological enterprise, gathered strength throughout the decades following Lausanne 1974 and [the publication of *Christian Mission in the Modern World*] in 1975.

Lesslie Newbigin, who returned to the United Kingdom in 1974 after a long missionary career in India and within the World Council of Churches, spoke and wrote prolifically for the next twenty years on the need for missional engagement with Western culture, and for a fully biblical, trinitarian understanding of mission itself . . . The influence of Newbigin has been immense, and many of those who are now involved in current efforts to develop a missional hermeneutic of Scripture are consciously in his debt (Newbigin, 1986, and more) . . .

That influence is seen in two outstanding contributions to the theology of mission in recent years – both of which comprehensively expound the essentially missional nature of the whole canon of Scripture, as the narrative of the mission of God, from which all human mission must be derived: Michael Goheen (2014), *Introducing Christian Mission Today*, and Scott Sunquist (2013), *Understanding Christian Mission*. Sunquist combines a strong articulation and defense of a missional hermeneutic with an equally passionate trinitarian lens through which to see the whole Bible in relation to the person and mission of God.

. . .

Evangelism and social action belong together within our exercise of biblical mission

[Stott maintained], throughout his life, that Christian mission in obedience to the Great Commission could not be confined, in definition or in practice, to the verbal proclamation of the gospel (evangelism) alone, but that mission legitimately and biblically includes the practical involvement of Christians in society in the wide variety of good works that constitute social responsibility, service and action. He insisted that both were inseparable partners in the task of Christian mission . . .

But in [*Christian Mission in the Modern World*] he characteristically argues not from experience but from the Bible. He had come to a fuller understanding of the Great Commission from all four Gospels.

> It is not just that the Commission includes a duty to teach baptized disciples everything Jesus had previously commanded (Matthew 28:20 [RSV]), and that social responsibility is among the things that Jesus commanded. I now see more clearly that not only the consequences of the Commission but the actual Commission itself must be understood to include social as well as evangelistic responsibility, unless we are to be guilty of distorting the words of Jesus.

Those two sentences are very significant and could do with a lot of unpacking, but they have not found universal agreement by any means. The question of how evangelism and social responsibility are to be related to each other continued to be a divisive issue among evangelicals, from the years immediately following Lausanne until today. For example, in their book *What Is the Mission of the Church?* Kevin DeYoung and Greg Gilbert (2011) quote John Stott in his use of the Johannine form of the commission ('As the Father has sent me, even so I send you,' John 20:21, along with John 17:18 [RSV]), but they disagree with his view that it means our mission (like Christ's) must be characterized by serving (not just evangelizing), with an 'incarnational' model of costly involvement in people's lives. In their view, the Great Commission is narrower and does not include or imply good works and social action *as part of the mission of the church* (though they do insist strongly that such practical works of love and compassion are indeed very important as part of our Christian obedience). 'The mission consists of preaching and teaching, announcing and testifying, making disciples and bearing witness. The mission focuses on the initial and continuing verbal declaration of the gospel, the announcement of Christ's death and resurrection and the life found in him when we repent and believe' (DeYoung and Gilbert 2011, p. 59).

During the 1980s, the Lausanne movement continued to debate and explore what the Lausanne Covenant had affirmed, in an effort to sustain its commitment to a holistic understanding of mission on a firm biblical and theological foundation. John Stott, as chair of Lausanne's Theology Working Group, . . . convened a landmark International Consultation on the Relationship between Evangelism and Social Responsibility, under the auspices of both Lausanne and the World Evangelical Alliance.[1] It met in Grand Rapids, Michigan, in 1982.

---

1 For the full report, see Lausanne Occasional Paper 21. In addition, one might add, Stott built up a model of gospel-centred, holistic mission in his own church, All Souls Langham Place, London, that still characterizes its ministry. Stott not only pioneered various fruitful

The lengthy report of that event speaks of three kinds of relationship ... between social action and evangelism. Social activity can be, first, a *consequence* of evangelism, and second, a *bridge* to evangelism. But the third, and most important, point of the report is the one Stott makes in [*Christian Mission in the Modern World*]. They are *partners*.

They are like the two blades of a pair of scissors or the two wings of a bird. This partnership is clearly seen in the public ministry of Jesus, who not only preached the gospel but fed the hungry and healed the sick. In his ministry, *kerygma* (proclamation) and *diakonia* (service) went hand in hand ... His words explained his works, and his works dramatized his words. Both were expressions of his compassion for people, and both should be of ours ... Indeed, so close is this link between proclaiming and serving, that they actually overlap.

This is not to say that they should be identified with each other, for evangelism is not social responsibility, nor is social responsibility evangelism. Yet, each involves the other.

To proclaim Jesus as Lord and Saviour (evangelism) has social implications, since it summons people to repent of social as well as personal sins, and to live a new life of righteousness and peace in the new society which challenges the old.

To give food to the hungry (social responsibility) has evangelistic implications, since good works of love, if done in the name of Christ, are a demonstration and commendation of the gospel ...

Thus, evangelism and social responsibility, while distinct from one another, are integrally related in our proclamation

forms of local church evangelism but also initiated ministries among the poor and the homeless, as well as stressing the importance of equipping Christian laypeople for ministry and mission in and through their daily work. Fascinating details of his systematic structuring of the whole life and work of All Souls around such a comprehensive missional agenda are recorded in *Our Guilty Silence* (Stott [1967] 1997).

of and obedience to the gospel. The partnership is, in reality, a marriage.

. . .

At the end of the decade, the Second Lausanne Congress in Manila, in 1989, made essentially the same affirmations . . . :

> The authentic gospel must become visible in the transformed lives of men and women . . .
>
> Evangelism is primary because our chief concern is with the gospel, that all people may have the opportunity to accept Jesus Christ as Lord and Saviour. Yet Jesus not only proclaimed the Kingdom of God, he also demonstrated its arrival by works of mercy and power. We are called today to a similar integration of words and deeds . . . It has been said, therefore, that evangelism, even when it does not have a primarily social intention, nevertheless has a social dimension, while social responsibility, even when it does not have a primarily evangelistic intention, nevertheless has an evangelistic dimension.
> (Lausanne Congress on World Evangelization, Second (1989), The Manila Manifesto, A.4, 'The gospel and social responsibility')

The language of 'dimension' and 'intention' is significant here, and almost certainly (since the Manila Manifesto was drafted by John Stott) reflects Stott's awareness of the origin of that distinction in a 1959 book by Lesslie Newbigin, whose writings on mission Stott admired. The distinction helps to protect us from Stephen Neill's famous (and much quoted) warning that if everything is mission, then nothing is mission. Simply put, everything the church does has a missional dimension, since the church exists for the sake of God's mission, but some things the church does have specific missional intention . . .

[Stott's] most worked-out defense of a holistic understanding of Christian mission followed . . . in 1992, in his chapter

'Holistic mission' in *The Contemporary Christian* (1992, pp. 337–355). There, he explains the context, surveys the biblical foundations for his position, answers some common objections and gives some historical examples.

By the time of the Third Lausanne Congress in Cape Town in 2010, the phrase 'holistic mission' was already being somewhat overtaken by the phrase 'integral mission' . . . So, rather than seeing the two activities (evangelism and social action) as simply partners that happen to stand or work alongside each other, this conception sees mission as an integrated system of interrelated activities – in which the proper functioning of each is essential to the functioning of the others, and to the health and 'success' of the whole enterprise.

. . .

The Micah Declaration on Integral Mission (2001) put it like this:

> Integral mission is the proclamation and demonstration of the gospel. It is not simply that evangelism and social involvement are to be done alongside each other. Rather, in integral mission our proclamation has social consequences as we call people to love and repentance in all areas of life. And our social involvement has evangelistic consequences as we bear witness to the transforming grace of Jesus Christ. If we ignore the world, we betray the Word of God which sends us out to serve the world. If we ignore the Word of God, we have nothing to bring to the world.

. . .

The Cape Town Commitment (I.10.b) integrates mission around that gospel core:

> *The integrity of our mission.* The *source* of all our mission is what God has done in Christ for the redemption of the whole world, as revealed in the Bible. Our evangelistic task is to make that good news known to all nations. The *context*

of all our mission is the world in which we live, the world of sin, suffering, injustice, and creational disorder, into which God sends us to love and serve for Christ's sake. All our mission must therefore reflect the integration of evangelism and committed engagement in the world, *both being ordered and driven by the whole biblical revelation of the gospel of God.*

That final phrase in (added) italics is crucial. It evokes the image of a wheel. The driving wheel of a car is an integrated object in which the hub (which is connected to the source of power, the engine), is integrated with the rim or tire (which is connected to the road). Every point of connection with the road (the context) has to be energized by the power transmitted from the engine through the hub (the gospel). The hub and the rim must be integrated with each other, and through their integration both are connected to, and driven by, the engine.

[Using this analogy, it seems preferable] to speak of the *centrality of the gospel* rather than the *primacy of evangelism* . . .

[The Cape Town Commitment (IID.1.e, italics added)] says, 'Let us keep evangelism at the centre of the fully integrated scope of all our mission, inasmuch as *the gospel itself is the source, content and authority of all biblically valid mission.* All we do should be both an embodiment and a declaration of the love and grace of God and his saving work through Jesus Christ.' . . .

Among those who conceive the mission of the church in this holistic or integrated way are some with outstanding qualifications in both practical missionary experience and extensive missiological reflection and teaching, both in the West and the Majority World . . . [including] Dean Flemming, Michael Goheen, Scott Sunquist, Samuel Escobar, René Padilla, Rosemary Dowsett, John Dickson, Vinay Samuel and Chris Sugden.

An interesting point that both Goheen and Sunquist make is that the effort expended in struggling to relate or integrate the two aspects of Christian mission (evangelism and social engagement) would have been unnecessary if we had not pulled them apart in the first place. The hostile dichotomy that Stott laments in [*Christian Mission in the Modern World*], as between the ecumenical emphasis on the sociopolitical realm (to the neglect of evangelism), and the evangelical emphasis on evangelism (to the neglect of social engagement – at least in the first half of the twentieth century), may owe its power and longevity to the dominance of Enlightenment dualism – in *both* camps. That is, we have imported into our thinking distinctions and rankings that do not really reflect the wholeness of the biblical worldview and teaching. We insist on taxonomies where the Bible calls for simple obedience to the totality of its mandates on the lives of God's people – or in Jesus' simpler words, 'to obey *all that I have commanded you*.' . . .

[There is another] area of integration in evangelical theology of mission that has developed since the initial publication of [*Christian Mission in the Modern World*] in 1975. That is the embracing of *creation care* as a dimension of Christian responsibility, and something that can legitimately be included in the overall category of Christian mission. There is still, of course, a wide variety of opinion on this, amounting to rejection of the whole environmental agenda in some evangelical quarters. But increasingly evangelicals are realizing that the Bible itself includes creation (here meaning specifically the earth in which we live) in the consequences of sin, in the redemptive purposes of God and in the reconciling accomplishment of the cross.

The earliest hint of awareness of the ecological dimension that I [Chris Wright] can find in the Lausanne documents is in the Manila Manifesto (1989), where, in paragraph 4 on 'The Gospel and Social Responsibility', we read that 'among the evils we deplore are . . . all forms of exploitation of people *and of the earth*' (italics added). Already, however, evangelicals were responding to the growing awareness of ecological crisis through humble but prophetically significant organizations such as the Au Sable Institute (founded in 1979) and A Rocha (founded in 1983). The Evangelical Environmental Network was founded in 1993 and later published the Evangelical Declaration on the Care of Creation (Berry 2000 [see Appendix 1 in this volume]). Indeed, since Lausanne 1974 there has been steady and increasing flow of serious evangelical and biblical writing on the issue . . . [Stott] endorsed the way the Cape Town Commitment went beyond the integration of only the two spheres of evangelism and social concern to embrace creation as well. Notice, in the following quote, how the integration is clearly done around the centrality of the gospel, focusing on the lordship of Jesus Christ – the first and crucial affirmation of the Great Commission itself.

'The earth is the Lord's and everything in it.' The earth is the property of the God we claim to love and obey. We care for the earth, most simply, because it belongs to the one whom we call Lord [Psalm 24:1; Deuteronomy 10:14 [RSV]].

The earth is created, sustained and redeemed by Christ [Colossians 1:15–20; Hebrews 1:2–3 [RSV]]. We cannot claim to love God while abusing what belongs to Christ by right of creation, redemption and inheritance. We care for the earth and responsibly use its abundant resources, not according to the rationale of the secular world, but for the Lord's sake. If Jesus is Lord of all the earth, we cannot separate our relationship to Christ from how we act in relation to the earth. For to proclaim the gospel that says 'Jesus is Lord' is to proclaim the gospel that includes the earth, since Christ's Lordship is over all creation. Creation care is thus a gospel issue within the Lordship of Christ . . .

The Bible declares God's redemptive purpose for *creation* itself. Integral mission means discerning, proclaiming, and living out, the biblical truth that the gospel is God's good news, through the cross and resurrection of Jesus Christ, for individual persons, *and* for society, *and* for creation. All three are broken and suffering because of sin; all three are included in the redeeming love and mission of

God; all three must be part of the comprehensive mission of God's people.
(Lausanne Congress on World Evangelization, Third (2010) The Cape Town Commitment, I.7.a–b)

[Since Cape Town 2010, the Lausanne Movement, in partnership with the World Evangelical Alliance, now also sponsors the Lausanne/WEA Creation Care Network, which produced the 'Jamaica call to action' (2012) after its international consultation in that year.]

Mission and ministry are for all disciples in all areas of life

My final reflection on Stott's chapter on mission picks up comments he makes in the first part of the section on practical implications. He affirms that mission and ministry are the privilege and responsibility of all believers, not only for those called into cross-cultural missionary work or ordained pastoral ministry. He argues that we need 'to gain a truer perspective in this matter of vocation,' and of ministry. All Christians are called into ministry, and for some that will mean cross-cultural missionary service or ordained pastoral ministry. But ministry – serving God and others – applies to all forms of work and service that a Christian may be engaged in, whether in an employed capacity or not. Although Stott had a very serious personal commitment to the biblical validity of ordained pastoral/teaching ministry within the church, he passionately believed that it was damagingly unbiblical to confine the concept of 'ministry' to the clergy. He affirmed that ministry and mission were the calling of all disciples of Christ – in all their varied vocations.

He was calling, though not in so many words at the time, for the eradication of that toxic sacred–secular dichotomy that has so infected Christian thinking, namely the view that God is interested in the religious area of life (church, worship, prayer, evangelism and so on), whereas the rest of life as it is lived in the 'secular' world of work and leisure is of little or no relevance to God or to the mission of the church. In place of that he wanted a return to the strong theology of work and vocation found in the Reformers and Puritans, in which every kind of honest work can be done for the service of others, for the benefit of the community *and for the glory of God and in a way that 'adorns the gospel'* – which of course is the clear teaching of the apostle Paul (Ephesians 6:5–8; Colossians 3:22–24; Titus 2:9–10 [RSV]).

Stott expanded on this theme in *The Contemporary Christian* (1992). It is worth quoting some sections at length, to sense the passion of Stott's conviction on this point . . . :

We do a great disservice to the Christian cause whenever we refer to the pastorate as 'the ministry', for by our use of the definite article we give the impression that the pastorate is the only ministry there is . . . I repented of this view, and therefore of this language, about twenty-five years ago, and now invite my readers, if necessary, to join me in penitence. Nowadays, whenever somebody says in my presence that 'So-and-so is going into the ministry,' I always ask innocently, 'Oh really? Which ministry do you mean?' And when my interlocutor probably replies, 'The pastoral ministry,' I come back with the gentle complaint, 'Then why didn't you say so?!' The fact is that the word 'ministry' is a generic term; it lacks specificity until we add an adjective . . .

It is a wonderful privilege to be a missionary or a pastor, *if God calls us to it*. But it is equally wonderful to be a Christian lawyer, industrialist, politician, manager, social worker, television script-writer, journalist, or home-maker, *if God calls us to it*. According to Romans 13:4 an official of the state (whether legislator, magistrate, policeman or policewoman) is just as much a 'minister of God' (*diakonos theou*) as a pastor . . .

> There is a crying need for Christian men and women who see their daily work as their primary Christian ministry and who determine to penetrate their secular environment for Christ.
> (Stott 1992, pp. 140–142, italics as in the original)

It was precisely this conviction about the missional import-ance of lay Christians in their everyday workplaces that led Stott to found the London Institute for Contemporary Chris-tianity, in 1982, 'with the core belief that every part of our lives comes under the Lordship of Christ, and that all of life is a context for worship, mission, ministry and active Chris-tian engagement' (from London Institute for Contemporary Christianity) . . .

> The Bible shows us God's truth about human work as part of God's good purpose in creation. The Bible brings the whole of our working lives within the sphere of ministry, as we serve God in different callings. By contrast, the falsehood of a 'sacred–secular divide' has permeated the Church's think-ing and action. This divide tells us that religious activity belongs to God, whereas other activity does not. Most Chris-tians spend most of their time in work which they may think has little spiritual value (so-called secular work). But God is Lord of *all* of life. 'Whatever you do, work at it with all your heart, as working for the Lord, not for men,' said Paul, to slaves in the pagan workplace [Colossians 3:23 [RSV].
> (Lausanne Congress on World Evangelization, Third
> (2010) The Cape Town Commitment, IIA.3)

I have no doubt that John Stott endorsed the robust missional theology and practical relevance of this paragraph, and would have seen it as entirely in line with, and the fruition of, the insights and summons he put forward in his book in 1975. (Wright, in Stott [1975] 2016 (updated and expanded by Wright), pp. 34–57)

5

Doctrine and relevance

Lifestyle, double listening
and creation's goodness

The meetings at Berlin, Keele, Uppsala and Lausanne were significant steps in Stott's personal pilgrimage. He was also a key figure in
the second National Evangelical Anglican Congress (at Nottingham
in 1977) and this further influenced his subsequent thought. Keele
provoked a move from the pietism and ghetto mentality of older
evangelicals. At Nottingham, the issue of hermeneutics challenged
evangelicals to examine their preconceptions when interpreting
the Bible, discomforting some traditional expositors, even though the
challenge was to interpretation and not in any way to scriptural
authority. The organizers had learnt their lesson from Keele, and
three volumes of essays under the overall title of *Obeying Christ in
a Changing World* (Stott 1977a) and general editorship of Stott were
issued before the meeting. One of the essays dealt with the environment, but it was really on lifestyle. It was called 'Global stewardship'.
Nevertheless, the lasting message of Nottingham was about hermeneutics. After the meeting, Stott wrote in his diary:

> It is increasingly clear to me that hermeneutics is Issue No.1 in
> the church today, and not least to evangelical Christians. Our
> differences are largely due to different ways of reading and
> understanding Scripture.
> (Stott quoted by Chapman 2012, p. 105)

These differences still persist over many issues. The long-standing
tradition of the sufficiency of 'appealing to the plain teaching of

Scripture' and claiming the key to exegesis is establishing the original intention of the biblical writer continues to divide evangelicals (see, for example, Wright 2009). It could explain the failure of many evangelicals to accept the discipline and consequences of 'double listening'; it could explain why the interpretation of the early chapters of Genesis still confuses many evangelicals (Halton 2015; Walton 2015) and leads them to disregard the doctrine of creation (Ruse 2001; Berry 2013).

The triad of Berlin, Keele, and Uppsala marked a reorientation of Stott's thought. They certainly propelled Stott to develop his advocacy of the importance of 'double listening', which he expounded at length in his book *The Contemporary Christian* (1992). They increased for him the importance of expert advice and criticism. The reaction of Norman Anderson to the discussions at Keele has already been noted. Anderson was a good friend of Stott's and a member of his All Souls congregation. Another friend and All Souls member was Oliver Barclay, who had been at Cambridge with Stott, and, by the time of Keele, was General Secretary of the University and Colleges Christian Fellowship. In 1972, Barclay published another plea for involvement with the 'world', titled *Whose World?* (written under the pseudonym 'A. N. Triton', lest his ideas were thought to be UCCF policy). Barclay took his stand firmly on the idea of God as creator. He wrote:

> We have tended to neglect some aspects of the Old Testament . . . for example that God is sovereign Creator and Upholder of His world . . . Evangelical Christians have often been a little unsure of themselves. Their grand and entirely biblical stress has been on the gospel of the grace of God in the death of Christ. This is the main theme of the New Testament. But . . . if we follow the apostles, [we must] make the doctrines of creation and providence the first stage in our argument. A failure to do this is responsible in large measure for an un-biblically negative attitude to what God has given us in nature and in society.
> (Triton 1970, pp. 10 and 13)

These are words that anticipate and perhaps encouraged Stott's assertion, reiterated in later years, that evangelicals tend to have a much stronger doctrine of redemption than creation.

Stott's gathering concern for creation care was also expressed in his support for Christian lifestyles to be characterized by simplicity. The Lausanne Covenant (paragraph 9) named the connection between poverty and injustice, and noted that '[t]hose of us who live in affluent circumstances accept our duty to develop a simple lifestyle in order to contribute generously to both relief and evangelism'. Stott went on to co-convene (with Ron Sider) an International Consultation on Simple Lifestyle. The five-day gathering was held outside London in March 1980, bringing together eighty-five evangelical leaders from twenty-seven countries (Sider 1982), and produced the 'An evangelical commitment to simple lifestyle', a document that Stott chose to include in its original entirety in his final book *The Radical Disciple* (2010b, pp. 64–82). An expanded version with substantial commentary is available as Lausanne Occasional Paper 20 (1980).

In describing the background to this work, Sider noted that as:

John R. W. Stott (one of the key framers of the Lausanne Covenant) travelled throughout the world after that 1974 congress, he was asked by Third-World Christians if Western Christians really meant the statement on simple lifestyle in the Lausanne Covenant. So John Stott proposed an International Consultation on Simple Lifestyle. Subsequent discussion between Stott's Lausanne Theology and Education Group [which Stott chaired] and the Unit on Ethics and Society (of which I serve as convenor) of the Theological Commission of the World Evangelical Fellowship led to a decision to have these two groups cosponsor [the International Consultation in 1980. The London Consultation was preceded by] scores of local study groups around the world . . . [and] a preparatory U.S. Consultation in 1979.
(Sider 1980, p. 15)

These included theological reflections from Old and New Testaments; a substantial number of concrete guidelines and models that recount participants' pilgrimages in family, church and professional arenas; and insights from William E. Pannell on how the African-American community and others who have long experienced the limitations and demands of basic standards of living may interpret the new calls for simpler lifestyles.

The first two sections of the 1980 'An evangelical commitment to simple lifestyle' are on creation and stewardship:

1 Creation

We worship God as the Creator of all things, and we celebrate the goodness of his creation. In his generosity he has given us everything to enjoy, and we receive it from his hands with humble thanksgiving (1 Timothy 4:4; 6:17). God's creation is marked by rich abundance and diversity, and he intends its resources to be husbanded and shared for the benefit of all.

We therefore denounce environmental destruction, wastefulness and hoarding. We deplore the misery of the poor who suffer as a result of these evils. We also disagree with the drabness of the ascetic. For all these deny the Creator's goodness and reflect the tragedy of the fall. We recognise our own involvement in them, and we repent.

2 Stewardship

When God made man, male and female, in his own image, he gave them dominion over the earth (Genesis 1:26–28). He made them stewards of its resources, and they became responsible to him as Creator, to the earth which they were to develop, and to their fellow human beings with whom they were to share its riches. So fundamental are these truths that authentic human fulfilment depends on a right relationship to God, neighbour and the earth with all its resources. People's humanity is diminished if they have no just share in those resources.

By unfaithful stewardship, in which we fail to conserve the earth's finite resources, to develop them fully, or to distribute them justly, we both disobey God and alienate people from his purpose for them. We are determined, therefore, to honour God as the owner of all things, to remember that we are stewards and not proprietors of any land or property that we may have, to use them in the service of others, and to seek justice with the poor who are exploited and powerless to defend themselves.

We look forward to the restoration of all things at Christ's return (Acts 3:21). At that time our full humanness will be restored, so we must promote human dignity today.
(Stott 2010b, pp. 69–71)

Subsequent sections of the Commitment discuss poverty and wealth, generosity and sharing among believers, and a section on personal lifestyle that includes this note on a life of obedient, faithfulness integrity echoed throughout *The Radical Disciple*: 'Our Christian obedience demands a simple lifestyle, irrespective of the needs of others. Nevertheless, the facts that 800 million people are destitute and that 10,000 die of starvation every day make any other lifestyle indefensible' (Stott 2010b, pp. 75–76).

The section on evangelism conveys the Lausanne Covenant's connection between proclaiming and living Christ's good news, and linking the broader work of the church to everyday, personal commitments:

We are deeply concerned for the vast millions of unevangelized people in the world. Nothing that has been said about lifestyle or justice diminishes the urgency of developing evangelistic strategies appropriate to different cultural environments. We must not cease to proclaim Christ as Saviour and Lord throughout the world. The church is not yet taking seriously its commission to be his witnesses 'to the ends of the earth' (Acts 1:8).

So the call to a responsible lifestyle must not be divorced from the call to responsible witness. For the credibility of our message is seriously diminished whenever we contradict it by our lives. It is impossible with integrity to proclaim Christ's salvation if he has evidently not saved us from greed, or his lordship if we are not good stewards of our possessions, or his love if we close our hearts against the needy. When Christians care for each other and for the deprived, Jesus Christ becomes more visibly attractive.

In contrast to this, the affluent lifestyle of some Western evangelists when they visit the Third World is understandably offensive to many.

We believe that simple living by Christians generally would release considerable resources of finance and personnel for evangelism as well as development. So by our commitment to a simple lifestyle we recommit ourselves wholeheartedly to world evangelization.

(Stott 2010b, pp. 80–81)

It was probably around this time that Stott realized more clearly than ever that Christian understanding and acceptance were commonly rejected because of their perceived irrelevance rather than conscious disbelief. A conversation he had with two young men obviously made a deep impression on him. He referred to it on a number of occasions and spelt it out in *I Believe in Preaching*:

I was talking with two students who were brothers, one at Oxford University and the other at Edinburgh. They had been brought up in a traditional Christian home, both their parents being practising Christians. But now they had renounced their parents' faith and their Christian upbringing. One was a complete atheist, he told me; the other preferred to call himself an agnostic. 'What had happened,' I asked? 'Was it that they no longer believed Christianity to be true?' 'No', they replied, 'that's not our problem. We're not really interested to know whether Christianity is true. And if you were able to convince us that it is, we're not at all sure we would embrace it.' 'What is your problem, then?' I asked with some astonishment. 'What we want to know', they went on, 'is not whether Christianity is *true*, but whether it is *relevant*. And frankly we don't see how it can be. Christianity was born two millennia ago in a first-century Palestinian culture. What can an ancient religion of the Middle East say to us who live in the exciting, kaleidoscopic world of the end of the twentieth century? We have men on the moon in the seventies, and shall have men on Mars in the eighties, transplant surgery today and genetic engineering tomorrow. What possible relevance can a primitive Palestinian religion have for us?' I have often thanked God for that conversation. Nothing has brought home to me more forcefully the gulf which people perceive between the Bible and themselves, and so the challenge which confronts Christian preachers today.

(Stott 1982, pp. 138–139)

These experiences came together to impress on Stott the need to insist on 'double listening'. He wrote, 'it is comparatively easy to be faithful if we do not care about being contemporary, and easy also to be contemporary if we do not bother to be faithful. It is the search for a combination of truth and relevance that is exacting' (Stott [1975] 2016 (updated and expanded by Wright), p. 64). Stott developed his ideas on double listening in *The Contemporary Christian*:

The main reason for every betrayal of the authentic Jesus is that we listen with exaggerated deference to contemporary fashion, instead of listening to God's Word. The demand for relevance becomes so imperious that we feel we have to capitulate to it, at whatever cost. We are familiar with this kind of pressure in the business world, in which it is the marketing people who determine the firm's product by discovering what will sell, what the public will buy. It sometimes seems as if market forces rule in the church as well. We become obsequious to the modern mood, slaves to the latest fad, even idolaters who are prepared to sacrifice truth on the altar of modernity. Then the quest for relevance has degenerated into a lust for popularity.

For the opposite extreme to irrelevance is accommodation, which is a feeble-minded, unprincipled surrender to the *Zeitgeist*, the spirit of the time . . . The people of God live in a world which is often unfriendly and sometimes actively hostile. We are constantly exposed to the pressure to conform. Yet throughout Scripture the summons is given to a vigorous nonconformity, and warnings are sounded to those who give in to worldliness. In the Old Testament the Lord said to his people after the exodus: 'You must not do as they do in Egypt, where you used to live, and you must not do as they do in the land of Canaan, where I am bringing you. Do not follow their practices. You must obey my laws . . .' (Leviticus 18:3–4a, [NIV 2011]). Yet the people said to Samuel: 'Now appoint a king to lead us, such as all the other nations have' (1 Samuel 8:5). And later Ezekiel had to rebuke them for their idolatry: 'You say, "We want to be like the nations, like the peoples of the world, who serve wood and stone"' (Ezekiel 20:32). It was similar in New Testament days. In spite of the clear commands of Jesus, 'Do not be like them' (Matthew 6:8), and of Paul, 'Do not conform . . . to the pattern of this world' (Romans 12:2), the constant tendency of God's people was, and still is, to behave 'like the heathen' (1 Thessalonians 4:5; cf. 1 Corinthians 5:1; Ephesians 4:17), until nothing much seems to distinguish the church from the world, the Christian from the non-Christian, in convictions, values or standards.

Thank God, however, that there have always been some noble souls who have stood firm, sometimes alone, and refused to compromise. I think of Jeremiah in the sixth century BC, and Paul in his day ('everyone . . . has deserted me' (2 Timothy 1:15; cf. 4:11, 16)), Athanasius in the fourth century and Luther in the sixteenth. C. S. Lewis wrote his tribute to Athanasius, who maintained the deity of Jesus and the doctrine of the Trinity, when the whole church was determined to follow the heretic Arius: 'It is his glory that he did *not* move with the times; it is his reward that he now remains when those times, as all times do, have moved away' (Lewis 1953, p. 9).

So today, we are resolved to struggle to present the gospel in such a way as to speak to modern dilemmas, fears and frustrations, but we are equally determined not to compromise the biblical gospel in order to do so. Some stumbling-blocks are intrinsic to the original gospel and cannot be eliminated, or even soft-pedalled, in order to render it more palatable to contemporary taste. The gospel contains some features so alien to modern thought that it will always appear 'folly' to intellectuals, however hard we strive (and rightly) to show that it is 'true and reasonable' (Acts 26:25). The cross will always constitute an assault on human self-righteousness and a challenge to human self-indulgence. Its 'scandal' (stumbling-block) simply cannot be removed. Indeed, the church speaks most authentically to the world not when it makes its shameful little prudential compromises, but when it refuses to do so; not when it has become indistinguishable from the world, but when its distinctive light shines most brightly.

Thus Christian people, who live under the authority of God's revelation, however anxious they are to communicate it to others, manifest a sturdy independence of mind and spirit. This is not obstinacy, for we are willing to listen to everybody. But we are determined to be faithful, and if necessary to suffer for it. God's word to Ezekiel is an encouragement to us: 'Do not be afraid of them ... You must speak my words to them, whether they listen or fail to listen, for they are rebellious' (Ezekiel 2:6–7 [NIV 2011]). So we have to apply the Word, but not manipulate it. We must do our utmost to ensure that it speaks to our time, but not bowdlerize it in order to secure a fake relevance. Our calling is to be faithful and relevant, not merely trendy.

How, then, can we be both conservative and radical simultaneously, conservative in guarding God's revelation and radical in our thoroughgoing application of it? How can we develop a Christian mind which is both shaped by the truths of historic, biblical Christianity, and acquainted with the realities of the contemporary world? How can we relate the Word to the world, understanding the world in the light of the Word, and even understanding the Word in the light of the world? We have to begin with a double refusal. We refuse to become either so absorbed in the Word, that we *escape* into it and fail to let it confront the world, or so absorbed in the world, that we *conform* to it and fail to subject it to the judgment of the Word. Escapism and conformity are opposite mistakes, but neither is a Christian option.

In place of this double refusal we are called to double listening, listening both to the Word and to the world. It is a truism to say that we have to listen to the Word of God, except perhaps that we need to listen to him more expectantly and humbly, ready for him to confront us with a disturbing, uninvited word. It is less welcome to be told that we must also listen to the world. For the voices of our contemporaries may take the form of shrill and strident protest. They are now querulous, now appealing, now aggressive in tone. There are also the anguished cries of those who are suffering, and the pain, doubt, anger, alienation and even despair of those who are estranged from God. I am not suggesting that we should listen to God and to our fellow human beings in the same way or with the same degree of deference. We listen to the Word with humble reverence, anxious to understand it, and resolved to believe and obey what we come to understand. We listen to the world with critical alertness, anxious to understand it too, and resolved not necessarily to believe and obey it, but to sympathize with it and to seek grace to discover how the gospel relates to it.

Everybody finds listening difficult. But are Christians for some reason (perhaps because we believe ourselves called to speak what God has spoken) worse listeners than others? Our symbol is rather the tongue than the ear. Yet we should have learned a lesson from Job's garrulous comforters. They began well ... [But] they did not really listen to what Job had to say. They merely repeated their own thoughtless and heartless claptrap, until in the end God rebuked them for not having spoken about him what was right ...

These voices will often contradict each other, but our purpose in listening to them both is to discover how they relate to each other. Double listening is indispensable to Christian discipleship and Christian mission.

It is only through the discipline of double listening that it is possible to become a 'contemporary Christian'. For then we see that the adjectives 'historical' and 'contemporary' are not incompatible, we learn to apply the Word to the world, and we proclaim good news which is both true and new. In sum, we live in the 'now' in the light of the 'then'.
(Stott 1992, pp. 24–29)

Double listening was not, of course, Stott's invention or exclusive practice. John Newton wrote, 'I read the newspapers that I may see how my Heavenly Father governs the world'. Charles Spurgeon scoured the newspapers daily to find relevant themes for his preaching. Karl Barth urged, 'Take your Bible and your newspaper, and read both, but interpret newspapers from your Bible.' Rowan Williams advised that his successor as Archbishop of Canterbury needed to preach with a Bible in one hand and a newspaper in the other. A distinguishing characteristic of Stott's practice was the rigour with which he approached the challenge of biblical interpretation and secular understanding. He developed this in many areas. His book *Issues Facing Christians Today* (2006), which he regarded as a companion volume to *The Contemporary Christian* (1992), is really a working-out of double listening. It was an answer to one of the resolutions of the Keele Conference, that 'we have not thought sufficiently deeply or radically about the problems of our society' and that we must do better.

In *Issues Facing Christians Today*, Stott deals with twelve major issues that he saw as facing Christians in three groups: global, social and sexual. He was well aware of his own limitations, especially his lack of understanding of modernity. His practice, therefore, was to gather a group of a dozen or so young graduates and professional people to debate and to inform him. In all the twelve areas, Stott made significant analyses and proposals, but as Alister Chapman says in his examination of Stott's ministry and lasting influence:

There was one issue where Stott took a lead, namely ecology. Stott's love of birds was old and deep ... Environmental concern was more a conservative than a progressive preoccupation in England during the mid-twentieth century, so it is not a surprise that this was one of [his father] Arnold Stott's gifts to his son ... In 'Our human environment', the chapter on the subject in *Issues Facing Christians Today*, Stott called his readers to 'think and act ecologically'. He argued that 'the root of the ecological crisis is human greed,' and in words that sounded like a prayer, he wrote: 'We repent of extravagance, pollution and wanton destruction. We recognize that man finds it easier to subdue the earth than he does to subdue himself' (Stott 2006, pp. 119–120) ... Stott's advocacy of environmental concern long before it became fashionable stands out as his most important contribution to evangelical ethics. (Chapman 2012, pp. 125–126)

Stott's approach to ecology is encapsulated in a harvest thanksgiving sermon that he preached at All Souls on 25 September 1988, based on the goodness of creation as set out in 1 Timothy 4:1–5. He begins with one of his often-repeated themes, that Christians have a much stronger doctrine of redemption than of creation, and how often we misdirect our understanding and worship. He then puts Paul's words in the context of creation, calling, as so often, on Psalms 103 and 104.

I wonder if you would agree with me that many of us Christians – many, particularly, those who call ourselves or are called by others evangelical Christians – tend to have a good doctrine of redemption and a bad doctrine of creation. I think that is true. You can tell it in our prayers. For many of us, ours is a Jesus religion. We are so preoccupied with the second person of the Trinity, maybe with the third person as well because he glorifies Jesus, but there is little room in our prayers for God the Father, almighty maker of heaven and earth. No wonder Tom Smail (2001) found it necessary a few years ago to write that well-known book, *The Forgotten Father*.

You can also see it in our hymns. Except at harvest thanksgiving, our hymns are normally Jesus hymns. 'How sweet the name of Jesus sounds in a believer's ear', 'Jesus calls us', 'Jesus, thou joy of loving hearts', *et cetera*. And seldom, by comparison, do we celebrate the love, the power, and the wisdom of our creator God.

I remember many years ago, while I was still, I think, a theological student, that I was introduced to a very fascinating book by a man called Bernard Manning (1942), called *The Hymns of Wesley and Watts*, that is Charles Wesley and Isaac Watts. Both those men, I'm sure all of you know, were very great evangelical hymn writers at the beginning of the 18th century and both of them sang the praises of Jesus, with this interesting difference: now Charles Wesley focused exclusively on the redeemer, almost exclusively, for example, 'And can it be that I should gain an interest in the Saviour's blood.' Or again, 'Jesus lover of my soul let me to thy bosom fly.' Or again, 'Oh for a thousand tongues to sing thy great redeemer's praise.' It's all about the redeemer.

Now Isaac Watts also sang the praises of the redeemer, but always set his redemption in the wider context of creation. So he is the one who composed 'I praise my maker while I've breath,' and 'Oh God, our help in ages past.' And even when he's celebrating the redemption of Jesus Christ, he does not forget the cosmic context of the redemption.

Let me give you two examples. I wonder if you have ever noticed these. We sing 'Jesus shall reign where'er the sun,' and so on. And you know its last verse: 'Let all creation join in singing his praises.' Well, take that greatest of all hymns, 'When I survey the wondrous cross upon which the prince of glory died.' You know the last verse? 'Were the whole realm of nature mine, that were an offering far too small.'

Do you think about that sometimes while you're singing hymns, how many of our hymns are Jesus hymns, forgetting the cosmic context of the creation of the universe? Well, I want to plead today for a more biblical perspective, so that when we come to worship God, we worship him both as our creator and as our redeemer.

The Bible is very clear about it. Have you ever thought of Psalm 103 and 104 as a neat couple? Both begin 'Bless the lord, O my soul.' But Psalm 103 goes on: 'forget not his benefits, who forgives all your sins, heals all your diseases, *et cetera.*' [He is] the God of salvation. Psalm 104 begins with the same words – 'Bless the lord, O my soul' – but it goes on 'O Lord, O my God, you are very great. You cover yourself with light as with a garment.' Psalm 103 is about the God of redemption; Psalm 104 is the God of creation.

And you have the same balance in Revelation 4 and 5. When in Revelation 4, the whole company of heaven sing, 'You are worthy, O Lord God, to receive honour and glory and majesty, because you have created all things, and by your will all things were created.' But in Revelation 5, the heavenly company change their tune, and sing a different hymn. They sing, 'Worthy is the lamb who is slain to receive honour and glory and might and majesty and dominion, for by your blood you have ransomed man for God.' So, you see, if the songs of the heavenly host focus both upon the creator *and* upon the redeemer, we need to get used to it on earth. If we're going to have to sing praises to the creator/redeemer in heaven, I think we need to do it more often on earth.

My text is 1 Timothy 4:1–5, but particularly verse 5:

Now, the spirit expressly says that in later times some will abandon the faith, apostatize, by giving heed to deceitful spirits and doctrines of demons through the pretensions of liars who are false teachers, whose consciences are seared, forbid marriage and enjoin abstinence from foods, which God created to be received with thanksgiving by those who believe and know the truth. Everything created by God is good, and nothing is to be rejected if it is received with thanksgiving. Then it is consecrated by the word of God and by prayer.

Now these false teachers [described by Paul] were manifesting what we usually call Gnostic tendencies. Under the influence of a false Greek dualism, they despise the material creation. They were embarrassed by the human body. They regarded their body as an encumbrance, and the sooner they could get rid of it the better. They regarded their body as a kind of tomb in which the soul had become imprisoned. They were embarrassed by the body's two major appetites, namely sex on the one hand, and hunger and thirst on the other. They even declared that matter and the material were evil, and all they could dream of was escape from the material order.

Gnosticism has never been completely eradicated from the Christian church. There are many Christians, and I don't doubt there are some here this morning, who, even if they have never heard of Gnosticism, are actually semi-Gnostics, because they despise the material order which God has created. They are ascetics. They are world-denying instead of world-affirming. They pride themselves on their super-spirituality. They want to escape from the material into the spiritual. They never learned what the Archbishop William Temple said, that Christianity is the most material religion in the world. He was thinking about creation, and about the resurrection of the body, and about the new universe, and about water, and bread, and wine. There is a great deal of the material in Christianity, but many of us have forgotten that. We're looking forward to heaven, and the more immaterial, the more ethereal heaven is, the better. And we forget that God is not going to give us a heaven; He's going to create a new heaven and a new earth. We are going to have new bodies. We are going to live in a resurrection body in a resurrection universe. And this is because God has created the material order, and he's going to recreate it and redeem it.

I'm afraid some of us deserve the scorn of Ibsen, [who] in his play about the Emperor Julian, said, 'Have you looked at these Christians closely? Hollow-eyed? Pale-cheeked? Flat-breasted all? They brood their lives away, unspurred by ambition. The sun shines for them but they do not see it. The earth offers them its fullness, but they desire it not. All they desire is to renounce and to suffer, so that, as soon as possible, they may come to die.'

Well, in the light of that, I bring you my text: 'Everything created by God is good, and nothing is to be rejected if it is received with thanksgiving.' I think that's a marvellous verse. It's a marvellous everything/nothing verse. *Everything* created by God is good, *nothing* is to be rejected. And I think if we get hold of this verse, it is calculated to liberate us from all negative, narrow understandings of creation, because it declares that the whole world is God's, and one day he is going to make it again, free from everything that has come to contaminate it through the Fall, I'll come to that in a moment.

Well here is the first thing we need to focus on – that word 'everything'. Everything. We need a broader understanding of creation. Paul of course is referring to Genesis 1 and to its refrain after each stage of creation, behold, it was good, it was good, it was good, until finally it was very good. Everything created by God is good. But what is involved in the good creation? When you hear that phrase, what do you think about? What is this creation that is good?

Most of us of course will think of the harvest, the material order, the galaxies, of space, our own solar system in the Milky Way, the planet Earth that God prepared as a habitation for human beings created in his own image, and all the amazing creatures that inhabit the earth, the sky, and the seas. The biblical authors are fascinated by the variety, the colours, the shapes, the skills, the habits of the material creation. The biblical authors invite us to study the creation. Psalm 111 verse 2: 'Great are the works of the LORD, studied by those who take pleasure in them.' We ought to take pleasure in the things God has made. And you know they tell us to enjoy the creation: 'Oh Lord, how manifold are your works, in wisdom you have made them all.'

And they even tell us that we may make pets of the creatures that God has made. You know, in Psalm 104, we read about Leviathan, that great sea monster. And some English versions say that God has made it to play *there* in the sea. But other English versions believe that the right translation is that God has made it to play *with*. Leviathan is the divine pet. God plays with his creatures. If you see dolphins playing, you'll have no doubt about it any longer. God intends us to enjoy his creation which he has made. I believe every Christian ought to be interested in the world God has made, and in some branch of natural history, though I forbear to make any suggestions as to which . . .

Now I want to move on from the material order as part of the creation to our own humanness. Do we thank God that he has created us in his own image, [as] human beings, our rationality so that we can think God's thoughts after him, and our moral sense that we distinguish between right and wrong, and our social life, that he has made us male and female, and that we can create communities of love and peace and justice and freedom? Because all that is part of the created order.

And then there is our sexuality, because sex is God's creation, and marriage is God's institution, and sex in the Bible is celebrated, within the context of the commitment of marriage, in a most uninhibited way. It's part of the creation, for which we are to be grateful. Then there is the joy of family and friends.

And another part of creation is our stewardship of the good earth. The primeval command was to fill the earth and subdue it. And to fill it doesn't only mean to populate it, but to decorate it: to fill it with architecture and art and music and all the other things with which human beings have filled the earth. And subdue it: developing its resources for the common good. The whole scientific and artistic enterprise is a fulfilment of God's purpose in Genesis 1, and it's part of the creation.

Then there is our capacity for worship. God has created us [as] worshipping beings. Henri Blocher, in his great exposition of the first three chapters of Genesis called *In the Beginning*, I believe rightly says that the climax of the created purpose of God is not work, but worship. It's not that Adam was put in the garden to till the soil and to beautify the garden and so on. It is that, on one day in seven, he is to lay aside his toil in order to rest and worship. The climax of God's creation of human beings is what we're doing this morning, that we've laid aside our work in order to come to worship. That too is part of the creation.

Let us determine, then, to live according to Scripture, to be more positive towards the created world and not so negative, to be world-affirming and not world-denying, to accept the good things that God has given us and rejoice in them. And if we don't, Paul says here, we've denied the faith. We've given heed to the doctrines of demons. Everything God has created is good.

Now . . . a qualification, in case you are following me carefully and this has come into your mind. When Paul castigates those who forbid marriage, he has not forgotten what he has written previously in 1 Corinthians 7, that he calls some people to remain single. And when Paul castigates those who forbid certain foods, he has not forgotten, and is not contradicting, what Jesus said in the Sermon on the Mount about the proper place of fasting. So even when he is telling us, as he does in chapter 6 of 1 Timothy, that we are to enjoy the good things that God has given us with such liberality, we need to balance that by saying that out of solidarity with the world's poor, we may feel it right to simplify our lifestyle and not enjoy everything that God has given, but to renounce some of the things that we could have enjoyed in order to share with those who are less fortunate than ourselves. The point is that, if we do renounce marriage or foods or possessions, it is not because they are evil. They are part of the good creation. They ought to be rejoiced in, as part of the good creation, and the only right reason for renouncing them is because of a particular calling of God and the rationale of such renunciation is not asceticism, as if they were evil, but sacrifice, the surrender of what is good in itself.

Now, we have been focusing on that word everything, but now secondly I want to ask you to notice that it is everything *created by God* that is good. Paul does not say that everything in the world is good. It isn't all good, because after the creation came the fall, and the creation has been tarnished, and the creation has been twisted, and therefore not everything in the world around us by any means is good. Indeed, as Paul writes elsewhere, the whole creation groans in pain longing for its redemption.

. . . So we cannot appeal to the creation in order to justify all the disorders of our human being. Are we prepared to justify our bad temper and our covetousness and our malice and our irritability because we say, 'Well, that's my temperament, God made me that way?' No, no, no. God did not make us that way. That is the twist of the Fall, and these things within us are due to the Fall, and they are not due to the creation. They are symptoms of the Fall. They are signs of disorder, and not of order, and they don't belong to the category of 1 Timothy 4: 'Everything created by God.' It isn't created by God, these things. They ought to be rejected because they are incompatible with the created order.

So far then, firstly, we have concentrated on the word 'everything', then second we concentrated on 'everything created by God is good.' We have to exercise discernment as what is created by God and what isn't – what is due to the creation and what is due to the Fall.

And then thirdly, just before I finish: everything created by God is *good*, nothing is to be rejected *if it be received with thanksgiving*. Thanksgiving is a prominent ingredient in the religion of the Bible. There were those three annual harvest festivals in Jewish national life. They weren't content with one a year, they had three a year: at the beginning of the grain harvest, at the end of the grain harvest, and at the end of the fruit harvest, when the produce of olive yard and vineyard had been gathered in. But it wasn't only annually that they gave thanks. They also had, as we have, a weekly remembrance in worship of God, our Creator.

And then there is daily thanksgiving. Do you thank God first thing in the morning when you wake? For the safety of the night, and that he's given back to you your powers of mind and body? Do you sit on your bed as you breathe deeply, and enter into the world of reality out of the world of fantasy? Do you thank God that he has given you back all the powers that he has created and given to you, and thank him for your life and your breath and all things? And do you say grace before meals? To me it is one of the great tragedies that this habit has been discontinued by so many Christians who ought to know better. Jesus gave thanks. When I think of that next week, He took the bread and he gave thanks for it.

Don't be like the pigeons. Do you know anything about pigeons? You know, don't you, that there are twenty-six Orders of bird in the world, and, of those twenty-six Orders, all of them but one drink by gravity feed. That is why they have in Ghana a proverb that says, 'Even the chicken, when it drinks, lifts its head to heaven to thank God for the water,' while the water trickles down by gravity. Only the pigeons feed by suction. You look at them the next time you're in Trafalgar Square: they put their beak into the puddle and suck; and they never lift their head to heaven to thank God for the water. Don't be like the pagan pigeons, and lift your head to heaven, and thank God for food and breath and everything else. Thank Him for his creation gifts, for the joys of marriage, sex, family, friends, and children; the daily work, and for laying it aside on the Lord's day; the peace, freedom, and justice in the community and for good government; for food, drink, clothing, and shelter; for music, literature, painting, and sport; for birds, beasts, flowers, butterflies, the glories of the creation. Everything created by God is good, nothing is to be rejected if it be received with thanksgiving. We need to be much more thankful.

I give the last word to G. K. Chesterton. He once said, 'You say grace before meals, alright, but I say grace before the play and the opera, and grace before the concert and the pantomime, and grace before I open a book, and grace before sketching, painting, swimming, walking, playing, dancing, and grace before I dip the pen in the ink.' God give us grace to say grace more often.

(Stott 1988b)

6
Clergy-naturalists and learning from birds

Where did Stott get his environmental expertise? He was a passionate birdwatcher, but simply ticking birds off on a list does not necessarily mean that a person has a wide knowledge about them. Was Stott really unusual in his interest and concern for the environment? In one sense he could be regarded as following a strong tradition, particularly in the UK, for clergy to study the natural world.

The best-known example of this must be the Reverend Gilbert White (1720–1793), for many years curate of the Parish of Selborne in Hampshire. His 1789 book the *Natural History and Antiquities of Selborne* has never been out of print and was said to be the fourth most-published book in the English language (after the Bible, the works of Shakespeare and *Pilgrim's Progress*). In fact, White regarded another clergyman, John Ray (1627–1705), as his mentor, both scientifically and theologically. Ray's *Wisdom of God Manifested in the Works of Creation*, based on addresses given in the Chapel of Trinity College, Cambridge (the College attended three centuries later by Stott), was published in 1691. According to historian Peter Harrison (1998, pp. 1–2), Ray powerfully influenced the discipline of biblical interpretation in post Reformation times by insisting that the study of the natural world should be based on observation rather than using it as little more than an allegory for the human condition, as in mediaeval times.

Ray and White may be seen as setting a pattern for a host of 'parson-naturalists', some of whom made significant contributions to theology or science, sometimes both (Armstrong 2000). In the nineteenth century William Buckland (1784–1856) moved from being Professor of Geology at Oxford University to becoming Dean of Westminster Abbey. Charles Kingsley (1819–1875), author of *The Water Babies*, was Rector of the Parish of Eversley in Hampshire for sixteen years before becoming Regius Professor of Modern History at Cambridge. Robert Rawnsley (1851–1920), Rector of Crosthwaite, was one of the founders of the National Trust, and was said to be a 'whole environment' man. More recently, the Reverend William Keble Martin (1877–1969) served in two Devonshire parishes for thirty years and wrote and illustrated with 1,400 paintings a *Concise British Flora* (1965), which was a bestseller. Edward Armstrong (1900–1978) was vicar of a Cambridge parish for nearly a quarter of a century. He was an international authority on bird behaviour and of wrens, and also authored three books of theology. Charles Raven (1885–1964) was Professor of Divinity at Cambridge and wrote three books on birdwatching; he wrote that his passion for birdwatching arose because he could see in birds 'Jesus in nature'. The Reverend Peter Harris (a keen bird-ringer – or 'bander') established a mission station in southern Portugal that gave rise to the charity A Rocha ('Christians in Conservation'), now working in twenty countries. Another devoted ringer, Dave Bookless, moved from the incumbency of a multicultural parish in west London to set up the UK centre of A Rocha.

Probably most 'clergy-naturalists' do not fully link their theology with their study of nature. Some are almost professional biologists, with their Christian ministry kept in a separate part of their lives. For others, nature study is a hobby, which they may justify to themselves because they are studying the work of God in creation.

How, then, should we regard John Stott? He was an Anglican clergyman par excellence, incumbent of an important London parish for twenty-five years (and, subsequently, Rector Emeritus), DD, CBE, Extra-Chaplain to Her Majesty the Queen – faithful churchman, pastor, counsellor, scholarly Bible expositor, evangelist, skilled communicator in both person and prose. He had a global influence and was respected around the world as a church leader. He wrote more than fifty books, many with a very wide circulation.

On top of all this, he can certainly be called a clergy-naturalist, albeit a clergy-naturalist extraordinaire. The clearest expression of this was his authorship of a beautifully illustrated book *The Birds Our Teachers* ([1999] 2007), subtitled *Essays in orni-theology*. It was an instant success when it appeared. In it, Stott expounds eleven 'truths' of the Christian life, each illustrated by the behaviour of a different species of bird. A reviewer in *Christianity Today* commented:

> Stott nixes any temptation to anthropomorphize. When comparing birds' breeding and parenting habits to those of humans, he notes, 'Human love is unique, because it is a reflection . . . of the eternal, selfless love of God himself, revealed on the cross, affirming the worth of its human objects, and leading to the "steadfast love" of his covenant pledge to his people.' . . . *The Birds Our Teachers* is an unusual mix of theology and ornithology. Stott pulls together quotes from Martin Luther, G. K. Chesterton, C. H. Spurgeon, and scenes from John Bunyan's *Pilgrim's Progress*, mixing them with mentions of famous birdwatchers Roger Tory Peterson and John James Audubon, Woody Allen's movie *Manhattan*, and pop novels such as *Jonathan Livingston Seagull*. Where else could you see photos of pioneer missionary Hudson Taylor mixing with the comic puffins, or of All Souls Church (where Stott is rector emeritus) across from facts about the osprey? Or Bishop John Jewel of Salisbury a page away from a photo spread of cotton-candy-pink flamingoes? It's all quite intriguing.
> (Crosby 2008)

Stott described the background to his interest in birds in his introduction to *The Birds Our Teachers*:

> It is largely to my father that I owe my commitment to birdwatching. He was a physician (a cardiologist, to be precise), and like most scientists, although we lived in the heart of London, he took a lively interest in all branches of natural history. In particular, he was a good amateur botanist. So during the summer holidays, beginning when I was a boy of

only five or six years old, he used to take me out for walks in the countryside, telling me to shut my mouth and open my eyes and ears. It was excellent training in observation. I was soon hooked.

When in 1945 I was ordained into the pastoral ministry of the Church of England, I returned to London and was surprised to discover that birdwatching was possible even there. Winter-visiting duck patronized the reservoirs, which supply Londoners with their water, and the Royal Parks harbour many species in both summer and winter. In addition, London's bombed buildings provided birds with excellent feeding and nesting sites. Kestrels hunted for mice in the war-torn ruins and reared their young on the ledges of precipitous walls. Black Redstarts availed themselves of convenient holes in which to nest, and, while I was serving Holy Communion early on Sunday mornings in All Souls Church, and there was no roar of traffic, I could distinctly hear the Black Redstart's rasping song while it perched on the top of Broadcasting House next door, the headquarters of the BBC.

Ten years later I began to travel overseas, to lecture and to preach, and of course I took my binoculars with me, for there are birds everywhere. The widely accepted estimate is that there are about 9,000 different species in the world. They occur in every zone and every terrain, from arid desert to tropical rainforest, in town and country, and from the Arctic to the Antarctic. Moreover, the variety of birds – in size and shape, plumage and diet, habits and habitat – is truly astonishing. Take size and weight as an example. The tiniest bird is the Bee Hummingbird, which is endemic to Cuba. From the tip of its beak to the tip of its tail it is 2.25 inches long, and without beak or tail only 1 inch. When it flies, it is easily mistaken for an insect. In fact, I have myself watched a Tody in the Caribbean chasing a diminutive hummingbird under the illusion that it was an insect, and suddenly giving up the chase when it realised that its prey was a bird not a bee! The Bee Hummingbird weighs 0.056 ounces, whereas a flightless ostrich can weigh up to 200 kg (30 stones). The largest flying bird in the world is the Wandering Albatross; its wingspan averages about twelve feet.

Roger Tory Peterson, who in his prime was the leading American birdwatcher, and who died in 1996, claimed after a long life-time of observing that he had seen about 4,500 species, just over half. Peter Winter, however, in his book *The Adventures of a Birdwatcher*, describes his nearly 100 expeditions, which took him to all six continents and led to sightings of 7,208 species. But the record was held by Ms. Phoebe Snetsinger whose tally, when she died in 1999, was more than 8,000. For myself, although I have had the privilege of travelling in many countries and habitats, I have seen only about 2,500 species.

At all events, only one person has seen them all, and that of course is God himself, their creator. '"Let birds fly above the earth", he commanded, "across the expanse of the sky." So God created . . . every winged bird according to its kind. And God saw that it was good' (Genesis 1:20, 21 [NIV 1984]). In consequence, he is able to claim: 'I know all the birds of the air, and the creatures of the field are mine' (Psalm 50:11, literally). More than that, since Jesus said that not a single sparrow falls to the ground without the knowledge of God (Matthew 10:29; Luke 12:6, 7), he must know not only every species of bird but every individual member of each species as well. And that would mean many thousands of millions.

It was Jesus Christ himself in the Sermon on the Mount who told us to be birdwatchers! 'Behold the fowls of the air' is how the King James' Version renders his command (Matthew 6:26). Translated into basic English, however, his instruction becomes 'watch birds!' So we have the highest possible authority for this activity. Moreover, he meant more than that we should notice them. For the Greek verb employed here means to fix the eyes on or take a good look at. This will certainly include our study and appreciation of their plumage and behaviour. But the Bible tells us that birds have lessons to teach us as well.

As a matter of fact, Scripture bids us go beyond birds and include in our interest everything God has made: 'Great are the works of the Lord, studied by all who delight in them' (Psalm 111:2, NRSV). Since 'the works of the Lord' refer to his works of both creation and redemption, it seems to me that nature study and Bible study should go together. Many Christians have a good doctrine of redemption, but need a better doctrine of creation. We ought to pursue at least one aspect of natural history.

So over the years I have been trying to develop a new branch of science, which a friend and I have jocularly called 'ornitheology', or the theology of birds. It is founded on an important biblical principle, namely that in the beginning God made man, male and female, in his own image, and gave us dominion over the earth and its creatures (Genesis 1:26–28). Because we alone among all God's creatures bear his image, we are radically different from animals, even though we share with them the same dependence on our Creator for our life. But as we are different, Scripture expects us to behave differently. At times, we are rebuked for behaving like animals (e.g. 'do not be like the horse or the mule,' Psalm 32:9). At other times Scripture chides us because animals do better by instinct than we do by choice (e.g. 'go to the ant, you sluggard, consider its ways and be wise!', Proverbs 6:6).

Martin Luther, in his fine exposition of the Sermon on the Mount, became quite lyrical when he commented on Jesus' teaching about the birds. He wrote:

> You see, he is making the birds our schoolmasters and teachers. It is a great and abiding disgrace to us that in the Gospel a helpless sparrow should become a theologian and a preacher to the wisest of men. We have as many teachers and preachers as there are little birds in the air. Their living example is an embarrassment to us . . . Whenever you listen to a nightingale, therefore, you are listening to an excellent preacher . . . It is as if he were saying 'I prefer to be in the

Lord's kitchen. He has made heaven and earth, and he himself is the cook and the host. Every day he feeds and nourishes innumerable little birds out of his hand'.
(Luther 1521, pp. 197–198)
(Stott [1999] 2007, pp. 7–10)

A few months before the publication of *The Birds Our Teachers*, Stott showcased what he called his 'orni-theology' on 1 August 1999 in an All Souls sermon called 'The feeding of ravens: faith'. Much of it was material that appears again in *The Birds Our Teachers*. Omitting overlap in his introduction (see above), in his sermon he said:

I'm sure we all know that there are many, many references to birds in the pages of Scripture, probably far more than we have ever noticed.

Let's begin with creation – way back in Genesis 1, v. 20: 'God said "Let the birds fly above the earth, across the expanse of the skies."' So the text goes on 'God made the creatures that inhabit the earth and the sea and every winged bird to fly across the sky and having done it, God saw that it was good.' Let me now jump to Psalm 50 where God says, 'I know every bird in the mountains and the creatures of the field are mine.' 'I know them all,' God says. It's a bold claim because it's generally accepted that there are between 8,600 and 9,000 species of birds in the world. And birds are to be found everywhere, in the desert and in the tropical rain forest, in the Arctic and in the Antarctic and in the countryside and in the town, yes and even here in the centre of the city in which All Souls Church is situated. I don't know if you know that kestrels, that are little falcons, have nested on the ledges of the Langham Hilton across the street from this building . . . It's amazing how many birds there are even in the city . . .

The Bible recognises what some of us may never have recognised, that birds add an important dimension of pleasure to our life on earth, so much so that according to the prophet Jeremiah, one of the signs of God's judgment upon the apostate nation of Judah was that there would be a total disappearance of birds. I looked, said Jeremiah, at the earth and it was formless and empty. It had reverted to its pre-creation chaos. I looked at the heavens, I looked at the mountains, I looked everywhere and there were no people and every bird in the sky had flown away. So, you see part of the judgment of God was the disappearance of birdlife on the earth.

Well, in the light of these biblical references, it should not be surprising that our Lord Jesus Christ drew attention to these birds because his mind was steeped in Old Testament Scripture and he was an acute observer of what was going on around him. So, 'consider the birds of the earth,' he said in the Sermon on the Mount. It's a command which, when translated into basic English, means 'Watch birds.' So Jesus himself told us to be birdwatchers; birdwatching is an occupation commended by the highest of all authorities. So beware, you may be living in disobedience . . .

My text today is Luke 12:22, 'then Jesus said to his disciples, Don't worry about your life, what you'll eat. Don't worry about your body and the clothes you're going to wear. Life is more than food and the body is more than clothing. Consider the ravens, they don't sow or reap, they have no storeroom or barn and yet God feeds them. How much more valuable you are than birds.' And then jump to the phrase in v. 28, 'how much more will he clothe you than he clothes the lilies – oh you of little faith.'

So, the first lesson that the birds teach us, and ravens in particular, is the lesson of faith. In other words, to trust God in all circumstances and in particular to trust him for the supply of everything that we need. We are not to worry, Jesus said. We're not to worry about our life or about the food and drink that nourish our life. We're not to worry about our body or what we are to wear to clothe our body, because life is more important than food and drink and our body is more important than the clothes we wear. So that if God looks after the life and the body, we can surely trust him to look after the food and drink and clothing. How much more of an argument is it that if God looks after the greater, that is the life and the body, can we not trust him to look after the lesser, the food on the one hand and the clothing on the other? So consider the birds. Jesus said learn this lesson from them, they don't sow or reap, they don't harvest. But God feeds them and you're much more valuable than they are so if he feeds them, can't you trust him to feed you? See, it's logical, isn't it, from the greater to the lesser and from the lesser to the greater. Perhaps you know this little doggerel, one could hardly call it poetry, which records an imaginary conversation between a robin and a sparrow. A little doggerel that is entitled, 'Overheard in an orchard':

> Said the robin to the sparrow 'I should really like to know why these anxious human beings rush about and worry so. Said the sparrow to the robin 'Friend, I think that it must be they have no Heavenly Father such as cares for you and me.'

Well it's a delightful sentiment but it's not a strictly accurate one as you may have noticed for Jesus did not say that birds have a Heavenly Father, he said that we have and if the Creator looks after his creatures like the little birds, can we not trust our Heavenly Father to look after his children? That's the argument. Well, according to Luke, Jesus refers specifically not to birds but to ravens, which are the largest of the crow family. Ravens have already figured quite prominently in the Old Testament narrative. You know, don't you, which the first creature was to be released from Noah's Ark – yes, it was a raven. And you know what God used to feed Elijah when he was in flight from King Ahab – yes, ravens. And twice in the wisdom literature of the Old Testament, in Job and in one of the Psalms we are specifically told that God provides food for the ravens and for their young. So with all this background about ravens in the Old Testament Jesus was perfectly justified in choosing ravens as his example of faith. Jesus argued that if God feeds the ravens you can surely trust him to feed you who are much more valuable than they.

Now, friends, from this point, we move on and say, it's very important for us not to misunderstand the teachings of Jesus. There are three common misinterpretations about faith which need to be corrected and which birds will help us to correct. And I hope we will try to remember these three things because we often forget them.

1 Faith, true faith, genuine faith, authentic faith does not prohibit forethought. The familiar King James Version 'take no thought for the morrow', is seriously misleading because what Jesus said was 'take no *anxious* thought for the morrow'. In other words, do not worry. It was anxiety that he was prohibiting and not prudence. Because faith is incompatible with worry but it is not incompatible with forethought, because of course we must take thought for the future, it would be very stupid of us not to take thought for the future, the Bible urges us to do so. For example, the reason we are to imitate the behaviour of ants in Proverbs chapter 6 is not because they are busy when we are often lazy, it is rather because they store provisions in the summer in preparation for the winter. In other words they are filled with prudence and forethought, thought for the future. As a matter of fact there are some birds which like ants do the same thing – they store up provisions although less systematically. Some of you I know are from the United States. If you have been in California and watched a dapper little bird called the Acorn Woodpecker – let me tell you about it. The Acorn Woodpecker chips a hole in a tree or a telephone pole which is precisely the shape and size of an acorn. And when he's dug this little hole he gets an acorn and just fits it into the hole so that he has a larder ready for when he needs it. And then the whole shrike family that stock their larder by impaling insects on convenient

thorns. So in the light of this, Paul's instruction to Timothy is relevant. Do you know 1 Timothy 5:8? We should do. Paul writes that if anybody does not provide for his relatives, and especially for his immediate family, he has denied the faith and is worse than an unbeliever. So here you see a biblical warrant for a life assurance policy whose purpose is simply to be a self-imposed way of saving in order to make sensible provision for the future after your death and for your family. What Jesus forbade was worry, not prudence. Authentic faith is not incompatible with making sensible provision for the future. Now we all admire those people in East Africa who are called the revival brethren. But you may not know that they had a split in the 1970s and one branch called the *kufufuka* meaning, I understand (I don't have any knowledge really of Swahili) but I understand that *kufufuka* means the re-awakened ones, and those re-awakened ones don't have any insurance policies because they believe, mistakenly, that to have an insurance policy is incompatible with faith. Faith does not prohibit forethought – have you got that one?

2 Then secondly, faith does not guarantee safety or immunity. When Jesus tells us to trust our Heavenly Father he is not promising that God's children will enjoy immunity to all accidents, illnesses and death. Now it's quite true that Jesus said 'Not a sparrow falls to the ground without the knowledge and permission of your Heavenly Father' but sparrows do fall to the ground as Jesus knew very well – as when a little chick falls out of its nest and perishes and human beings also fall and injure themselves from time to time and aeroplanes of course sometimes crash. So what Jesus promises is not that the law of gravity would be suspended for our benefit but, rather, that nothing can harm us or our loved ones without our Heavenly Father's knowledge and permission. So faith neither forbids forethought nor

guarantees immunity to suffering, accident, illness or
death.

3 And now, thirdly, faith does not exclude the use of means.
Now I was talking about this a month or two ago, and I
hope if you were there, you'll forgive me if I repeat it, but
it's a good example that we need to learn. Jesus is not
telling God's children to sit back and do nothing because
God would do everything. True salvation, because Christ
died to secure everything for us is a totally free, unmerited
and non-contributory gift of God. Salvation is a free gift.
We can do nothing but receive it but on the other hand, in
every other sphere, we have to co-operate with God just as
birds do. Because Jesus says here that God feeds the ravens,
he feeds the birds, but how does God feed the birds?
Some say he doesn't or at least he doesn't do so directly.
We mustn't imagine God feeding birds as we feed our pets
at home, filling our hand or a plate with food and inviting
them to come and take it. God doesn't feed us like that,
and he doesn't feed birds like that. No, Jesus was a keen
observer of nature and he knew very well that birds feed
themselves. Some are insectivorous, some eat berries or
seeds or fruits, others are flesh eaters, others are fish
eaters, others are predators and pirates, some suck nectar
from flowers and others find worms to their taste and
even snails. As for ravens, you know, they are omnivorous,
they eat anything, they are opportunistic scavengers. They
pick up anything they find, they forage along the seashore,
they forage in the local rubbish tip or by the abattoir. So,
what did Jesus mean when he said that God feeds the
ravens, when they don't but feed themselves? Well what
he meant is that God feeds the birds indirectly. That is
to say he provides the wherewithal with which they feed
themselves. But they still have to forage as the Psalmist
in 104 writes 'these all look to you to give them their food
at the proper time, and when you give it to them they
gather it up'. So faith in God is not incompatible with

co-operation with God. Thus we acknowledge that our food comes out in a different [way from] God, we're right to say grace before meals in order to acknowledge that our food comes from him and we're right to pray the Lord's Prayer and ask for our daily bread. But at the same time we know that we are not just dependent directly on God but indirectly on farmers and fishermen and on the whole retail and wholesale trade and similarly when we're ill of course we pray to God for healing but we also go to the doctor and, if we are wise, we accept whatever medication or treatment he prescribes. The other day I mentioned Hudson Taylor, and I would like to mention him again, the founder in the middle of the last [nineteenth] century of the China Inland Mission as it then was [now the Overseas Missionary Fellowship] when he first sailed to China in 1853. His boat was caught in the Irish Sea in a terrific storm. And the captain ordered the passengers to put on their life belts. Hudson Taylor refused. He reckoned at that time, that he couldn't trust in a life belt and trust in God at the same time. But later he came to understand his folly and this is what he wrote: 'the use of means (in this case a life belt) ought not to lessen our faith in God and our faith in God ought not to hinder our using whatever means God has given us for the accomplishment of his purpose' (Broomhall, 1929:53).

So let me sum up and conclude: if we take the birds as our teachers the best lesson they teach us is faith, trust in God and not worrying. At the same time true faith in God does not prohibit forethought, it does not guarantee immunity and it does not exclude the use of means. So let's have a mature biblical understanding of the meaning of faith and the birds can help us to gain one. Faith is a living trust in God but it does not stop us taking all the precautions we can, taking all the pains we can, using all the means we can so long as our confidence is not in them but in Him who makes these things

available to us in the life of faith. Thank God for the ravens and the lesson of faith which they teach us.
(Stott 1999)

Another lesson in *The Birds Our Teachers* is that to be learned from owls, who teach us to look both back to Christ's first coming and forwards to his second coming. Stott used this particular lesson as an opportunity to describe his decades-long search for Snowy Owls:

What is it about owls which inclines us to develop a love–hate relationship with them? They both fascinate and frighten us. On the one hand, their upright posture, fixed forwards stare, ability to blink with their upper eye-lid, and facial discs like huge spectacles remind us of a rather pompous scholar and may be the origin of their 'wise old owl' reputation. On the other hand, they are mostly nocturnal, some of them have a penchant for cemeteries and ruins ('I am . . . like an owl among the ruins', Psalm 102:6), and they have an eerie repertoire of spine-chilling hoots and shrieks, so that in many cultures they are regarded as birds of evil omen.

Yet owls are superior to human beings in at least one import-ant respect. I am not referring to their excellent eyesight, not to their amazingly sensitive hearing, which enables them to locate a small rodent under leaves or snow, but rather to this: an owl's head is mounted on such flexible bearings that it can rotate at least 180° and even (in the case of the Long-eared Owl, it is claimed) 270°. So an owl's body can face one way, while its head is looking in the opposite direction. That is a gymnastic of which we humans are quite incapable.

Nevertheless, what we cannot do physically we can and should do spiritually. In John Bunyan's famous seventeenth-century allegory *Pilgrim's Progress*, the main character, Christian, who is on his way to the Celestial City, meets a number of interesting people. Their names tell us whose side they are on. Some of them are good guys like Faithful, Hopeful and Evangelist. Others, however, are evidently bad guys like Mr. Malice, Mr. Liar and Mr. Nogood. And one day Christian hears of a character called Mr. Facing-Bothways. He is a bad guy. He is neither a Christian nor a non-Christian. He sits on the fence. He tries to be what Jesus said we cannot be, namely the slave of two masters.

Yet in another sense every Christian should be owl-like or a Mr. Facing-Bothways, because all the time we should be looking back to the past with gratitude and on to the future with expectation. It is not easy to do both simultaneously. Some Christians are such avid futurists that they welcome only what is new and have no respect for the past, the old or the traditional. Others make the opposite mistake. They are such ardent traditionalists that they are resistant to all change. They are stuck in the mud, and the mud has set like concrete. Their favourite formula is 'as it was in the beginning, is now and ever shall be, world without end, Amen.' In contrast to these, according to the Preface to the Prayer Book, it has always been the church's wisdom 'to keep the mean between the two extremes, of too much stiffness in refusing, and of too much easiness in admitting any variation . . .'

Then there is another sense in which Christians are always facing both ways, for we are always looking back to the first coming of Christ on the original Christmas Day, when he came to the stable in great humility, and looking forward to his second coming at the end of the world, when he will come in power and great glory. Meanwhile, we are living in between times, between his two appearings, between kingdom come and kingdom coming, between kingdom inaugurated and kingdom consummated, between the 'already' and the 'not yet' of our salvation.

The Lord's Supper, or Holy Communion, constantly reminds us of these things for, as the apostle Paul wrote, 'Whenever you eat this bread and drink this cup, you proclaim the Lord's death until he comes' (1 Corinthians 11:26 [NIV 1984]). It is truly remarkable that, within the compass of a single verse,

Paul should refer both to the Lord's death (which is past) and to the Lord's coming (which is future), and should indicate that the Lord's Supper is a bridge between them. For when he comes in person, and the reality has arrived, the signs and symbols will no longer be needed.

So we must learn to imitate the owls, which swivel their heads right round. For then we can perform our essential spiritual contortion, looking back to Christ's death and resurrection with enormous gratitude, and looking on to his return with eager expectation. This is the only right way in which to be a Mr. (or Ms.) Facing-Bothways.

There are said to be about 140 owl species in the world . . . North America too is quite rich in owls. I have been fortunate to see the Barred Owl in Florida, the Spotted Owl in Oregon, the Burrowing Owl in California, and the Northern Hawk Owl in Alaska. Then once on the same day in Yosemite National Park I saw both a Great Grey Owl and a Pygmy Owl, which are respectively amongst America's largest and smallest owls.

But none of these is the owl I most wanted to see. I have had a life-long romantic fascination, which I cannot rationalize, for *Nyctea scandica*, the Snowy Owl . . . [In six trips to the Canadian Arctic between 1971 and 1991, I had] sightings of Rock Ptarmigan, Brent Geese, Grey Phalaropes, King Eiders, Grey Plovers, Sabine's Gulls, Tundra Swans, a pair of nesting Roughlegged Hawks, and three species of Skuas or Jaeger (Arctic, Long-tailed and Pomarine) . . . [b]ut still no Snowy Owls.

In 1996, however, to celebrate my 75th birthday, I had the chance to return to Cambridge Bay [in the Canadian Arctic, where my] friend Keith Todd was now in charge of St. George's Anglican Mission. So, soon after his appointment, I had the temerity to write to him and suggest that one of his first pastoral duties would be to find a breeding pair of Snowy Owls! . . . How can I capture in words the excitement of sitting in a hide, or blind, for hour after hour only a few yards from the bird of my dreams?! ... Because the Canadian Arctic is 'the land of the midnight sun', it was light enough to take photographs round the clock, including the early hours of the morning. It was a fantastic experience to eavesdrop on the domestic life of this majestic but elusive bird. She stared at me (although of course she could not see me), and I stared back. I could even watch mosquitoes crawling on her feathered face until she blinked and shook her head vigorously to dislodge them ... It was the culmination of a twenty-five-year search for a truly sensational bird. I felt I could now say my *Nunc Dimittis*: 'Lord, now lettest thou thy servant depart in peace ... for my eyes have seen ...' (Luke 2:29, 30).

(Stott [1999] 2007, pp. 23–25 and 31–32)

A postscript to the snowy owl search showing something of Stott's birdwatching passion is given by Keith and Gladys Hunt of the US InterVarsity Christian Fellowship, who described a month's holiday with Stott in Alaska, birdwatching and exploring this frontier area. They wrote:

During the third week, we travelled by station wagon far north toward the Arctic Circle until the road ended at the Yukon River ... [One evening,] returning after dark to our cabin, we sat around the small table by the light of candles and a lantern to talk about the day. We suggested that John read to us from the travel diary he was keeping. It was a perfect setting for hearing him give us his record of our adventure. It was mesmerizing. It was riveting. We saw our travels with fresh eyes. It was descriptive, full of observations (he had watched the drama of a goshawk with a rabbit in its claws), full of information, full of movement – it was alive. And furthermore, it was publishable just as he read it to us! Listening to him read was one of those 'Wow!' moments. Our diary, full of half-sentences and half-information, was fit only for the trash heap by comparison. Who could not love this fellow traveller in his wrinkled shirt and jacket, glasses on the end of his nose, with a

battered hat on his head, using the same well-chosen words in the candlelight to enrich our memories of this journey as he used in Bible exposition.
(Hunt and Hunt 2011, pp. 100–101)

Other 'orni-theological' lessons Stott draws in *The Birds Our Teachers* are as follows.

- Repentance, illustrated by the migration of storks, drawing on Jeremiah 8:4–7, 'for when birds "observe the time of their migration" (Jeremiah 8:7) and do so . . . by instinct (by inbuilt, inherited navigational skills which scientists have not yet fully fathomed), we human beings should do by deliberate choice, returning from our self-centred ways to the living God our Creator . . . Wise Christians will not procrastinate, but repent, confess, and seek restoration immediately. The penitential psalms (especially 51 and 130) will help us to express our contrition. Birds can challenge us here, too, for in addition to their annual migration, many of them have a highly developed homing instinct. Even when they are taken to an unfamiliar place and released, they can still find their way home. Pigeons, for example, have been famous for this for centuries, indeed ever since Noah's dove found its way back to the ark (Genesis 8:8–12). During World War II "pigeon post" became so valuable that the British Air Ministry initiated a register of carrier pigeons and sought to destroy all Peregrine Falcons, which are the principal predators of pigeons . . .
  'Another example of the "homing" instinct of birds is of special interest to me. Since 1954 I have had a cottage on the coast of Pembrokeshire in south-west Wales. Off shore are the islands of Skomer and Skokholm, on which more than 200,000 pairs of Manx Shearwaters (half the world's population) are believed to breed. Manx Shearwaters are birds of the open ocean, which winter as far south as the coast of Argentina. They come to land only to breed, and lay their single egg underground at the end of a rabbit burrow. In 1952 one was

taken from Skokholm and released inland in Cambridge, about 240 miles away; it was back in its burrow seven hours later. On another occasion a Manx Shearwater was flown 3,000 miles from Skokholm across the Atlantic, and released at Boston's Logan International Airport. Twelve and a half days later it had returned to its burrow home, having travelled an average of 250 miles a day.

'Would that we had as strong a homing instinct spiritually as birds have physically! The more we come to recognize that God is the true home of the human spirit, and that we are waifs and strays without him, the more quickly and painfully will we become aware of even the smallest estrangement from him, and the more eagerly will we return to him. For when we come back, we have come home' (Stott [1999] 2007, pp. 20–22).

- '[T]he biblical symbol of true freedom is not the flight of the seagull [as portrayed in the runaway bestseller *Jonathan Livingston Seagull*, by Richard Bach] but the flight of the eagle . . . [F]light in Scripture is not a symbol of self-effort but of salvation. The picture it presents is not the strenuous flapping of wings, but the spreading of wings to catch the wind, and effortless soaring into the sky.

'There are two notable references to the flight of eagles in the wisdom literature of the Old Testament, both of which emphasize its mystery and majesty. "Does the eagle soar at your command", God asks Job, "and build his nest on high?" (Job 39:27). The expected answer is plain. The flight of eagles is beyond human understanding and control. So one of Israel's wise men confessed that, of four things which were "too amazing" for him, one was "the way of the eagle in the sky" (Proverbs 30:18 and 19).

'Nevertheless, in spite of the enigmatic nature of eagle flight, it remains a visual emblem of strength. It illustrates the saving power of God displayed in the experience of both the nation and the individual. In describing his rescue of the Israelites from their Egyptian bondage, God said he had carried them "on eagle's wings" and brought them to himself (Exodus 19:4). And when even his own people are conscious of their weakness, they can have no higher aspiration than to "soar on wings like eagles" (Isaiah 40:31; compare Psalm 103:5). This does not represent self-effort, however. For the only people who "renew their strength", who walk and run without growing tired and who even fly like eagles, are those who wait patiently for the Lord, and put their trust in him (Isaiah 40:29–31).

'C. H. Spurgeon, a nineteenth-century Baptist preacher in London, expressed this challenge to faith with his customary eloquence in an address to ordained ministers and ministerial students:

> Brother, your failure, if you fail, will begin in your faith. The air says to the eagle, "Trust me; spread thy broad wings; I will bear thee up to the sun. Only trust me. Take thy foot from off yon rock which thou canst feel beneath thee. Get away from it, and be buoyed up by the unseen element." My brethren, eaglets of heaven, mount aloft, for God invites you. Mount! You have but to trust him.
> (Spurgeon 1960, p. 29)'

(Stott [1999] 2007, p. 57)

- The territorial behaviour of robins: '"I need space", we sometimes say. "Please don't invade my personal space." . . . The demand for personal space . . . is particularly a symptom of adolescence when we emerge out of childish dependence on our parents into a necessary independence . . . And what "space" is to humans, "territory" is to birds . . . [E]ven colonial nesters are still territorial . . . I think of the huge number of King Penguins which lay their single egg in their "rookeries" on South Georgia in the South Atlantic, and of the 30,000 pairs of gannets which build their nests on Grassholm, [an] island off the coast of West Wales. In both cases the sitting birds, the penguins and the gannets, look like a well laid-out orchard, as each is just beyond pecking distance from its neighbour.

'Thus these seabirds are both colonial and territorial at the same time. And so are many modern city-dwellers. Our high-rise apartment blocks sometimes resemble the perpendicular sea cliffs; the thousands who occupy the apartments somewhat resemble the densely populated seabird colonies; and as these close colonies enjoy a measure of protection against predators, so the large numbers of apartment block residents offer them a measure of mutual security. Both situations combine the colonial (massed numbers) and the territorial (individual space to be defended).

'Christians are anxious to preserve this combination of colony and territory, and to avoid extremes. Although the ratio between the two varies from culture to culture, authentic human existence must include both; for either without the other would be destructive of our created humanness.

'On the one hand, to surrender to the pressures of mass culture, to have no privacy, no time for reflection on the fundamental issues of life, and no opportunity to grow into the unique person God has made each of us, is to lose a vital part of ourselves.

'On the other hand, as solitary confinement is regarded as a peculiarly cruel punishment, so to live a hermit's life is to deny both our creation as social beings and our Christian calling into *koinonia* (fellowship). The eastern mystic looks forward to ultimate absorption into the Divine, as a droplet of water is absorbed into the ocean. But Christians know that God's purpose for us is not to lose but to retain our created individuality. The Christian life begins when Christ stands at the door of our heart and knocks (Revelation 3:20). He will not invade our space. Only when we open the door to admit him will he come in' (Stott [1999] 2007, pp. 60–66).

- In *The Birds Our Teachers*, Stott also has chapters on shelter, drawing on verses referring to the protective wings of a hen (Ruth 2:12; Matthew 23:37), and joy as heard in the song of the lark (Psalm 96:1, 2; 148:7, 10 and 13). He writes of the beak-lifted drinking of most birds as illustrating gratitude.

Stott concludes *The Birds Our Teachers* by returning once again to Psalms 103 and 104 and their 'early allusion to ecology' ([1999] 2007, p. 94). He urges us to participate avidly in preserving and restoring healthy habitats that all creatures need in order to flourish, not least the fascinating birds that God created.

> Psalms 103 and 104 make a significant pair. Both are invitations to worship. And both begin and end with the same formula: 'Praise the LORD, O my soul'. But Psalm 103 celebrates the goodness of God in salvation, forgiving our sins and keeping his covenant, whereas Psalm 104 celebrates the greatness of God in creation, establishing heaven, earth and sea, and sustaining their creatures with life and food.
>
> In his rehearsal of wildlife in Psalm 104 the psalmist twice makes an honourable mention of 'the birds of the air'. He refers to their main activities, singing and nesting, and relates them to the Lord's well-watered trees in verses 12 and 17:
>
> > The birds of the air nest by the waters;
> >   they sing among the branches . . .
> > There [that is, in the trees] the birds make their nests;
> >   the stork has its home in the pine trees.
>
> Here, then, is an early allusion to ecology – that is, to living creatures in their natural environment. God both plants and waters the trees; the birds both sing and nest in them. Indeed, all creatures are dependent on their environment, and loss of habitat is the major cause of loss of species.
>
> It was Jeremiah in the seventh century BC who foretold of the evils of habitat destruction. He combined the roles of patriot and prophet, and it caused him great anguish. He was torn between his patriotic love for his own country and his prophetic warning of God's coming judgment on it. If the people stubbornly maintained their refusal to repent, he cried, the Babylonian army would invade from the north and would devastate the land. Four times he repeated his statement

'I looked'. He looked at the earth and the heavens, at the mountains and the hills, at city and sky, at orchard and town, and each time he saw only destruction. The earth had again become 'formless and empty', having returned to the primeval chaos of Genesis 1:2; the heavens had become dark, as they were before God had said 'let there be light' (Genesis 1:3); the mountains were quaking and the hills swaying. Worst of all, there were no people, and there were no birds, for 'every bird in the sky had flown away'. Why? Because 'the fruitful land was a desert' and 'all its towns lay in ruins before the LORD, before his fierce anger' (Jeremiah 4:23–26 [NIV 1984]). The tragic disappearance of 'the birds of the air' as a result of divine judgment is a regular theme of the prophets (see Jeremiah 9:10 and 12:4; Hosea 4:3 and Zephaniah 1:3).

We would do well to reflect on Jeremiah's warning of a possible return to pre-creation chaos, darkness and devastation. One of God's creation blessings was the appearance of birds to 'fly above the earth across the expanse of the sky' (Genesis 1:20 [NIV 1984]); one of his judgments would be their disappearance.

So let's resolve to do all we can to protect and preserve our unique God-given environment, and so continue to enjoy its God-given 'biodiversity', not least its fascinating birds.
(Stott [1999] 2007, pp. 94–95)

7

The works of the Lord

Creation care in
Christian discipleship

A reference that Stott makes in his introduction to *The Birds Our Teachers* is to the different 'works of the Lord'. He pointed out that 'the works of the Lord' refer to his works of both creation and redemption. He returned to this distinction on a number of occasions, and enlarged on it in a seminar entitled 'Caring for creation' he prepared to lead at the InterVarsity Urbana Student Missions Conference in 2003, but could not present due to ill health just before the planned trip.[2] The following extract is from an unpublished manuscript of Stott's, in the Stott archive in the Lambeth Palace Library:

> I begin with a note of serious evangelical self-criticism, namely that, although we have a good doctrine of redemption, we tend to have a bad doctrine of creation. This is all the more regrettable because the same God is the author of both, and both are called the 'works of the Lord'. This expression which recurs about 100 times in the Psalms refers sometimes to his mighty works of creation, bringing the universe into being and sustaining it by his power. At other times 'the works of Yahweh' are his mighty works in salvation, rescuing his people Israel

2 Peter Harris noted (email to Laura Yoder, 9 February 2021) that when John Stott could not travel to Urbana 2003 on short notice, Cheryl Bear, Nadleh Whut'en First Nation, then a member of the A Rocha Canada board, kindly agreed to present the seminar in his place. However, unlike the plenary message text that was delivered by Joshua Wathanga (available online at: <https://urbana.org/message/john-stott-message-read-joshua-wathanga>), Cheryl Bear (2003) did not receive Stott's notes, and she presented an exquisite seminar on her own understanding and experience of creation as a First Nations woman (her talk is available online at: <https://urbana.org/seminar/caring-creation>).

from their slavery in Egypt and establishing them in the promised land. Both these works, of creation and of salvation, are said to be the 'works of Yahweh'. For example, 'How many are your works, O Lord! In wisdom you made them all; the earth is full of your creatures' (Psalm 104:24). This is clearly a reference to creation. But 'Many O Lord my God, are the wonders you have done . . .' (Psalm 40:1–5) in the context refers to David being rescued from the horrible pit of sin and guilt.

Since both creation and redemption are termed 'the works of Yahweh' it is evident that we should hold them together and not acquiesce in their separation. How then should we redress the imbalance between them? I propose to take four aspects of our Christian discipleship and show that in each case neglect of the truth of creation causes a serious loss of equilibrium.

My first example [applies] to meditation and study. It is natural for Christians to reflect on God's saving works and to say 'I will meditate on your works and consider all your mighty deeds' (Psalm 77:12), especially on the death and resurrection of Jesus. But it should be equally natural to reflect on the wonders of God's creation as implied in Psalm 111:2, 'Great are the works of the Lord; they are pondered (RSV 'studied') by all who delight in them'. These words were inscribed in Latin over the entrance of the old Cavendish Laboratory in Cambridge, probably at the instigation of the great physicist James Clerk Maxwell who became the first Cavendish Professor of Experimental Physics at Cambridge University and who ushered in the new era of post-Newtonian physics. He was a Christian believer.

Moreover when the new Cavendish Laboratory came to be built in 1976, it is said to have been Christian influence which persuaded the authorities to inscribe the same text over the front door, this time in Miles Coverdale's English. Again, the very same text was adopted by Lord Rutherford as his motto. His pioneering work in nuclear physics led to the first splitting of the atom in the 1930s. These were Christian men, godly scientists who heeded the biblical admonition to study the works of the Lord.

It was the 17th-century British philosopher, statesman and essayist, Francis Bacon, who first said that God had written not one book but two, namely the book of his works (nature) and the book of his words (Scripture). The former is the general revelation of God's glory in nature, while the latter is the special revelation of God's grace in Scripture. Both are self-disclosures of God. And what Johan Kepler, the 17th-century German astronomer said about his explorations of the universe, we could equally say about our explorations of the Scriptures, namely that in both we are 'thinking God's thoughts after him'. Since God has given us two self-revelations, nature study and Bible study should go together.

The second aspect of Christian discipleship in which creation and salvation should be seen to belong together, is that of thanksgiving and worship. Of course gratitude for our salvation should be taken for granted. Paul prays that the Colossians would be 'joyfully giving thanks to the Father' who had qualified them 'to share in the inheritance of the saints in the kingdom' (1:12). But is it equally natural to thank our heavenly Father for our 'creation, preservation and all the blessings of this life'? It should be. 'For everything God created is good, and nothing is to be rejected if it is received with thanksgiving' (1 Timothy 4:4 [NIV 1984]).

And thanksgiving naturally turns into worship, and God's mighty works in creation and salvation are to be the main two subjects of our worship. It is surely no accident that Psalms 103 and 104 stand side by side in the Psalter, for they beautifully complement one another. Both are Hallelujah psalms, that is, they both begin and end with Hallelujah, the Hebrew invitation to praise the Lord. I like to call them Hallelujah sandwiches, because between the two Hallelujahs is the meat, the doctrinal meat, telling us why we are to praise the Lord. Psalm 103 celebrates all God's benefits – forgiveness, healing, deliverance from death, together with love and compassion. In other words, it praises God the Redeemer. Psalm 104 begins with the same invitation to worship God, but continues with the blessings not of redemption but of creation: 'The trees of the Lord are well-watered ... there the birds make their nests, the stork has its home in the pine trees'. This is a sample of what is perhaps the earliest essay in ecology in the literature of the world. It depicts the animals in their living environment. Thus Psalm 103 invites us to worship God the Redeemer and Psalm 104 invites us to worship God the Creator – and in each case an account of his mighty works.

Now this double worship of God is only a stammering anticipation of the full-throated chorus of heaven, in which angels, animals and humans will join in and say:

'You are worthy, our Lord and God,
    to receive glory ...
for you created all things,
    and by your will they were created
    and have their being.'
(Revelation 4:11)

'Worthy is the Lamb who was slain to receive power ...
honour, glory and praise.'
(Revelation 5:12)

Thus the worship of heaven also recognizes the double nature of the works of the Lord, as Creator and Redeemer.

Thirdly, the works of the Lord are to be the subject of our witness. Worship and witness belong inseparably together. We cannot possibly worship God, that is articulate his infinite worth, without longing to go out into the world to persuade people to come and worship him. Witness leads inevitably to worship, but witness leads to worship as people are brought to Christ and begin to worship him too. It is a continuous cycle of worship leading to witness, leading to worship, and so on. They cannot be separated.

In both worship and witness, the works of the Lord are paramount. Of course we are used to the idea that we are to bear witness to what God has done in Jesus Christ for the salvation of the world, but the scripture says we are also to witness to the wonderful works of our Creator. Here are two examples:

> 'Give thanks to the LORD, call on his name;
>   make known among the nations what he has done.
> . . . sing praise to him;
>   tell of all his wonderful works.'
> (Psalm 105:1–2)

Then there is also Psalm 145:4:

> 'One generation will commend your works to another;
>   they will tell of your mighty acts.'

So God's mighty acts in creation and redemption are to be made known throughout the world. We are not to be afraid to bear witness to the Creator as well as to the Redeemer. Just as the apostle Paul did when confronted by the philosophers in Athens, we are to hold together in our evangelistic witness the Creation and the Cross; the God who made us and who has redeemed us in Jesus Christ. If either is omitted, our gospel has been truncated.

The fourth aspect of Christian discipleship in which creation and redemption are both involved is that of cooperation with God. We are 'God's fellow-workers', Paul wrote to the Corinthians (2 Corinthians 6:1), referring to their partnership in spreading the gospel. The notion of divine–human collaboration is yet more striking in the field of the creation. For the God who made the world could easily have managed it by himself. But he chose not to. Instead, he deliberately humbled himself to require human cooperation.

Some outspoken critics of Christianity have tried to fasten the blame for ecological irresponsibility on the Genesis command to 'rule' and 'subdue' the earth. True, these are strong words. But the meaning of words is fixed by their context, and it would be absurd to suppose that the Creator of the world should have handed it over to men to destroy it. A more accurate word for our responsibility for the earth would be 'stewardship'. God has delegated the care of his world to us. Once we grasp this, we will be conscientious in avoiding waste, protecting the delicate biosphere and preserving resources.

It is noteworthy in Genesis 2 that God put the man he had made into the garden he had planted in order 'to work it and take care of it' (Genesis 2:15). This partnership has been perpetuated in the distinction between 'nature' (what God has made) and 'culture' (what we make of it). It also gives us a Christian philosophy of work, namely of cooperation between us and God. I like the story of the Cockney gardener who was showing the local pastor round his magnificent herbaceous flower garden. The pastor kept mentioning how marvellous God's flowers were. No credit was being given to the gardener, until he exploded – 'you should have seen this 'ere garden when God 'ad it all to 'isself'. He was right. Without the skill of the gardener, the flower bed would have been nothing but a wilderness. Work is a partnership with God.

So I return to where I began. We need as strong and biblical a doctrine of creation as we do of redemption. Then we would care for creation more conscientiously than we usually do. (Stott 2003b)

Stott made the same distinction between God's works in redemption and creation in a sermon he preached on 25 September 1993 to mark the tenth anniversary of the A Rocha Trust, an interest close to Stott's heart and on whose Council of Reference he served until his death. The text of the sermon was reprinted in Stan LeQuire's edited volume, *The Best Preaching on Earth: Sermons on caring for creation*. In it Stott returns once again to his favourite Psalms, 103 and 104.

A Rocha is committed to a partnership of Christian responsibilities – evangelistic, on the one hand, and environmental, on the other. It may be called 'earthbound' in the double sense that it cares for the earth and it is also concerned that the good news of Jesus Christ is carried to the ends of the earth.

I invite you to reflect with me on a phrase that occurs about a hundred times in the Psalter. Although I understand that the Hebrew words are somewhat different, nevertheless the idea is repeated again and again in the expression 'the works of the Lord', the mighty works of Yahweh. What is vital to notice, because it is often missed, is that sometimes 'the works of the Lord' are his mighty works of *creation*, bringing the universe into being and sustaining it by his Word of power. But at other times, the works of Yahweh are his mighty works of *salvation*, rescuing his people, Israel, from their slavery in Egypt and establishing them in the Promised Land. Both these works, of creation and of salvation, are said to be works of Yahweh. Let me give you an example of each.

The first, the works of creation, are described in Psalm 104:24:

> How many are your works, O Lord!
> In wisdom you made them all;
> The earth is full of your creatures.

We read about his works of salvation in Psalm 40:5:

> Many, O Lord my God,
> are the wonders you have done . . .
> Were I to speak . . . of them
> they would be too many to declare.

The context of Psalm 40:5 is that the psalmist is being rescued from the horrible pit of sin and guilt, and his feet are being established on the rock.

Now, with this double understanding of the works of Yahweh in our minds, I want to ask a question: what is our Christian responsibility in light of, and in response to, the works of the Lord?

The subjects of our study

First, the works of the Lord are to be the subjects of our study. Listen to Psalm 111:2 (RSV), to which I will refer again later: 'Great are the works of the Lord, *studied* (NIV says 'pondered') by all who have pleasure in them.' Alternatively, Psalm 77:12, 'I will *meditate* on all your works and consider all your mighty deeds.'

I think it was Sir Francis Bacon, the seventeenth-century essayist, who was the first to say that 'God has, in fact, written two books, not just one. Of course, we are all familiar with the first book he wrote, namely Scripture. But he has written a second book called creation.' That is to say, God has revealed himself both in the created order and in Christ and the biblical witness to Christ. To be sure, there are a number of important differences between the two books of God, between the *general revelation* of his glory in nature and the *special revelation* of his grace in Scripture. Yet both are divine revelation. Now here is the point: what God has revealed, we are to study, to explore, to ponder, to meditate on, to make our own and to rejoice in. We should be fascinated by the self-revelation of God and want to study his mighty works.

Seventeenth-century astronomer Johann Kepler said that, when he was studying the universe, he was 'thinking God's thoughts after him.' Those words are equally applicable to Bible readers. Bible study and nature study are *both* Christian obligations, a necessary response to God's double self-revelation in creation and in Christ. This brings me back to Psalm 111:2 (RSV): 'Great are the works of the Lord, studied by all who have pleasure in them.'

(Stott 1996, pp. 78–80)

Stott then recounts the aforementioned illustration of the words inscribed over the entrance of the old Cavendish Laboratory at the instigation of the first Cavendish Professor, James Clerk Maxwell, who was a Scottish Presbyterian. After his death, a prayer was found among Maxwell's papers: 'Almighty God, who created man in Thine own image, and made him a living soul that he might seek after Thee and have dominion over Thy creatures, teach us to study the works of Thy hands, that we may subdue the earth to our use and strengthen the reason for Thy service; and so to receive Thy blessed Word, that we may believe on Him Whom Thou hast sent, to give us the knowledge of salvation and the remission of our sins.' Maxwell's successor as Cavendish Professor was Lord Rayleigh, who was also a keen Christian and had the words of Psalm 111:2 inscribed on the cover of his collected science publications. [A fuller account of the Cavendish Laboratory and the text is in Berry 2008.] Stott continued:

> These were Christian men, godly scientists, who were anxious not only to recognize the works of the Lord but to *study* his revelation. Bible study and nature study are twin obligations.

The subjects of our worship

Second, the works of the Lord should be the subject, though not the object, of our worship. We are to rejoice in the works of the Lord, just as, we are told, he rejoices in his *own* works (Psalm 104:31). When we rejoice in the works of the Lord, our rejoicing quickly slides into praising him for them. For God's mighty works in creation and salvation are to be the main subjects of our worship. It is not, I believe, an accident that Psalms 103 and 104 stand side by side in the Psalter, for they are beautifully complementary. Both of them begin and end with an invitation to praise the Lord. Psalm 103 (NIV) begins: 'Praise the LORD, O my soul,' and it goes on:

> all my inmost being, praise his holy name.
> Praise the LORD, O my soul,
>   and forget not all his benefits.
> (vv. 1–2)

What are these benefits? The Revised Standard Version says:

> who forgives all your iniquity
>> and heals all your diseases;
> who redeems your life from the Pit,
>> who crowns you with steadfast love and mercy.
> (vv. 3–4)

In other words, it is praise of God the Redeemer.

Psalm 104 begins with the same words: 'Praise the LORD, O my soul.' Again, we hear the invitation to worship Yahweh, but why should we?

> O LORD my God, you are very great;
>> you are clothed with splendour and majesty.
> He waters the mountains . . .
>> the earth is satisfied by the fruit of his work . . .
> The trees of the LORD are well watered . . .
> There the birds make their nests;
>> the stork has its home in the pine trees.
> (vv. 1, 13, 16 and 17)

Psalm 104 is perhaps the earliest essay in ecology in the literature of the world. It depicts the animals in their living environment. Psalm 103 is an invitation to praise God the Redeemer; Psalm 104 is an invitation to praise God the Creator. In each case, we praise God on account of his mighty works.

Now this double worship of God – for his mighty works in creation and salvation, for his glory revealed in creation and his grace revealed in Scripture – is only a stammering anticipation of the full-throated chorus of heaven, in which angels, animals, and humans will join in unison and sing:

> You are worthy, our Lord and God,
>> to receive glory and honor and power,

for you created all things,
    and by your will they were created
    and have their being.
(Revelation 4:11 [NIV])

And again,

Worthy is the Lamb, who was slain
to receive power and wealth and wisdom and strength
and honor and glory and praise!
(Revelation 5:12 [NIV])

Thus, the worship of heaven also recognizes the double nature of the works of the Lord, as Creator and Redeemer.

The subject of our witness

Third, the works of the Lord are to be the subject of our witness. Worship and witness belong together. We cannot possibly worship God – that is, acknowledge his infinite worth – without longing to go out into the world to persuade other people to come and worship him. Worship inevitably leads to witness, but witness leads to worship too. It is a continuous cycle of worship leading to witness leading to worship and so on. The two cannot be separated.

In both worship and witness, the works of the Lord are paramount. Of course, we are used to the idea that we are to bear witness to what God has done in Jesus Christ for the salvation of the world, but Scripture says we are also to witness to the wonderful works of our Creator. Here are two examples. Psalm 105:1–2 says:

Give thanks to the LORD, call on his name;
    make known among the nations what he has done.
Sing to him, sing praise to him;
    tell of all his wonderful acts.

We hear in Psalm 145:4: 'One generation will commend your works to another; they will tell of your mighty acts.'

So God's mighty acts in creation and redemption are to be made known throughout the world. I hope, sisters and brothers, that we will not be afraid to bear witness to the Creator, as well as the Redeemer. Just as the apostle Paul did when confronted by the philosophers in Athens, we need to hold together in our evangelistic witness the creation and the cross – the God who made us and the God who has redeemed us in Jesus Christ. If either is omitted, our gospel has become truncated.

And so, I wish to conclude by encouraging those who honor the Lord by studying and pondering his works. I am thankful for those Christians who lead us to a deeper worship of the Creator God and who make known his works to others throughout the world – all to the glory of the one true God, Creator and Redeemer, the Father, the Son and the Holy Spirit.

(Stott 1996, pp. 81–83)

In 1974, Stott inaugurated an annual series of lectures under the general title 'London lectures in contemporary Christianity', coordinated by a committee with representatives from Stott's own Langham Trust, the International Fellowship of Evangelical Students, the University and Colleges Christian Fellowship, the Scripture Union and All Souls Church. He wrote in the All Souls church magazine in May 1974:

The Christianity which most of us prefer is more ancient than modern, more biblical than contemporary . . . What Scripture plainly teaches we gladly receive and hold fast, but it is not congenial to us to develop a Christian mind, informed with Christian presuppositions, and with this mind of Christ to grapple with the great problems of the day, so as to develop a Christian worldview.

(Stott quoted in Dudley-Smith 2001, p. 168)

The annual London lectures series continued for three-and-a-half decades, most of them being subsequently published in book form. They continue as individual 'John Stott lectures', reflecting on current contemporary and biblical issues under the auspices of four groups that were important to Stott: A Rocha, All Souls Langham Place, the Langham Partnership and the London Institute for Contemporary Christianity.

By the mid 1970s, it seems clear that Stott had come to have a much broader vision of our relationship with the Creator than previously (Stott called it 'cooperation'). It was a very fruitful period for Stott. He was the main author of the Covenant agreed at Lausanne in 1974 and its vision came to dominate his ministry. He was much influenced by two books – one by Carl Henry (*The Uneasy Conscience of Modern Fundamentalism*, 1947) and the other by Harry Blamires (*The Christ Mind: How should a Christian think?*, 1963) – and by the vision of Regent College, which was established by his friend Jim Houston in Vancouver in 1968 to educate the laity theologically.

In 1980 he began to plan an Institute for Contemporary Christianity in London, based partly on the pattern of Regent College and partly inspired by René Padilla and Samuel Escobar, who had set up the Kairos Community in Argentina as an educational institute to explore the embodiment of the gospel in public life (Kirk 2011). The Institute opened in 1982 in the deconsecrated church of St Peter's, Vere Street, which was previously a Chapel of Ease for the nearby All Souls. Its genesis and purpose have been described by Mark Greene:

> John Stott was 61 years old when the London Institute for Contemporary Christianity (LICC) was founded. At that point in his life he could instead have pastored a church, or taught in almost any seminary or theological college in the world. He could have concentrated only on his global itinerant preaching and teaching ministry, or accepted an episcopal call, with a seat in the House of Lords. But instead he chose to focus much energy around this new, small institute for contemporary Christianity.

John and a few friends (including Oliver Barclay, [Lord] Brian Griffiths, Jim Houston, Os Guiness and Andrew Kirk) saw with searing clarity how hard evangelicals found it to apply the word of God to issues we encounter. Evangelical preaching was beset by the sacred–secular divide, which left pastors and lay people with a narrow concept of mission, and a narrow vision for discipleship and disciple-making. One of John's major contributions to this area shortly after the London Institute was founded is his book *Issues Facing Christians Today* (Stott 2006) . . .

John was one of the greatest preachers of his generation, but he never elevated his own calling above any other. He was interested in raising up a new generation of missional Christian disciples in every area of life, not just a new generation of preachers.

He taught and wrote and preached at All Souls and all round the world, and he also discipled . . . John saw discipling in a wide context. For example he met with a group of business people in London for a regular prayer breakfast. And he met with young professionals in diverse fields to engage biblically with the key books, films, exhibitions, events. He listened carefully to everyone but, as one of them put it, 'he was really teaching us to engage with culture.'

John was essentially a disciple-maker, making disciples for ministry in the church, for ministry in business, for ministry in every area of life. This is a goal and a practice that very few church leaders have emulated. The inseparability of proclaiming the gospel and practically pursuing social justice has now been grasped in principle by large sections of the global evangelical church. But there is more work to do in helping to equip the laity for whole-life mission and whole-life discipleship.

John recruited a rich mix of people to come to LICC for its unique ten-week residential course, 'The Christian in the Modern World' (CMW), which combined listening to the word and the world: understanding culture, mission and discipleship. He taught double listening: listening to the word and listening to the world. But the course actually engaged in triple listening: listening to the word, listening to the world, and listening to one another in humility, seeking to help one another fulfil our diverse callings, individual and corporate, in the diverse settings where God has placed us. A teacher, lawyer or a mechanic should go to work with a sense of representing the body of Christ, supported in prayer and fellowship, and able to draw on the wisdom of a local body of believers, to the glory of the Father. It was a radical vision back in 1982, and it still is. LICC's team is now much larger and our range of activity broader, but the focus remains the same as that of our founders – namely envisioning and equipping God's people, lay and ordained, for whole-life mission.

(Greene 2020, pp. 68–71)

Stott's 360-page book *Issues Facing Christians Today* was first published in 1984. It could almost have been a textbook for the early LICC courses. In his preface to the first edition, Stott wrote:

For approximately fifty years (*c.*1920–1970) evangelical Christians were preoccupied with the task of defending the historic biblical faith against the attacks of theological liberalism, and reacting against its 'social gospel'. But now we are convinced that God has given us social as well as evangelistic responsibilities in his world. Yet the halfcentury of neglect has put us far behind in this area. We have a long way to catch up.

(Stott 2006, pp. xi–xii)

Stott's starting point was:

a commitment to the Bible as 'God's Word written', which is how it is described in the Anglican Articles and has been received by nearly all churches until comparatively recent times … But we Christians have a second commitment, namely to the world in which God has placed us … Some Christians, anxious above all to be faithful to the revelation of

God without compromise, ignore the challenges of the modern world and live in the past. Others, anxious to respond to the world around them, trim and twist God's revelation in their search for relevance. I have struggled to avoid both traps . . . I have sought with integrity to submit to the revelation of yesterday within the realities of today . . . This is our Christian calling: to live under the Word in the world.
(Stott 2006, pp. xi–xii)

Issues Facing Christians Today first appeared in 1984, but it had a long gestation. Much of its text was tried out in a series of sermons preached by Stott in All Souls Langham Place, in 1978 and 1979, on 'Issues facing Britain today', following a suggestion by Michael Baughen, Stott's successor as Rector. Stott has described their preparation:

Before each sermon, I got Tom Cooper [his study assistant at the time] to bring together a little research group of about eight people. I remember particularly that for the one on work and unemployment we got a trades union leader to come, two un-employed younger people, an employer and an economist, all Bible-believing Christians. I had done some preliminary reading, and I then told them, 'These are my questions, these are my problems; can you throw light on them for me from your point of view and from your expertise? I've studied the biblical aspect; I want you to give me the practical.' Then I sat back and listened for two hours, taking notes, and of course it was very fascinating.
(Stott, taped interview, quoted in Dudley-Smith 2001, p. 338)

Stott dealt with thirteen different topics in *Issues Facing Christians Today*. On some he was resolutely conservative. He accepted critiques of capitalism because the Old Testament prophets repeatedly con-demned those who ignored or exploited the poor. But he took a very definite and positive lead on ecology in a chapter he originally called 'Our human environment' and which became 'Caring for creation' by the fourth edition of the book (2006). It expanded Stott's 1977 sermon on the subject (see page 257) and remains his most extensive treatment of the subject. Between the first and fourth editions of the book, the chapter doubled in length (from thirteen to twenty-six pages), the main change being in the first major section, 'Reasons for change', which increased five-fold (from two to ten pages). This changed the balance of the chapter from Stott's original drafting and presumably his intention of a largely biblical basis for creation care. In this respect the chapter became much more like more conventional treatments of the subject: a statement of the problems to be faced, followed by a biblical justification for action.

The names of the 'experts' Stott consulted on the environment are not known. Because of his own expertise with birds and years of contact with like-minded enthusiasts, he may not have had a formal group of environmental advisers. He had read Rachel Carson's *Silent Spring*, which appeared in 1962. His 1983 notes in the book drew on the journal of the Audobon Society (the US equivalent of the Royal Society for the Protection of Birds), citing how:

A Harvard Medical School professor defended [Carson's] case as accurate. As direct result of publication of *Silent Spring*, President J. F. Kennedy set up a special panel of his Science Advisory Committee to study the problem. Their report entirely vindicated Rachel Carson's thesis. Thus did a single book, whose authoress died 2 years after its publication, influence public policy for good.

Stott had also read (with approval) *Only One Earth: The care and maintenance of a small planet*, the background document prepared by Barbara Ward and René Dubos for the first UN conference on the environment in Stockholm in 1972. Intriguingly, he nowhere cites *Pollution and the Death of Man: The Christian view of ecology*, by Francis Schaeffer (1970), which is often described as the first analysis of the subject by an evangelical, though generally regarded as immature. Stott must have known it.

Stott's friend Oliver Barclay, who had a doctorate in zoology and knew a fair amount about ecology, is thanked for his help with the first edition of *Issues Facing Christians Today*. Barclay was the secretary of the Research Scientists' Christian Fellowship (now Christians in Science) and had acted as rapporteur for a 1972 conference on 'The abuse of the environment' (see below). Stott would certainly have known about this and may have used material from it. In the preface to the second edition of the book (1990), Stott notes that new material had been added on the green movement and its warnings about ozone depletion and the greenhouse effect, and on the Brundtland report (World Commission on Environment and Development, 'Our common future', 1987) and the concept of sustainable development, but he does not acknowledge the help of any environmentalists. For the third edition, John Houghton (formerly Director of the Meteorological Office and Chairman of the Royal Commission on Environmental Pollution) is thanked and the 1992 'Earth Summit' in Rio noted. Ex-civil servant at the Department of the Environment, Neil Summerton is credited for his help in the third and fourth editions. The fourth edition (2006) names Peter Harris of A Rocha as a helper.

Additional input may have come via Stott's ongoing involvement with university colleagues. Spanning two decades, he served four one-year terms as President of the Universities and Colleges Christian Fellowship (UCCF), 1961–1962, 1971–1972, 1977–1978 and 1981–1982 (Dudley-Smith 2001, pp. 274 and 486). UCCF issued a press release following the Research Scientists' Christian Fellowship conference, 'The abuse of the environment', in October 1972. The statement was published in the *Journal of the American Scientific Affiliation* in March 1973; italics in the extract are as in the original source).

Man has a positive responsibility to manage nature

1 The Christian's positive mandate

A. Man has *a positive responsibility to manage 'nature'* and to mold it for his own good (Genesis 1:28, 2:5 and 15).

This was as true before the Fall as after it. Man has still an ongoing responsibility, or mandate, to control and use natural resources for his own *corporate* good and for posterity.

B. *Since the Fall* there is added a lack of some degree of harmony between man and his environment which makes the task harder and at times distasteful. The environment is not entirely friendly and it needs to be tamed as well as used. This, however, only alters man's role in *degree* and not in principle. For most purposes the principle (A) is an adequate rule. However well man had behaved it is hard to see how he could have avoided an ultimate problem of population and use of scarce resources.

C. The Christian should hold any constructive *work as honorable*. Jesus was a carpenter, the apostles mostly fishermen and Adam was a gardener even before the Fall. Most constructive work is, in the end, deriving from 'nature' what we would not otherwise have without molding it to our purposes. Such work is good and, since the Fall at least, essential.

D. In an imperfect world, in which many do not have a proper standard of living, the Christian must have a *compassionate aim of material progress* as a part of his desire for the good of all men. As long as people suffer from diseases, lack of basic education, food, physical facilities for family and personal life, etc. we must work for progress, within the limits outlined below.

E. The Christian cannot therefore accept a call to revert to a state of 'nature'. That is animal not human. We must boldly insist that man is intended to rule his environment and mold it for his own good. That in itself is not selfish; it is a duty. The back-to-nature movement is like asceticism in sex. It denies our God-given calling.

F. The Christian's outlook will in these respects differ from that of non-Christians in each of the above points. His view will also differ as to what is the '*good* of all men'.

The Christian cannot see it as merely material. Most non-Christians will agree, in theory at least, but will value things in a different way. Because Christians value the family so highly, for instance, it will alter any view of 'progress' that may disrupt family life.

2 Limitations and priorities in that mandate

In Genesis 1:28 man is commanded to multiply without qualification. The qualifications, such as marriage and the family, come later. In the same verse he is called to have dominion without qualification but qualifications are later given in the Bible.

A. *We are to love the Lord our God* and we are *stewards* of *His* world (Genesis 9:1–9, Psalm 8, Leviticus 25:23). This means:
   1 That we must not waste God's wealth; we are to use His gifts as He does and as He commands us.
   2 We are His vice-regents (Psalm 8) and we are to make a *constructive* use of nature consistent with *respect* for it as His.
B. *We are to love our neighbor as ourselves.* The Christian's mandate is for the whole of mankind. It is not sectional and it includes future generations. This limits us severely but constructively.
C. We *must beware of love of self.* Many abuses have arisen from *selfishness* and *greed*, etc. Some are due to *ignorance* and in that case only become blameworthy when we discover our fault and do nothing about it. The Christian must constantly speak out, especially when his own group or society or country is guilty of greed, luxury and selfishness. (Man's fallen nature is very evident here.)
D. *The methods used must be ethical.* Not everything that can be done should be done. Wholesale abortion for instance is not a Christian option. The break up of family

life or euthanasia are not methods that we can accept any more than war, famine or genocide.

E. Everything created by God is good (1 Timothy 4:4). Therefore our management must be conservative. The creation has a wonderful balance and richness which is all too easily destroyed thoughtlessly. We want to *preserve a natural state and balance as far as these are compatible with other positively good aims.* Like the ideal of physical health (which may involve sanitation, extermination of certain species, etc.) there is an ideal of human well-being which includes for the Christian at least a recognition that man, if he is to be altogether *healthy*, needs beauty, contact with trees and birds and animals, human community, mental and physical recreation, etc. and a life which can be open to God and His truth. If not all are available then we must compensate by art, etc. We therefore want to change nature as little as possible and to preserve the diversity of nature and a state of balance. Man's aesthetic sense is not altogether misplaced. What men value as beautiful should be highly prized.

3 Some practical applications

A. We must use the best knowledge and methods available to avoid destruction and establish a reasonably natural state of equilibrium. Biological resources (e.g., whales) should be managed as long-term assets. Mineral resources must be used economically.

B. Scarce resources especially, but all natural resources, should be used as a trust. Conservation and recycling of many waste products should have a much higher priority than at present.

C. The extinction of species and of natural habitats is a cause for concern; they represent a loss of natural diversity and often upset the balance of nature more than is expected. Even if tigers have to be confined to game parks and yellow fever mosquitoes extirpated from areas where they might carry yellow fever, we should hope to preserve the species if possible. Even malaria has its medicinal uses against other diseases. There is here a question of balance and even if *Bacillus tuberculosis* has its uses we would all be glad to see it extinct unless we can completely control it.

D. Population growth may need to be checked artificially if natural falls in reproductive rates do not operate adequately. If we cannot give the next generation a wholesome life if their number is too large, we should avoid their increase. This is a corporate responsibility. As nearly all parents at some stage say 'Enough! We cannot adequately look after more children', so the community must do the same.

E. Governments will need great reinforcing in their resolves to do good because every government is tempted to find favor by taking more out of 'nature' than is necessary at the expense of future generations. Christian opinion is needed to help to create a whole attitude to natural resources that will enable governments to do what in their responsible moments they would like to, but dare not, because of popular greed. There is a stage between personal motivation and legislation in which Christian opinion should be influential. This stage is the creation of public opinion on which legislation can be based. The existentialist mood of living only in and for the present has to be fought here. Rational long-term planning is necessary.

F. Christians will need to set an example of abstemiousness in consumption (i.e., standard of living), perhaps in family size, and in respect and love for the creation, even when it requires extra effort and self-sacrifice to do so.

(UCCF 1973, pp. 3–4)

Creation care became a regular theme in LICC teaching, with lectures by Ron Elsdon, Rowland Moss, Andrew Kirk and John

Houghton. In 1985, Stott organized a joint conference of LICC and the Christian Ecology Group (now Green Christian) on 'People, technology and the environment'; it was chaired by Rowland Moss (author of *The Earth in Our Hands* 1982) and involved Sam Berry (author of *Ecology and Ethics* 1972) and Ron Elsdon (author of *Bent World* 1981). LICC produced a study pack in 1991 with a succinct account of creation care by Stott, with two main headings: the trinitarian work of God in creation, and God's delegation of his creation to us, interpreted as cooperation with God rather than deification (as in Gaia or the New Age movement) or exploitation. Its framework is very similar to that of the keynote talk he gave at a conference in 1989, 'Caring for God's world', organized by A Rocha with Christian Impact in Reading (published in 1990 as A Rocha Occasional Publication Number 2).

The chapter 'Caring for creation' (which was entitled 'Our human environment' in the original edition) in *Issues Facing Christians Today* had four sections: 'Reasons for environmental concern' (under five headings: 'Population growth', 'Resource depletion', 'Reduction in biodiversity', 'Waste disposal' and 'Climate change'); 'Biblical perspective' (subdivided into 'Dominion over the earth', 'Cooperation with the earth' and 'Entrusted with the earth'); 'The conservation debate'; and 'Contemporary awareness'. The five topics described in the section 'Reasons for environmental concern' were the same as those cited by Stott in the first edition of *Issues Facing Christians Today*, although their details were updated in successive editions of the book. The contents of the section are necessarily fluid, as new discoveries are made and fresh damage discovered. Useful summaries by Christian authors are given by Martin and Margot Hodson (2015, 2017) and James Hindson (2016). The five reasons for concern are continually changing and developing. For completeness, they are reproduced in Appendix 2. Encouragingly, the 'Biblical perspective' section remained exactly the same throughout the revisions of the book, implying that it was Stott's settled conclusion. Indeed, Stott uses a framework that he repeated in later works (the 'LICC study guide' of 1991 and his address to an A Rocha conference in 1989). His starting point is that the earth belongs to God but its care is delegated to us. This gives us dominion over the earth as divinely appointed trustees under God and in cooperation with him, a dominion that we are charged with exercising. The whole chapter is not reproduced here because the 1989 A Rocha address was really an expanded version of the 'Biblical perspective' section of the book, and the expanded A Rocha version is reprinted in Appendix 2 in this volume. 'The conservation debate' and 'Contemporary awareness' sections were only slightly changed between the 1984 and 2006 editions and these are reproduced here, together with the introduction to the chapter (all from the fourth edition, published in 2006).

Issues Facing Christians Today, chapter 5: 'Caring for creation' (2006)

In September 2002 world leaders, with the notable exception of President George W. Bush, assembled in Johannesburg for the follow-up conference to the first United Nations Conference on Environment and Development which had been held in Rio de Janeiro in June 1992. Popularly known as the 'Earth Summit', this original gathering of more than 100 heads of state with representatives of other governments, of the scientific community and of special interest groups is thought to have been the largest conference ever held. A decade later, the Johannesburg conference seemed to many to reveal the intractable difficulties we currently face in trying to address problems that had only intensified since 1992. The 2002 agenda focused on sustainable development, biodiversity, resource depletion, pollution and climate change, but all, with the possible exception of water conservation, were discussed in an atmosphere of growing controversy and disappointment that led to few definite proposals. Even the conventions initiated at Rio ten years earlier had subsequently been ratified by few national governments. Despite this, there was perhaps a more positive development as a result of the growing awareness that earlier, more confrontational approaches were giving place to new alliances between economic and social development and environmental concerns, and that in this creative process ways forward might be more easily found. Mark Malloch Brown, administrator of the United Nations Development Program (UNDP), said, 'The old environmental movement had a reputation of elitism. The key now is to put people first and the environment second, but to remember that when you exhaust resources, you destroy people.' For Brown, as for many others, sustainable development became the watchword of the new decade.

Meanwhile, the scientific community entered into vehement debate following the publication of statistician Bjorn Lomberg's *The Skeptical Environmentalist* in 2002, in which he challenged many of the more pessimistic scenarios of environmental groups and non-governmental organizations (NGOs). The violence of the argument revealed the central role that ideology and economic theory continue to play in the discussion of environmental issues, even when the subject is apparently restricted to data and its interpretation. A sad result has been the wariness of the Christian community in the wealthier world to face the urgent questions that impact the daily life of the poor, and the well-being of the wider creation.

Even so, in wider society, it is remarkable how quickly a dedicated, campaigning minority succeeded in the last decades of the twentieth century in alerting the general public to green concerns. Significant numbers of people in the wealthier world nowadays seem to be apprehensive about the destruction of the tropical rainforest, the depletion of the ozone layer, climate change and the imminent disappearance of a number of spectacular large mammals such as the Siberian tiger. The key is to translate these concerns into lifestyle changes and political action. Previously indifferent politicians have become obliged to add green issues to their agendas. Corporations have departments specializing in the ecological aspects of their businesses. Most petrol-engine cars on the road use lead-free petrol, and emissions laws are being tightened. In addition, householders are becoming 'green consumers', using more products that are environmentally friendly, eating more 'natural' or 'organic' foods and encouraging the recycling of paper, glass and metals.

There seem to be five (or seven, according to DeWitt in Berry 2000, pp. 61–62) main areas of widespread environmental concern which help to explain this rise in public awareness. They should be seen in relation to one another [Appendix 2 details the five reasons for environmental concern] (Stott 2006, pp. 135–136).

The conservation debate

Trusteeship includes conservation. The greatest threat to humankind may prove in the end to be not a wartime but a peacetime peril, namely the spoliation of the earth's natural resources by human folly or greed. All life on earth is dependent on the biosphere, the narrow layer of water, soil and air in which we live. Yet our record in conserving it, especially during the twentieth century, is not good.

At the same time, not all Christians have accepted the responsibility which Scripture lays upon us; some have even used the Genesis story to excuse their irresponsibility. Gavin Maxwell, author of books on otters, especially *Ring of Bright Water*, once wrote how he lost two lovely otter cubs he had brought back from Nigeria: 'A minister of the Church of Scotland, walking along the foreshore with a shotgun, found them at play by the tide's edge and shot them. One was killed outright, the other died of her wounds in the water. The minister expressed regret, but reminded a journalist that "the Lord gave man control over the beasts of the field"' (Maxwell 1963). As Professor C. F. D. Moule rightly comments, 'A crime against sense and sensibility cannot be defended by the appeal to mere texts' (Moule 1964, p. 1; see also Linzey 1988).

To be sure, the biblical texts have been variously interpreted. In the Middle Ages, for example, Thomas Aquinas taught that animals exist entirely for human pleasure and profit, whereas

Francis of Assisi treated them as his equals, his brothers and sisters. It was Jeremy Bentham, however, at the end of the eighteenth century, who first maintained that animals have rights, because they are sentient creatures which feel pain. In our day Dr Peter Singer, professor of bioethics at Princeton University, has gone much further. In his controversial book *Animal Liberation* (Singer [1975] 1990), although he concedes that there are differences between humans and animals, he yet argues for the extension of the 'basic principle of equality' to animals (or rather to 'non-human animals', as he calls them). He rejects what he calls 'species-ism' as vigorously as he rejects racism and sexism. He defines it as 'a prejudice or attitude of bias in favour of the interests of members of one's own species and against those of members of other species' (Singer [1975] 1990, p. 6). In consequence, the presupposition that 'the human animal' has the right to rule 'over other animals' is in his opinion 'now obsolete' (Singer [1975] 1990, p. 185).

This is an extreme overreaction, however. We cannot possibly surrender the fundamental truth that human beings alone of all God's creatures are made in his image and are given a responsible dominion over the earth and its creatures. It is more meaningful, therefore, to speak of our responsibilities to and for animals than of rights possessed by animals themselves. Since God created them (Genesis 1), since he shows his concern for them by giving them life, food and shelter (Psalm 104), and since Jesus spoke of their intrinsic 'value' (Matthew 10:31; 12:12), we too must be committed to their welfare. The Bible is quite clear on this point. According to the law, the benefits of the Sabbath rest were to be enjoyed by animals as well as humans (Exodus 20:10). According to the Wisdom Literature, 'A righteous man cares for the needs of his animal' (Proverbs 12:10).

Anxious public debate continues, not least among Christians, about the application of these biblical principles to such practices as vivisection, intensive farming, the shipping and slaughter of animals for food, their domestication for work and play and the keeping of pets. Christians should protest against all perceived cruelty to animals, and campaign for their humane treatment in all circumstances, asking ourselves whether each practice is consonant with their value (as God's creatures) and with our responsibility (as God's stewards).

What about the Genesis texts, however? Are we sure that we have interpreted them correctly? Or are the critics of Christianity right in saying that these verses are to blame for contemporary ecological irresponsibility? For example, the American historian Lynn White, of the University of California, Berkeley, has written: 'Christianity . . . not only established a dualism of man and nature, but also insisted that it is God's will that man exploit nature for his proper ends . . . Christianity bears a huge burden of guilt' (White 1967, pp. 1,203–1,207). More outspoken still is Ian L. McHarg. He is a Scot, who spent his childhood between the ugliness of Glasgow and the beauty of the Firth of Clyde and the Western Highlands and Islands. He became a town planner, an ecologist and the founder and chairman of the Department of Landscape Architecture and Regional Planning at the University of Pennsylvania. In 1969 he wrote that the Genesis story, 'in its insistence upon dominion and subjugation of nature, encourages the most exploitative and destructive instincts in man rather than those that are deferential and creative. Indeed, if one seeks license for those who would increase radioactivity, create canals and harbors with atomic bombs, employ poisons without constraint, or give consent to the bulldozer mentality, there could be no better injunction than this text' (i.e., Genesis 1:26, 28). 'When this is understood,' he continues, 'the conquest, the depredations and the despoliation are comprehensible' (McHarg 1969, p. 26). God's affirmation about man's dominion was 'also a declaration of war on nature'. He concludes with these words: 'Dominion and subjugation must be expunged as the biblical injunction of man's relation to nature' (McHarg 1969, p. 197).

In his Dunning Trust lectures in 1972–1973, Ian McHarg further extended his assault. He traced Western man's attitude to the natural world to 'three horrifying lines' in Genesis 1 about the dominion which God gave to man. 'Dominion is a non-negotiating relationship,' he said. 'If you want to find one text of compounded horror which will guarantee that the relationship of man to nature can only be destruction, which will atrophy any creative skill ... which will explain all of the destruction and all of the despoliation accomplished by Western man for at least these 2,000 years, then you do not have to look any further than this ghastly, calamitous text' (McHarg 1972–1973).

Ian McHarg uses very intemperate language to state his case. Some misguided people (e.g., Gavin Maxwell's minister) may have tried to defend their irresponsible use of Genesis 1. But it is absurd to call this text 'horrifying', 'ghastly' and 'calamitous', and then attribute to it two millennia of Western man's exploitation of the environment.

A much more temperate judgement is supplied by Keith Thomas, the Oxford University social historian. In his *Man and the Natural World*, he provides meticulously thorough documentation for changing attitudes towards nature in England between 1500 and 1800 (Thomas 1983; see also Echlin 1989; Russell 1994, pp. 86–93). His theme is that at the beginning of this period, 'human ascendancy' was taken for granted. People accepted 'the long-established view ... that the world had been created for man's sake and that other species were meant to be subordinate to his wishes and needs' (Thomas 1983, p. 17). Gradually, however, this 'breathtakingly anthropocentric' interpretation of the early chapters of Genesis was discarded (Thomas 1983, p. 18). It is true that some Christians did use the grant of 'dominion' over the creatures as a mandate even for such cruel sports as bear-baiting and cock-fighting (Thomas 1983, p. 22). But Dr Thomas also writes that Genesis 1 cannot be blamed for ecological problems, since (a) they exist in 'parts of the world where the Judaeo-Christian tradition has had no influence', (b) Genesis also contains a 'distinctive doctrine of human stewardship and responsibility for God's creatures', and (c) other parts of the Old Testament clearly inculcate care for the animal creation (Thomas 1983, p. 24; cf. p. 151). In fact he concedes that 'the modern idea of the balance of nature . . . had a theological basis before it gained a scientific one. It was belief in the perfection of God's design which preceded and underpinned the concept of the ecological chain, any link of which it would be dangerous to move' (Thomas 1983, p. 278). So let us look at the Genesis text again.

It is true that the two Hebrew words used in Genesis 1:26 and 28 are forceful. The verb translated 'have dominion' (RSV) means to 'tread' or 'trample' on, so that the paraphrase in Psalm 8 is 'you put everything under his feet'. It is often used in the Old Testament of the rule of kings. The other verb, 'subdue', was used of subduing enemies in warfare and of bringing people into subjection or bondage as slaves. So man was commanded to rule the creatures of the sea, sky and earth (v. 26) and to enslave the earth, bringing it into subjection (v. 28). Ian McHarg is right, then? No, he is not. It is an elementary principle of biblical interpretation that one must not establish the meaning of words by their etymology alone, but also and especially by the way they are used in their context. What I have written earlier about this biblical instruction is germane to the interpretation of these texts. We have seen that the dominion God has given us is delegated, responsible and cooperative; that it is intended to express the same sustaining care of the environment as its Creator's; and that, far from exploiting the earth and its creatures, we are to use them in such a way as to be accountable to God and to serve others. We have no liberty to do what Ian McHarg did in one of his lectures, namely to set Genesis 1 and 2 in opposition to each other as if Genesis 2 taught 'cultivation' and Genesis 1 'destruction'. On the contrary, the two passages interpret each other. The dominion God has given humankind is a conscientious and caring stewardship which involves the husbanding of the earth's resources. It would be ludicrous to suppose that God first created the earth and then handed it over to us to destroy it.

Contemporary awareness

Certainly our generation is taking environmental responsibility more seriously than our immediate predecessors did. Scientists are emphasizing the delicate balance of nature. God has established in nature almost unbelievable powers of recuperation and regeneration, and in particular a cycle for the renewal of energy (from sun to plants to animals to bacteria to earth, and back to plants again). It is an example of what Barbara Ward called 'the most majestic unity' of our planet. It is due to natural laws which produce a 'dynamic equilibrium of biological forces held in position by checks and balances of a most delicate sort' (Ward and Dubos 1972, p. 83). 'They are so intricate,' commented Dr John Klotz, the American conservationist, 'that they could not have developed by chance' (Ward and Dubos 1972, p. 45). But if we despoil the green surface of the earth, or destroy the plankton of the oceans, we will quickly reach the point of no return in the recycling process. Our immense modern scientific knowledge teaches us 'one thing above all', wrote Barbara Ward, namely the 'need for extreme caution, a sense of the appalling vastness and complexity of the forces that can be unleashed, and of the eggshell delicacy of the agents that can be upset' (Ward and Dubos 1972, p. 85).

There have been a number of encouragements in recent years. The environment has, once again, become an important agenda item at world summits. Yet it is easier to sign treaties than to live lives that are consistent with good trusteeship of God's world.

Have Christians a distinctive contribution to make to the ecological debate? Yes, we believe both that God created the earth, entrusting its care to us, and that he will one day re-create it, when he makes 'the new heaven and the new earth'. For 'the whole creation has been groaning as in the pains of childbirth right up to the present time'. Its groans are due to its 'bondage to decay' and its consequent 'frustration'. In the end, however, it will come to share in 'the glorious freedom of the children of God'. That is, its bondage will give place to freedom, its decay to glory, and its pain to the joy of a new world being born (Romans 8:19–22). These two doctrines, regarding the beginning and the end of history, the creation and the consummation, have a profound effect on our perspective. They give us an appropriate respect for the earth, indeed for the whole material creation, since God both made it and will remake it.

In consequence, we must learn to think and act ecologically. We repent of extravagance, pollution and wanton destruction. We recognize that human beings find it easier to subdue the earth than they do to subdue themselves. Ronald Higgins' book *The Seventh Enemy* is significant in this respect. The first six 'enemies' are the population explosion, the food crisis, the scarcity of resources, environmental degradation, nuclear abuse and scientific technology. The seventh enemy, however, is ourselves, our personal blindness and political inertia in the face of today's ecological challenge. That is why the sub-title of Ronald Higgins' book is 'The human factor in the global crisis'. The human race needs a new self-awareness, and fresh vision, a reawakening of its moral and religious capabilities (Higgins 1978). But is this possible? Yes, Christians are convinced it is.

One of the particular merits of the late Professor Klaus Bockmuhl's booklet *Conservation and Lifestyle* is that he goes beyond the 'Christian criteria' for environmental responsibility to the 'Christian motives'. In his conclusion he presses the challenge home: 'What is sought from Christians is the motivation for selfless service, which once distinguished the Christian heritage. We should be pioneers in the care of mankind . . . We should show whence the power and perspective for such a contribution come. We are charged to give an example.' We have to 'reawaken the heart of the gospel ethic' (Bockmuhl 1975, pp. 23–24; see also Elsdon 1992; Russell 1994;

Stott 1996). We may be thankful that there are now a number of Christian organizations working specifically in the area of care for creation. Among them are the John Ray Institute, the International Evangelical Environmental Network, A Rocha and the Au Sable Institute. At the root of the ecological crisis is human greed, what has been called 'economic gain by environmental loss'. Often it is a question of competing commercial interests (though some multinational corporations have an environmental department). It is only logical that the consumer should pay the cost of production without pollution, whether in increased prices or (through a government subsidy to the manufacturer) in increased taxes. Christians should not grudge this, if it is the cost of responsible, ecological stewardship.

Those who want to live responsibly in the light of the biblical vision for the environment and the current crises which are besetting it will find many practical suggestions in Ruth Valerio's recent book *L Is for Lifestyle* (2019), which is subtitled 'Christian living that doesn't cost the earth'. The book goes through the alphabet and looks at particular issues we are facing and offers indications of how we could change our lifestyle or be better informed about that particular issue. So, A is for activists, B is for bananas, H is for HIV, R is for recycling, S is for simplicity, T is for tourism and so on. The book is a combination of practical suggestions and thoughtful meditations on issues such as globalization and simplicity. It also contains suggestions of where to go for further information and help.

As Majority World countries struggle to raise their standards of living, the environment is often given less priority than the more immediate problems of undernourishment, disease and poverty. This is understandable, and these deeper issues must be addressed if we are ever to make headway in preserving and enhancing the natural environment. Furthermore, to insist on the protection of tropical forests in the Majority World, if we are unwilling to reduce CO_2 output in our own countries, is rank hypocrisy. We must also be willing both to share technologies which can help curb natural destruction and to create economic benefits for environmentally safe business practices. While the vast disparity between wealth and poverty remains, Christians are bound to have an uneasy conscience. We should strenuously avoid all wastefulness and greed, not only out of solidarity with the poor but also out of respect for the living environment.

(Stott 2006, pp. 151–157)

8

Commitment to nature conservation and Christian mission

Issues Facing Christians Today was first published in 1984. The previous year the A Rocha Trust had been established with the twin tasks of nature conservation and Christian mission. Stott shared the aims of A Rocha and was a strong supporter from its early days. Indeed, he helped to draft the five commitments that the growing global movement adopted as it grew beyond its first decade of work in Portugal:

- **Christian** a biblical faith in the living God, who made the world, loves it and entrusts it to the care of human society;
- **conservation** research for the conservation and restoration of the natural world, plus environmental education programmes for people of all ages;
- **community** through commitment to God, one another and the wider creation, to develop good relationships within both the A Rocha family and local communities;
- **cross-cultural** drawing on the insights and skills of people from diverse cultures, both locally and around the world;
- **cooperation** working in partnership with a wide variety of organizations and individuals who share A Rocha's concern for a sustainable world.

In 1983, Reverend Peter and Miranda Harris went to the Algarve in southern Portugal to test this vision. They were seconded to A Rocha by the Anglican missionary agency Crosslinks, which had come to accept, on scriptural grounds, that mission included the care of creation. In 1986, the trust bought the old farmhouse that became the centre of the work, situated on a peninsula by the Alvor estuary and its extensive salt marshes. The A Rocha staff continue to carry out systematic studies of the birds, insects and plants there. They have fought hard to protect the area from development and are the focus of a community welcoming students and others to share their vision.

A Rocha was close to Stott's heart from its beginning. He became a member of its International Council of Reference and took a close interest in its work. A Rocha is now active in twenty countries around the world. The story of its early years has been told by Peter Harris in a book, *Under the Bright Wings* (1983), and its further development in *Kingfisher's Fire* (2008). Stott wrote the foreword to the first book, repeating his familiar detestation of dualism and separating God's works of creation and redemption:

Peter [Harris] refuses to compartmentalise Christian discipleship. His overriding concern is to help break down the disastrous dualism which still exists in many Christians between the sacred and the secular, the spiritual and the material, the soul and the body, as if God were interested only in the former, in the 'religious' bits of our lives, and as if only they deserve to be called 'Christian'.

But the living God of the Bible is the God of both creation and redemption, and is concerned for the totality of our well-being. Put another way, the older theologians used to say that God has written two books, one called 'nature' and the other called 'Scripture', through which he has revealed himself. Moreover, he has given us these two books to study. The study of the natural order is 'science', and of the biblical revelation 'theology'. And as we engage in these twin disciplines, we are (in the words of the seventeenth-century astronomer Johann Kepler) 'thinking God's thoughts after him'.

Christian people should surely have been in the vanguard of the movement for environmental responsibility, because of our doctrines of creation and stewardship. Did God make the world? Does he sustain it? Has he committed its resources to our care? His personal concern for his own creation should be sufficient to inspire us to be equally concerned.

But can ecological involvement properly be included under the heading of 'mission'? Yes, it can and should. For mission embraces everything Christ sends his people into the world to do, service as well as evangelism. And we cannot truly love and serve our neighbours if at the same time we are destroying their environment, or acquiescing in its destruction, or even ignoring the environmentally depleted circumstances in which so many people are condemned to live. As by the incarnation Jesus Christ entered into our world, so true incarnational mission involves entering into other people's worlds, including the world of their social and environmental reality.

The gospel itself includes God's creation as well as his work of redemption. Certainly the apostle Paul, in his sermon to the Athenian philosophers, ranged much more widely than we usually do in our gospel preaching. He took in the whole of time from the creation to the consummation, and demonstrated from the truth of God as creator and sustainer of all things the sheer absurdity of worshipping idols made by human hands.

As for methods of evangelism, an activity which Peter Harris clearly and rightly distinguishes from both propaganda and proselytism, he lays his emphasis on the importance of the Christian community. Of course the gospel must be articulated in words. But so deeply alienated are contemporary Europeans from the traditional image of the church, that almost nothing is more important than that people should be able to *see* what we are talking about. In consequence, Peter and Miranda and their four children have opened their hearts and their home to people. They welcome virtually everybody who comes. It has been a costly commitment. The pressures have been relentless. And they recognise that there must be sensible limits to this kind of exposure. Nevertheless, they are determined that the gospel of God's love will be given visible and tangible expression at Cruzinha [A Rocha's base in Portugal].

Peter's account of the A Rocha odyssey is marked both by humility (although the centre has already had a remarkable influence on the conservation movement in Portugal) and by honesty (he neither exaggerates, nor portrays himself, his family and his colleagues as other than flawed and frail human beings). At times his narrative is also hilariously funny, as he laughs at the vagaries of the human scene and at himself. I hope many people will read his book. They are sure to be enriched by it.

It will be evident to readers that I love and admire Peter and Miranda, and enormously enjoyed a recent birdwatching expedition with them in north-west Turkey, as I had also enjoyed some previous birding with Peter in Portugal, west Wales and Morocco. I thank God for their vision, commitment, faith and perseverance, their love for the people they are seeking to serve, and their deep immersion in the Portuguese language and culture. In the developing ministry of A Rocha an exciting, contemporary form of Christian ministry has come alive.

(Stott in Harris 1983, pp. ix–xi)

Peter Harris shared Stott's vision for the natural world and became one of Stott's closest birdwatching friends. He has written his own memoir of Stott in a chapter, 'Birding before dawn around the world', in *John Stott: A portrait by his friends*, edited by Chris Wright.

It had all come as something of a surprise. Despite the fact that rather few British Christians seemed to be taking the known crisis in the world's ecosystems to heart, the Universities and Colleges Christian Fellowship (UCCF) had decided to sponsor our ornithological trip to southern Sweden, their first environmental initiative. It was 1982, and in the face of a certain amount of evangelical muttering, we thought it prudent to recruit some irreproachable theological support. I had only met John Stott once before, two years earlier, when he had come to bless the graduating class of ordinands and other students from Trinity College, Bristol, but his passion for birding was well known. Given his increasingly direct appeals for contemporary application of biblical Christian thinking, we had some hope that he would give us a sympathetic hearing for our ideas. I was, however, completely unprepared for the fact that he was so immediately interested. John's letters are the kind you keep, and so I still have this letter with the others: 'I am so glad the Falsterbo expedition to watch the raptor migration was such a success – I wish I could have joined you!'

So he never made it on that trip, but he did agree immediately to join the Council of Reference of the A Rocha Trust to which it gave birth. Once again, it was on conditions we had not expected, but which we came to know as characteristic. He wrote:

I made a decision some years ago that, as a matter of integrity, I would not be on any council of reference unless I was personally involved in the work concerned, and thus able to speak from personal knowledge about it. Indeed, only these last two or three weeks I have declined a couple of invitations on this ground . . . Perhaps I should insist on your inviting me to visit the field study centre and bird observatory in Portugal [A Rocha] at the earliest possible moment!! Will you be coming to London during the early months of the New Year? Then perhaps we could meet and talk and my conscience would permit me to accept your invitation.

We did meet. He did come to Portugal. And it proved to be the start of a friendship and a collaboration that lasted over a quarter of a century, even though it came at a time of his life when he was already deeply committed to many other organizations around the world.

At first we saw our role as perhaps providing the way for John to lay down some of the more major demands of his life.

In doing birding in the spare moments of his travels, he was able to keep his legendary mental powers in gear, but he was then applying it to problems such as how to determine the length of the Bee-eaters' nest hole, rather than the more intractable challenges of whether the Anglican Church was thinking straight about ordaining women bishops, or how evangelical Christian leaders around the world could reconcile their newly recovered social conscience with their convictions about the vital work of preaching and evangelism.

Even our own somewhat spontaneous family life seemed to be a welcome distraction on his first stay with us in our rented accommodation in Portugal. He arrived late one evening when our youngest daughter, Bethan, was just three weeks old, and Miranda's *feijoada* (a Portuguese dish of beans with beef and pork) was about to burn on the stove as John came over the doorstep. Miranda's request, 'Could you hold her a moment?' didn't prove a challenge to this particular bachelor. He simply called on years of baptismal experience and took Bethan in his arms. He showed equal abilities with small children and struck up rapid friendships with all of ours. He developed a series of competitions with our son Jeremy, who at the ripe age of four had just broken his arm by tripping over on the rough track by our house. They culminated in John secretly signing Jem's plaster cast while he slept on the morning John left at his accustomed early hour. I would have come close to burnout if I had ever attempted to keep up with the rhythms of life that were a simple routine for John.

However, John's ease with pre-dawn hours equipped him to be the perfect companion on a series of birding trips over successive years. The trick was to find a place at the end of one of his speaking tours and convene there for a week or so, usually with a couple of other friends, but with only one guiding principle – the birding came first in all the decisions. So the accommodation was frequently lamentable, the food infrequent and occasionally high risk, but John's delight in what he saw and his stamina in getting to the places where some of the more remote species were to be found made every-thing worthwhile. We were fortunate that experts such as Rick and Barbara Mearns could come with us to Turkey and Spain, and in the United States Rob and Helen Kelsh were able to join us. Colin Jackson of A Rocha Kenya also had a spectacular week in Ethiopia with John, continuing the tradition, and Ginny Vroblesky of A Rocha USA went down to Belize for another trip. But mostly it was Miranda and I who had the joy of planning an itinerary that would take John out of the stress of his normal travels and into the close study of what he taught us to understand as 'God's book of works' – the com-panion volume to God's book of words, the Bible, in God's revelation . . .

Over the years his involvement with A Rocha became steadily greater. He helped us formulate a solid theological basis for the work we were doing, and joined us in several countries to plead with Christian leaders the cause of caring for creation. He wrote articles and forewords for our publica-tions, and advised us on the wisdom of different alliances and against potential distractions. I believe his own thinking was able to take shape through the challenge of seeing several of the practical conservation projects that A Rocha people were undertaking in places as diverse as Lebanon, Kenya and Southall in the United Kingdom. He helped us identify some wonderful leaders from the non-Western non-white world, and he made it his business to turn them into what he called 'orni-theologians'.

We will miss him greatly – his gift for close friendship with Miranda and myself, his genuine interest in our family, the welcomes to his tiny London flat to plan the next trip over sandwiches provided by the equally indefatigable Frances [Stott's long-serving secretary], his knowledgeable delight in all he saw that was familiar, and his endless penetrating ques-tions about anything that was new to him. The simplicity of his lifestyle was a constant reminder of his many friends around the world who lived in tough and needy circumstances,

and whom he always kept in his mind and in his (meticulously organized) praying. He was a great field companion and a true Christian – probably more profoundly converted than anyone else I have known.
(Harris in Wright 2011, pp. 155–158 and 160–161)

Peter Harris was a welcomed birdwatching companion of Stott's for several decades. He was interviewed by Lowell Bliss, the Director of Eden Vigil, a US-based charity that provides help to church planters wanting to learn about creation care. Their conversation was published as a podcast in 2012. Harris takes us to the heart of Stott as human being and orni-theologian but, above all, as a dedicated believer. An edited transcript of Harris's replies reads:

John Stott had a remarkable gift of friendship. He was quite extraordinary that way. A Rocha was blessed over 25 years to have John Stott's friendship, and his support and guidance as well. And I think he formed our theology in a deep way, along with others from around the world. And I know that he retained a very close relationship with a number of A Rocha leaders around the world. He has left a remarkable legacy and we will be seeing the fruits of that for many years to come.

I don't think anyone who knew John would describe him as a moderate person. He strove for Anglican moderation, but whatever he did, he did extremely thoroughly, and birding was no exception. He was a very keen birdwatcher. It would be a little unkind to say he was obsessed, but he certainly took his birdwatching with a seriousness that other birders respected and recognize.

Our friendship began in 1982. I thought it was prudent to get some theological firepower to cover us in an expedition to the south of Sweden with a group of students from British universities, with the twin aims of watching the migration of birds of prey and studying the Psalms, in the face of some nervousness on the part of UCCF worried that people would worship nature. I contacted John; I think he was amused by some of the issues that the innocent pursuit of ornithology raised for people. He was somebody who constantly strove to hold all the bits of his life into one whole. And so his relationship with God and his understanding of God as Creator quite naturally gave him a particular kind of joy. Appreciating birds and wild places was quite a straightforward thing for him, something which was instinctive. In fact there is a tradition of Anglican clergymen and birdwatching that goes back at least to the 18th century. Gilbert White of Selborne and many great observers of nature and early scientists were Anglican ministers. But as awareness of ecological crises around the world grew, I think birdwatching moved in John's mind to become something of a missionary and activist issue.

Over the years we joined John in quite a number of birdwatching expeditions. Sometimes it was a simple bribe to get him to speak at one of the A Rocha founding conferences, as he did in Lebanon and Kenya. The deal was if he would do that, usually adding it to an existing programme, then we would go birding afterwards. Or, if he was speaking somewhere in the world and we were able either to get there easily or we were there too, we would put on some days at the beginning or end of his visit. There was an occasion when he was arriving for a speaking tour round the USA just as we were finishing some teaching in Vancouver, and so we agreed to meet in Oregon to take as much ornithological advantage as we could from this happy overlap. Despite his jet-lag, having just arrived from Europe, and having planned the usual 6 a.m. departure for the next day's search for Lewis' Woodpecker, he stayed up until well after midnight, talking over questions about Christian belief that were bothering one of our hosts.

There was also a sense in which my wife Miranda and I sometimes considered it something of a service to call John away from his busy schedule and out among the birds. He drove himself very hard. He would always try to understand those he didn't agree with, and that sort of act of understanding was intellectually and spiritually costly. Everybody writes about the extraordinary pace of life he used to keep and the discipline he maintained; he was usually up at 4.30 in the morning. On one trip we made to Turkey, he had promised himself he would write for an hour every day. He was writing his commentary on Romans and this meant he had to read around 24 or 25 commentaries, many of which he wouldn't have agreed with but he had to try to understand where people were coming from. A birding trip typically kicks off at about 6 in the morning, which meant he had to get his hour done before then, but John wouldn't accept any compromise on the scheduling. Once we had ended up late the previous evening in a fairly basic hostel. It was cold, and the rather public latrines gave the whole place a pervasively unhealthy smell. When Miranda and I stumbled out of bed around 6 a.m. next morning, it was to find John emerging glowing from his unheated room, wrapped head to foot in a blanket, deeply satisfied by the logic of the apostle Paul and content that his morning's writing had done it justice.

We had some very funny moments together. On that Turkish trip, we were up a mountain trying to find some particular species. Because he started so early, John used to take a half an hour out after lunch regardless of where he was. He called it his HHH ('Horizontal Half Hour'). Miranda and I had wandered off looking for different things, and John was always trying to photograph birds as well. When 2 o'clock came he just dug a hole on the hillside to put his hip in and went out like a light. He woke somewhat prematurely being prodded by a shepherd who thought he had found a corpse. John had this incredible capacity to just deflate out for a half hour completely and then come around.

Another memorable time was an incredibly hot time in Morocco towards the northern edge of the Sahara. We got back to the town where we were staying about nine o'clock in the evening; it was still extremely hot. Neither John nor I had eaten much during the day and he got it into his head that we needed to eat outdoors. He negotiated with the owner of the only café in the village (whose café was in a stuffy downstairs room). The poor restaurateur found himself part of an unstoppable mission to find some ropes from a neighbour and then haul table and chairs up on to the flat roof. We sat under the stars until about midnight. It was fantastic.

Then there was the time when Sunday worship conflicted gravely with raptor migration across the Straits of Gibraltar, the wind having swung to the west shortly after dawn, bringing low-flying Black Kites distractingly close as we went into the church. 'Don't I recognize you?' said the minister musingly and hospitably, as we tried to do a rapid exit after the early service. 'Just visiting birdwatchers . . .' muttered John Stott evasively, pulling down his cap and looking shifty as he tried to avoid recognition, thinking of the inevitable delaying conversation that would ensue.

John used to talk about 'orni-theology'. I think it was John's term. He was always trying to hold his birdwatching and his theology together. Many people less keen on birds as he was, were in his eyes subjects to be converted. Orni-theology was his language for saying: 'Well, you've been following me on the theology, so now you need to follow on the ornithology as well, and blend the two.' He used to refer to Matthew 6:26 ('study the birds of the air'), which he always said was a command. He didn't see a Christian had any wriggle room there.

One of the chapters in his book *The Birds Our Teachers* was 'The migration of the storks: repentance'. [It also formed the subject of an All Souls sermon on 8 August, 1999, with the text, Jeremiah 8:7 [NIV]: 'Even the stork in the sky knows her appointed seasons. Even the dove, the swift and the thrush observe the time of their migration. But my people do not know the requirements of the law.'] John commented that this could very well be one of the first written mentions of bird migration in all of literature since Jeremiah was writing in the 7th century before Christ. In the Bekaa Valley of Lebanon where we work, you can still see tens of thousands of storks going through on migration, and the prophet Jeremiah would have been very familiar with this phenomenon. He would have had this clear sense of the birds orientated by God's wisdom. It's interesting that people didn't believe in or understand migration at all until relatively recently; they thought swallows went down into reed beds for the winter, and re-emerged again in the spring. So, Jeremiah wasn't doing badly.

Palestine is a flyway for migrants and it's rather heart-breaking actually to think of the numbers that the people of Jeremiah's times would have seen, compared to what we see now. If you look at Psalm 104, most of the species that are listed there are now gone from the region altogether, and the numbers must be a fraction of what they were. The numbers of migration hotspots now are a fraction of what they were fifty years ago.

Everybody who knew him will tell you that one of the most remarkable things about John Stott was the way that he was constantly taking on new subjects, challenging himself with opinions from the professional worlds that he was in touch with. We had many conversations about key issues in the environmental world. He was always keeping his ideas under revision. He would think about things and reflect on them. He was an extremely good listener and an avid learner. It's not surprising that, as issues became more and more current and more and more in the public space, John was keen to engage with them. He would seek out people expert in their fields and probe their knowledge. I think one advantage was that those people were in return challenged to reflect theologically on what they were doing.

I described John in the book *John Stott: A portrait by his friends* (Wright 2011) as 'probably more profoundly converted than anyone else I have known.' He was quite fearless in following his understanding of Christ through to its logical conclusions. He didn't hold much back. If you were travelling with him, he would swing his legs over the bed in a determined fashion at half past four in the morning, just to make sure he didn't go back to bed. The guy was remarkably single-minded.

He was trained to have a very questioning mind; he came from a very rigorous academic tradition. C. S. Lewis said of himself, 'You won't see my like again; I'm a dinosaur.' John came from the same generation; its intellectual training was pretty demanding.

That applied also to John's spirituality, although he wouldn't have used the word. It meant he endeavoured to see what was Christlike in absolutely everything: what he ate, when he ate, what he wore, where he lived, the films he watched, the conversations he had, even the birds he watched. He consciously shared his life with people of all ages, and from many different cultures. He's well known for having remained single because he felt he had a particular calling that really wouldn't suit the married life. From the early days of Lausanne he opened himself to the criticisms and perspectives of Christians from the developing world. He had a tremendous integrity. The way he lived privately matched what he said publicly, and that's a fantastic thing when you see it in a Christian leader. I think that was why he was so authoritative. It wasn't that he was in any way dogmatic; it was just that what he said came across with great weight because he was living it, even if he hadn't got all the answers. There was a mixture of conviction and humility in John. That meant people weren't deterred from following him on the same paths.

By the time he wrote *The Radical Disciple* (Stott 2010b), his strength, both physical and intellectual, was clearly waning. That book was very important to him, and not least the final chapter about death and dying. In the book, John set out his path of discipleship – particularly the eight traits he called all of us to also take seriously. The first four are nonconformity, Christlikeness, maturity, and then chapter number four, creation care.

We often talked about the book when we went to see him in his last months. I think he was astonished that, given the urgency of the environmental issues we all faced and given the theological priorities that Scripture gives to creation,

creation care continued to be such an orphan child within the evangelical conscience and awareness. I wasn't surprised he put the creation care chapter so front and centre of what he was writing about in neglected issues. And yet John, one of our greatest theologians of our age, seems to base himself on just two verses: Psalm 24:1: 'The Earth is the Lord's' and Psalm 115:16: 'The Earth He has given to humankind.' I don't think he was trying to build a theology. I have heard him appeal to many other scriptures on creation over the years. His concern in the chapter was to avoid both the deification and the exploitation of nature. He sets out the best way to accomplish this was in cooperation with God. I wouldn't want to put words in John's mouth, but you could say that the affirmation in those two verses was sufficient. It certainly would take popular evangelical culture a long way further than it's gone, because both those affirmations challenge the way that most of us in the Western world live: as though the world is just here for us and for our material satisfaction, while rejecting – or at least marginalizing – the God-given responsibility to care for God's creation.

It's possible for Christians to borrow the narrative of the secular environmental movement, and merely gloss it with a bit of God language. But there are some very significant differences between secular environmentalism and a Christian approach to what we would call the care of creation. One of the most significant things is that the Christian engages in these things first and foremost because he believes that this is something that pleases God, that's coherent with a worshipping relationship of a loving Creator. It has been said that you can't say you love Rembrandt and then trash his paintings. So, Christians care for creation, not because they necessarily believe they are going to save the world or because they believe that this is the flavour of the times, but simply out of their response to a loving Creator. I think John was trying to draw attention to that simple truth and also to the sense that insofar as this pleases God, God himself is working. It is the work of

God's Holy Spirit to call the church to a loving relationship with other people and also to a concerned relationship with creation. This is made possible by the work of the Holy Spirit, because it's an extremely difficult work. And if it honours the creation, if it honours the Creator, it's a spiritual path. And in that sense we are cooperating with the Creator.

John repeatedly reminded us that peace with God and Christ extends from the person into their widest set of relationships with other people in the healing of communities. Romans 8 tells us that the whole creation, which is groaning, is waiting for the day when it is drawn into the glorious freedom of the children of God. I don't see how we can ignore that dimension of the gospel.

The scope of the gospel extends to the whole creation. John began his charge to the Third Lausanne Congress, 'we are facing new challenges. For example, there is the spectre of global warming, which adds new urgency to our evangelism'. John was entirely persuaded that climate change was a reality. He was very widely travelled. And anybody who's travelled in the poorer world is not left in much doubt that climate change is happening and that it is now expected to be the biggest driver of people movements globally, the biggest contributor to health issues globally, and certainly the biggest contributor to biodiversity loss globally; it will have profound consequences for human societies. And all of that kind of disruption necessarily poses acute problems and issues to those who are seeking to draw people to understand the love of God in Christ.

This is a conversation that should be with those who are qualified to talk about the issues. We need Christians who are working in climate science to be honest with us about what their data show and their conclusions show. We need those who are taking issue with some of these things to be clear about why they are doing that, because what we're hearing from Christians in the poorer world is that climate change, infrequent weather patterns, acute weather events, all of the things that the climate scientists have been talking about for

decades now, are happening in their lives and causing enormous suffering. And so we do need to have this debate conducted between those who are able to talk about this from their professional background. And I don't think that's what has happened. I often feel the Internet acts as an amplifier of discord, because we don't sit down and spend time with each other and realize that our brothers and sisters are our brothers and sisters even if we don't agree with them.
(Harris 2012, 'Bliss' podcast)

Stott was the archetype and exemplar of an orni-theologian. He took every opportunity to preach the gospel and he took every opportunity to watch birds. His delight in seeing remote species of birds easily overcame the difficulties and basic conditions involved. In his foreword to the American edition of *John Stott: A portrait by his friends* (Wright 2011), David Neff, the editor of *Christianity Today* recorded that when he mentioned that his parents lived in the birding mecca of the American southwest, Stott told him he had been there three times. In return, Stott clearly delighted in ministering to the birdwatching community, and particularly to the A Rocha Trust. In October 1989, he gave the below keynote address, 'The biblical imperative', at the conference 'Caring for God's world' organized by A Rocha in collaboration with the London Institute for Contemporary Christianity (then known as Christian Impact). It was published as A Rocha Occasional Paper No. 2. As noted above, it is an expanded version of the 'biblical perspective' section of the 'Creation care' chapter in *Issues Facing Christians Today*. It is his clearest exposition of our responsibility as Christians for the environment. Stott began with the same two affirmations that were at the heart of *The Radical Disciple* chapter on creation care.

The biblical imperative

My assignment is to attempt to expound the biblical imperative for environmental and ecological concern. There are two major biblical doctrines which together constitute this imperative and which have been neatly captured in the title for this conference – 'Caring for God's world'.

The first doctrine is that the world belongs to God. He is the Creator. It is God's world. The second is that he has committed it to us, so that we are responsible for caring for God's world. We are the caretakers of the environment. So the first doctrine is about God and the creation, while the second is about us and about his delegation to us of ecological responsibility.

1 The creation by God

Many of us when we come to church on the Lord's Day delight to affirm the first section of the Creed – *We believe in God the Father Almighty, maker of heaven and earth.* In saying this we affirm our faith not only in the fact that he is the Creator of all things, but that he is the Almighty, meaning the ruler of all things that he has made. This affirmation is common to all Christians who look to the Bible for their authority and who belong to the tradition of historic Christian orthodoxy. All true Christians are 'creationists' irrespective of whether they think the created earth is young or old and irrespective of whether they think that some form of evolutionary process was involved in the creative activity of God.

We must strenuously resist all attempts to narrow the definitions of 'creation' and 'evolution' in such a way as to make them mutually exclusive, so that if you believe in creation, you cannot believe in evolution and vice versa. Neither of these two words must be hijacked in the interests of a particular pressure group, either 'creation' by six-day creationists or 'evolution' by secular evolutionists. The doctrine of creation does not necessarily mean a six-day creation and the theory of evolution does not necessarily mean a process of random development by modification in which there is no room for God. All Christians believe that God is the Creator of all things, whatever mode or process he employed.

But I want to go beyond that in a way that may be a little less familiar to some of you. In affirming that God is the Creator and Ruler of all things, we need to develop a *trinitarian* understanding of his creative work; we are not only creationists, we are also trinitarians. We are very familiar with the truth that the Father, the Son and the Holy Spirit were together involved in our redemption. I think of 1 Peter 1:2, we 'have been chosen according to the foreknowledge of God the Father, by the sanctifying work of the Spirit, for obedience to Jesus Christ and sprinkling with his Blood.' There in one verse at the beginning of Peter's first letter is a plain reference to the part played by the Father, the Son, and the Holy Spirit in redemption. But we must also recall that the Father, the Son, and the Holy Spirit were together involved in the creation, and are involved in the conservation of the natural order as well.

So let us look at the part played by the three persons of the Trinity.

a) God the Father

We can say with Jeremiah 'Ah, Sovereign Lord, you have made the heavens and the earth by your great power and outstretched arm' (32:17). Similarly, the psalmist ascribes the creation to the fingers and hands of God (8:3, 6). But what in these texts is attributed to his arm, hands and fingers is elsewhere attributed to his bare Word as expressive of his creative will, 'He spoke and it came to be' (Psalm 33:9).

Very different was the grotesque concept of Creation prevalent in the Ancient Near East, such as the Babylonian Creation epic known as *Enuma Elish* with its crude and puerile polytheism. It describes the original struggle between Cosmos and Chaos. It dates from about the second millennium B.C. and was solemnly recited at the turn of every year. In the beginning, it says, nothing existed except the male deity Apsu, the begetter, and the female deity Mummu-Tiamat, the Mother Goddess. Together they formed a watery chaos and brought forth other gods who misbehaved disgracefully and fought one another in endless celestial battles. In the course of time Apsu was murdered in his sleep and Marduk (tall, handsome and powerful) with four eyes and four ears, the loftiest of the gods, resolved to avenge Apsu and attack Tiamat.

> 'Then joined issue Tiamat and Marduk, the wisest of the gods. They strove in single combat, locked in battle. The Lord (Marduk) spread out his net to enfold her. The evil wind . . . he let loose in her face . . . He released the arrow and it tore her belly. It cut through her intestines, splitting her heart. Having thus subdued her, he extinguished her life. He cast down her carcass in order to stand upon it . . . The Lord trod upon the legs of Tiamat. With his unsparing mace he crushed her skull. He split her like a shellfish into two parts. Half of her he set up and ceiled it as the sky. The other half became the foundation of the earth.'

Then in the end Marduk proceeded to create from other parts of her body the stars, the mountains and human beings.

Some foolish secularists say that they find remarkable parallels between *Enuma Elish* and Genesis 1, which makes me wonder if they have read either. It is a relief to turn from this crude polytheism with its unseemly battles between immoral gods. In the noble ethical monotheism of Genesis 1, the Creation is attributed to God's sovereign Will and Word. This is the place of God the Father in the Creation.

b) God the Son

We are very familiar with the central place occupied by God the Son in the redemption of human beings, but we need to see that he occupies a central place in creation and conservation too. Colossians 1:15–17 sums up his creative work in four propositions:

First, God the Son is the agent *through* whom the Creation was brought into being. Three times this truth is asserted in the New Testament. In the first, 'For through him all things were created' (Colossians 1:16a). Secondly 'All things were made through him, and without him nothing was made that has been made' (John 1:3). And thirdly he is the Son 'through whom he made the universe' (Hebrews 1:2).

Second, God the Son is the heir *for* whom the Creation exists. 'All things were created through him and for him' (Colossians 1:16b). So he is Creation's goal as well as its source; its end as well as its beginning. This is reiterated in Hebrews 1:2, that God appointed his Son 'heir of all things'. This one truth should be enough to make every Christian a conscientious environmentalist. If the universe, especially planet earth, is destined by the Father for the Son, and will one day be given to the Son, how can we presume to squander or spoil his inheritance?

Third, God the Son is the integrating principle *in* whom the universe coheres. 'He is before all things and in him all things hold together' (Colossians 1:17). Again, the Son is 'sustaining all things by his powerful word' (Hebrews 1:3). The same word of God by whom the Universe was brought into being, continuously holds it in being and prevents it from falling apart.

Fourth, God the Son is Lord *under* whom the Creation is in subjection. He is 'the firstborn over all creation' (Colossians 1:15). The expression means not that he himself was the first created being, but that he had the right of the first-born over the Creation itself. For he is 'before all things . . .' (not only in time but also in rank).

Indeed it is in the man Christ Jesus that the cultural mandate to subdue the earth is fulfilled. Thus, meditating on Genesis 1, the Psalmist wrote in Psalm 8:6, 'You (God) made him (man, male and female) ruler over the works of your hands; and you put everything under his feet.' Later the writer to the Hebrews, also meditating on Psalm 8, wrote 'Yet at present we do not see everything subject to him [that is under his feet], but we see Jesus . . . crowned with glory and honour' (Hebrews 2:8, 9). Similarly in Ephesians 1:22 we read that God placed all things under his feet and appointed him to be head over everything for the church.

Thus, even while human beings fail adequately to fulfil the environmental mandate which they have been given, Jesus Christ does not fail. For he is the agent, the heir, the sustainer and the Lord of the environment. He is the second Adam, the head of the new Creation, who exercises his sovereignty over it.

This truth that Creation is 'through', 'for', 'in', and 'under' Christ should give us a new attitude to the Creation.

c) God the Holy Spirit

The first indirect reference to the Trinity in the Bible occurs in the first three verses of Genesis. 'In the beginning God created the heavens and the earth . . . and the Spirit of God was hovering over the waters'; indeed it was God the Father through the word (the Son) and the Spirit who together reduced the primeval chaos into a cosmos. Thus 'By the word of the Lord were the heavens made; all their starry host by the breath (or spirit) of his mouth' (Psalm 33:6). Similarly '. . . when you take away their breath, they die and return to the dust, when you send your Spirit, they are created and you renew the face of the earth' (Psalm 104:29, 30).

It is a really wonderful truth that the Father, the Son and the Holy Spirit were together involved in the creation of the world and are together involved in its control and conservation. They brought it into being: they hold it in being. Then one day they will liberate it from its present bondage to decay and invest it with the freedom of the glory of the children of God. There will be a new heaven and a new earth, a renewed universe which will be suffused with the glory of God, and of which the glorified body of Jesus is the pledge.

2 The delegation to us

It is interesting to ask the question 'To whom does the earth belong?' for Scripture appears to give two contradictory answers. First, 'The earth is the Lord's and everything in it' (Psalm 24:1), and secondly 'The highest heavens belong to the

Lord, but the earth he has given to man (male and female)'
(Psalm 115:16). So does the earth belong to us or to God?

The only possible biblical answer is that it belongs to both. It
belongs to God by creation and to us by delegation. We have
been given the enormous privilege of caring for God's world.
Not that he has handed it over to us in such a way as to
relinquish his own rights over it, but that he has delegated to us
the responsibility to preserve and develop the earth on his
behalf. God remains the landlord; we are his tenants. God
remains the owner; we are his stewards, and it is required of
stewards that they be found faithful.

Let me now remind you of Genesis 1:26–28. First came
the divine resolve 'let us make man (male and female) in our
image . . . and let them rule [have dominion] over the earth
and its creatures'. This was followed by the divine action 'So
God created man (male and female) in his own image . . . and
said to them . . . 'fill the earth and subdue it'. Thus the divine
image and the earthly dominion belong together. Indeed our
dominion over the earth is due to our likeness to God. God has
set us human beings in between himself as Creator and the rest
of the natural creation, both animate and inanimate. In one
sense we are part of nature, because we share its dependence
on the Creator. But in another sense we are distinct from the
rest of creation because we have been given responsibility for
it. Physiologically we are like the animals, morally and spiritually we are like God.

There is no question, then, of human beings behaving like
Prometheus who, in the classical myth, stole fire from the
gods. There is no question of our invading God's private territory and wresting his power from him. No, human research
into the natural environment and human resourcefulness
in developing tools and technology, domesticating animals,
farming the land, extracting minerals from the earth, dam-
ming the rivers, and harnessing energy are all legitimate
fulfilments of the primeval command to subdue the earth.
God created the earth with fantastic animal, vegetable and

mineral resources and God has authorised us to use these resources, provided that we use them for the common good including our posterity.

3 Relations between humans and nature

How does Scripture envisage the relationship of human beings to nature? My answer is that, in the light of the truths that God created the earth and has delegated its care to us, we have to avoid two opposite and extreme views into which some people have foolishly lapsed, namely the deification of nature and the exploitation of nature, in favour of a third and better way which I will call cooperation with nature.

1) **Deification**. There are many ways in which human beings have divinized or deified 'nature' and to some degree worshipped it. Pantheists identify the Creator with the Creation and regard everything that exists as a part of God. Animists populate the natural world with spirits (e.g. the spirits of the forests, the rivers and the mountains) and believe that these spirits are quickly offended if we trespass into their territory and then need to be placated. Buddhists regard all life (not just human life) as sacred and therefore as inviolable. Next, contemporary believers in Gaia, the earth goddess, who are part of the New Age movement regard nature as invested in some mysterious and inexplicable way with its own intrinsic and self-perpetuating mechanisms with which we must not interfere.

In his book *Gaia: A new look at life on Earth*, published in 1979, Jim Lovelock argues that the earth 'constitutes a single system, made and managed to their own convenience by living organisms. We all know that life here is only made possible because of the right balance of gases in the atmosphere, but what we do not realize is that this balance is maintained not by chance [nor, he might have added, by a Creator!] but by the very process of life in itself' (1979, p. 249). In other words, the earth is a single self-regulating system which 'inexplicably' maintains the right level or balance of oxygen and methane.

Gaiaism is the mystical or religious strand in the Green Movement today. It is a kind of sophisticated Pantheism in divinizing nature as if it were responsible for itself and regulates itself.

Now Scripture rejects all these confusions which are derogatory to God the Creator. It insists on distinguishing between the Creator and his creation. It tells us to respect nature because God made it and it has therefore its own integrity, but not to reverence nature as if it were God and inviolable. So the de-sacralizing or the de-divinization of nature, which is the recognition that nature is creation and not creator, was an indispensable prelude to the whole scientific enterprise, and is essential to the development of earth's resources today.

If we reject the extreme of the divinization of nature, we must also reject the opposite extreme, namely the exploitation of nature. This is not treating nature as if it were God, but regarding ourselves as if we were God and free to do what we like with nature.

2) Exploitation. Christianity has been unfairly blamed for widespread environmental irresponsibility. Many of you will know the writings of Lynn White and Ian McHarg. Lynn White (1967) described Christianity as 'the most anthropocentric religion the world has seen.' Keith Thomas (1983) in his book *Man and the Natural World*, subtitled *Changing attitudes in England 1500–1800*, agrees that some Christian preachers in Tudor and Stuart England did interpret the biblical story in a breathtakingly anthropocentric spirit, implying that man's authority over the natural world was virtually unlimited. In the 17th century, for example, bear-baiting and cock-fighting were defended by reference to the dominion which God had given to man. But during the period 1500 to 1800, changes took place in the way in which human beings perceived the natural order. They came to see it in terms of stewardship. Lynn White postulated that the Judeo-Christian tradition was responsible for the environmental crisis. In an article in *Science* in 1967, entitled 'The historical roots of our ecological crisis,' he wrote

'Christianity . . . not only established a dualism of man and nature but also insisted that it is God's will that man exploit nature for his proper ends; Christianity bears a huge burden of guilt'.

This attack by Lynn White was continued by Ian McHarg, Chairman of the Department of Landscape Architecture in the University of Pennsylvania in the United States. In his book *Design with Nature* (1969) he wrote that the Genesis story 'in its insistence upon dominion and the subjugation of nature encourages the most exploitative and destructive instincts in man rather than those that are deferential and creative'. Indeed, he goes on, 'if one seeks license for those who would increase radioactivity, create canals and harbours with atomic bombs, employ poisons without restraint and give consent to the bulldozer mentality, there could be no better injunction than this text . . .' (i.e. Genesis 1:26–28). Then in his Dunning Trust Lectures of 1972/3 Ian McHarg traced Western man's attitude to the natural world to what he called 'three horrifying lines' in Genesis 1 about man's dominion. He wrote 'If you want to find one text of compounded horror which will guarantee that the relationship of man to nature can only be destruction . . . which will explain all of the destruction and all of the despoliation accomplished by western man for at least these two thousand years, then you do not have to look any further than this ghastly calamitous text.'

How shall we respond to White and McHarg? We have to say that they have misquoted, misapplied and manipulated Scripture to their own purpose. It is true that the Hebrew verbs used in Genesis 1 are forceful. The verb translated 'to have dominion' can mean 'to tread upon' or 'to trample on'; it is paraphrased in Psalm 8:6 'you put everything under his feet'. It is also true that the verb 'to subdue' is used of subduing enemies in warfare and even enslaving them. But it is an elementary principle of biblical interpretation that words have to be understood not by their etymology but by their context (i.e. how each author uses them). The context of Genesis 1 and 2 makes it plain beyond doubt that the kind of dominion God intended human beings to exercise was a responsible dominion, for God himself created the earth and then committed its care to us. It would be absurd to imagine that having arranged for its creation, God would then arrange for its destruction. No. The dominion he gave to human beings is one of stewardship.

My purpose in defending Genesis is not to exonerate all Christians (for some are to blame), but rather to exonerate the Bible from the accusation that it encourages the destruction of the environment. It does not. So we reject these two extremes, divinization and exploitation and instead we seek to develop a third and better way that I will call *co-operation*.

3) Co-operation. In order to grasp the co-operation that God intends between himself and us, we need to remember the distinction between 'Nature' and 'Culture'. Nature is what God has given us; culture is what we do with it, for example agriculture, horticulture and apiculture. Nature is raw materials; culture is commodities and manufactured goods prepared for the market. Nature is creation; culture is cultivation.

The beautiful truth is that God has deliberately humbled himself to make this divine–human partnership necessary. Of course having created the world he could have retained its conservation in his own hands. Having planted a garden, he could also have caused it to bear fruit. But he deliberately condescended to make us collaborators or co-workers with himself. He created the earth, but told us to subdue it. He planted the garden, but put Adam and Eve in it to 'work it and take care of it' (Genesis 2:15). This is rightly called 'the cultural mandate', the mandate or commission to human beings, not only to conserve the environment but to develop its resources for the good of all.

I wonder if you know the story about the Cockney gardener who was showing a pastor round his most beautiful herbaceous border at the height of the summer. The pastor, as pious pastors sometimes do, was waxing eloquent about the glories of Creation and the wonders of the Creator until the gardener got fed up because no credit was being given to him. So he turned to the pastor and he said, "You should 'ave seen this 'ere garden when Gawd 'ad it to 'imself".' When God had it to himself, it was a wilderness. It was the gardener who had transformed it into a garden. The Cockney's theology was correct. A garden is neither exclusively the work of God nor exclusively the work of human beings, but the product of both. And without a human cultivator every garden would quickly degenerate back into a wilderness.

We usually emphasise the necessity of God's part in the transaction, and at Harvest Festivals give all the Glory to God.

> 'We plough the fields and scatter the good seed
> on the land,
> but it is fed and watered by God's almighty hand.'

It would be equally correct, however, to lay the emphasis on our part. So I venture to give you a new verse for the same hymn.

> 'God plants the lovely garden and gives the fertile soil,
> but it is kept and nurtured by man's resourceful toil.'

God calls us to a privileged partnership with himself. It is a noble thing to be called to cooperate with God for the fulfilment of his purposes, and to transform the created order for his glory and for the pleasure and profit of all.

I end with a final thought or appendix. It is possible to overstate this emphasis on human work in the conservation and transformation of the environment. The climax of Genesis 1 is not the creation of man the worker but the institution of the Sabbath for man the worshipper; not our toil (subduing the earth) but the laying aside of our toil on the Sabbath day. For the Sabbath relativizes the importance of work. It protects human beings from a total absorption in their work as if it were the be all and end all of their existence. It is not. We human beings find our humanness not only in relation to the earth, which we are to transform, but in relation to God whom we are to worship; not only in relation to the Creation, but in relation to the Creator.

It is the Sabbath which pinpoints the difference between the Marxist and the Christian views of work and of man. Marxism sees man as *Homo economicus*, whose destiny is to be productive; Christianity, however, sees man as *Homo adorans*, whose destiny is to worship. Worship, not work, is the summit of human activity. At the same time this is to some degree a false distinction. For God intends our work to be an expression of our worship, and our care of the Creation to reflect our love for the Creator. Only then whatever we do, in word or deed, shall we do it to the Glory of God (1 Corinthians 10:31).
(Stott 1990)

Stott spent much of his writing time in south-west Wales. He shared something of this experience in a Sunday Worship Radio 4 broadcast from the Hookses on 18 April 2004, hosted by Nick J. Page:

I've been coming down here for 50 years – drawn mainly by the magnificent scenery and by the rich variety of birds, especially of course sea birds. Offshore are the islands of Skomer, Skokholm and Grassholm and these islands are world-famous bird sanctuaries. Indeed, this whole area is part of the Pembrokeshire National Park, and because of its wildlife it has recently been designated an 'SSSI' – that is, a Site of Special Scientific Interest. Looking across the bay and the headland beyond to the open Atlantic is a view of spectacular beauty, which prompts me (as I'm sure it would also prompt you) to worship the God of creation.
(Stott 2004)

He shared four of his 'orni-theology' lessons, and then gave this commentary on degradation and creation care:

It's really impossible to thank God for the blessings of his creation without at the same time remembering our responsibility to care for it. Down here in Pembrokeshire we are constantly reminded how fragile our living environment and its biodiversity are.

Just along the coast on the 15 February 1996, the huge tanker *Sea Empress* was grounded at the entrance to Milford Haven, which has a great reputation for cleanliness. More than half her cargo of 136,000 tons of oil was spilled. It was the third-largest oil spill ever in British waters. Being February it was fortunately still two to three months before the colonies of sea birds would occupy their nesting sites on Skomer and Skokholm islands. Nevertheless, it was a major disaster, polluting many miles of beautiful coastline and killing thousands of birds, especially Common Scoters and Guillemots.

Over against such horrors, we need to listen again to God's original intention for us. Some critics of Christianity try to fasten the blame for ecological disasters on God's instruction to us to subdue the earth and rule over its creatures. But really this is a serious misuse of the biblical text. It is absurd to suppose that God would first create the world and then hand it over to us to destroy it. No, our God-given responsibility is one of stewardship – that is, of caring for God's creation.

(Stott 2004)

The eight areas that Stott regarded as marking a radical disciple were nonconformity, Christlikeness, maturity, creation care, simplicity, balance, dependence and death. But joining them was his commitment to and proclamation of Jesus Christ as Lord. At the Keswick Convention in July 2007, Stott gave his final public address, 'The model: Becoming more like Christ'. In it he declared the result of a lifetime's reflection:

God wants His people to become like Christ. Christlikeness is the will of God for the people of God ... [He gave reasons for believing this was indeed God's will, and then concluded] I have spoken much tonight about Christlikeness, but is it [Christlikeness] attainable? In our own strength it is clearly not attainable, but God has given us his Holy Spirit to dwell within us, to change us from within. William Temple, Archbishop in the 1940s, used to illustrate this point from Shakespeare.

> It is no good giving me a play like *Hamlet* or *King Lear* and telling me to write a play like that. Shakespeare could do it – I can't. And it is no good showing me a life like the life of Jesus and telling me to live a life like that. Jesus could do it – I can't. But if the genius of Shakespeare could come and live in me, then I could write plays like this. And if the Spirit could come into me, then I could live a life like His.

So I conclude, as a brief summary of what we have tried to say to one another: God's purpose is to make us like Christ. God's way to make us like Christ is to fill us with his Spirit. In other words, it's a trinitarian conclusion, concerning the Father, the Son and the Holy Spirit.
(Stott 2007)

To Stott, 'creation care' was part of this, and in no way alien or additional to it. In *The Radical Disciple*, Stott expands on the traits that mark the mature disciple, which can otherwise be described as the fruit of the Spirit. This has already been referenced above on a number of occasions. Stott's chapter on creation care in *The Radical Disciple* repeats the arguments set out at greater length in the chapter in *Issues facing Christians Today*, but it is significant because it sets it out as an integral component of discipleship, not merely as one of a number of challenges facing the Christian believer. All the traits characteristic of a radical disciple are the fruit of the Spirit. Creation care can be regarded as the sword of the Spirit, which completes the armour of the Christian described by Paul in Ephesians 6:13–17.

In May 1999 I was privileged to take part in a day conference in Nairobi on Christians and the environment. Sharing the platform with me were Dr Calvin DeWitt of Au Sable Institute, Michigan, and Peter Harris of A Rocha International. Participants that day included both leaders in the Kenyan Government and representatives of churches, mission organizations and NGOs. The meeting received wide publicity. It was evident that creation care is neither a selfish interest of the developed 'north', nor a minority enthusiasm peculiar to birdwatchers or flower-lovers, but an increasingly mainline Christian concern. Soon afterwards, an Evangelical Declaration on the Care of Creation was published [see Appendix 1], and the following year a substantial commentary appeared, edited by R. J. Berry and titled *The Care of Creation* (IVP, 2000) . . . It is a noble calling to cooperate with God for the fulfillment of his purposes, to transform the created order for the pleasure and profit of all. In this way our work is to be an expression of our worship since our care of the creation will reflect our love for the Creator . . .

Reflecting on [our knowledge of] environmental hazards, one cannot help but see that our whole planet is in jeopardy. *Crisis* is not too dramatic a word to use. What would be an appropriate response? To begin with, we can be thankful that at last in 1992 the so-called Earth Summit was held in Rio and made a commitment to 'global sustainable development'. Subsequent conferences have ensured that environmental questions have been kept before the leading nations of the world.

But alongside these official conferences several NGOs have arisen. I will mention only the two most prominent explicitly Christian organizations, namely Tearfund and A Rocha . . . Tearfund, founded by George Hoffman, is committed to development in the broadest sense and works in close cooperation with 'partners' in the Majority World. The wonderful story of Tearfund has been documented by Mike Hollow (2008) in his book *A Future and a Hope*. A Rocha is different, being much smaller. It was founded in 1983 by Peter Harris, who has documented its growth in two books: *Under the Bright Wings* (the first ten years) and *Kingfisher's Fire* (bringing the story up to date). Its steady development is remarkable, as it now works in twenty countries, establishing field study centres on all continents.

It is all very well to give our support to Christian environmental NGOs, but what are our individual responsibilities? I leave Chris Wright to answer the question, what can the radical disciple do to care for the creation? Chris dreams of a multitude of 'Christians who care about creation and take their environmental responsibilities seriously':

> They choose sustainable forms of energy where possible. They switch off unneeded appliances. They buy food, goods and services as far as possible from companies with ethically sound environmental policies. They join conservation societies. They avoid overconsumption and unnecessary waste and recycle as much as possible.
> (Wright 2006, p. 412)

Chris also wants to see a growing number of Christians who 'include the care of creation within their biblical understanding of mission':

> In the past, Christians have instinctively been concerned about great and urgent issues in every generation ... These have included the evils of disease, ignorance, slavery and many other forms of brutality and exploitation. Christians have taken up the cause of widows, orphans, refugees, prisoners, the insane, the hungry – and most recently have swelled the numbers of those committed to 'making poverty history'.
> (Wright 2006, pp. 412–413)

I want to echo Chris Wright's eloquent conclusion:

It seems quite inexplicable to me that there are some Christians who claim to love and worship God, to be disciples of Jesus and yet have no concern for the earth that bears his stamp of ownership. They do not care about the abuse of the earth, and indeed by their wasteful and overconsumptive lifestyles they contribute to it.
(Wright 2006, p. 414)

'God intends . . . our care of the creation to reflect our love for the Creator.'
(Stott 2000, p. 9)

'To the LORD your God belong the heavens, even the highest heavens, the earth and everything in it' (Deuteronomy 10:14 [NIV 1984]).
(Stott 2010b, pp. 51–59)

9

Reflections

Influence of Stott's teaching
on creation care

Stott did not seek to develop a theology of creation care, but he laid down the grounds for one. Taking his cue from the conclusion of the creation care chapter in *The Radical Disciple*, Chris Wright, in his landmark exposition of *The Mission of God* (2006, pp. 393–395 and 397), identified some of the underlying themes woven through the Bible's grand narrative, the themes that are the foundational pillars of the biblical world-view. The following is taken from his discussion of the 'Arena of mission', which necessarily involves the earth (Bible extracts are from the NIV 1984, or Wright's own translations).

> The Lord God of Israel is also the God of all the earth and all nations, so now we need to . . . consider that grand arena within which the Bible's grand narrative takes place. For the mission of God is as universal as the love of God, and as Psalm 145:13 reminds us:
>
> > The LORD is faithful to all his promises
> > and loving towards all he has made.

> It is helpful to begin our reflection with the apostle Paul, that great missional interpreter of the Old Testament.
> Compare Paul's sermon in the Jewish synagogue in Pisidian Antioch in Acts 13:16–41 with his speech before the Areopagus in Athens in Acts 17:22–31. Both addresses have a common ultimate purpose – to introduce the listeners to Jesus. But the

conceptual frameworks are very different. In the first, before a Jewish audience, Paul speaks of 'the *God* of the people of *Israel*' and describes how God had overthrown the Canaanites and 'gave their *land* to his people as their inheritance' (13:17, 19, emphasis added). In the second, before a Gentile audience, Paul speaks of 'the *God* who made the *world* and everything in it' and describes how this God 'made *every nation of men*, that they should inhabit the whole earth' (Acts 17:24, 26, emphasis added).

If you will pardon [some] geometry, we could portray these two frameworks in the form of two interconnected triangles. On the one hand there is the triangle of God, Israel, and their land [see Figure 9.1].

Figure 9.1 **Conceptual framework of Paul's sermon in Antioch**

This is the conceptual framework of Paul's sermon in Antioch and, of course, it represents the self-understanding of Old Testament Israel. Their God, YHWH, had chosen and called Israel as a people in covenant relationship with himself, and had redeemed them out of slavery in the land of Egypt, and given them the land of Canaan in which they were to live in covenant obedience to him and thereby under his blessing . . . Insofar as Israel in the Old Testament understood itself as a people with an identity and mission, this was the context of such thinking. The uniqueness of their election, redemption, covenant and ethic was grounded in this triangle of interconnected relationships. The mission of Israel was to live as God's people in God's land for God's glory. And the God in question was YHWH.

But . . . this triangle of relationships did not exist for its own sake. It was part of a wider set of relationships that frame the mission of God for all nations and the whole earth. It is this outer triangle (God, humanity and the earth [see Figure 9.2]), that Paul has in mind when he speaks to the Gentile audience in Athens – a group of people to whom the inner triangle of God's dealings with Israel in their land would not have made sense as yet. So Paul presents to them what is in effect a scriptural (Old Testament) doctrine of creation, but without directly quoting Old Testament texts.

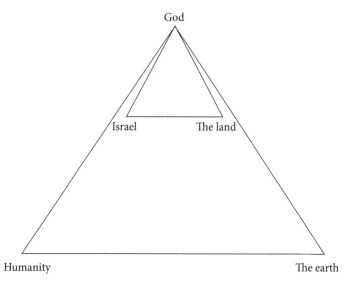

Figure 9.2 **Conceptual framework of Paul's sermon in Athens**

That outer triangle, however, although it is still the basic platform of all God's dealings with humanity in history, has been twisted and fractured as a result of human rebellion and sin. All three primary relationships have been affected: human beings no longer love and obey God as they ought, and they live under his wrath; humanity is at odds with the earth; and the earth is subject to God's curse and to the frustration of not being able to glorify God as it ought until humanity is redeemed. Such are the grim realities of our fallen human condition that Paul expounds in Romans. We live as fallen humanity in a cursed earth.

But the outer triangle is also the platform or arena of God's mission. All that God did in, for and through *Israel* (the inner triangle) had as its ultimate goal the blessing of all nations of *humanity* and the final redemption of all *creation* (the outer triangle) . . .

Mission and God's earth

To the LORD your God belong the heavens, even the
    highest heavens,
  the earth and everything in it.
(Deuteronomy 10:14 [NIV 1984])

This bold claim that YHWH, the God of Israel, owns the whole universe is echoed in the familiar assertion of Psalm 24:1, 'To YHWH belongs the earth and its fullness' (author's [CW] translation), and in the less familiar claim that God himself makes to Job in the context of the grand recital of all his works of creation: 'Everything under heaven belongs to me' (Job 41:11).

The earth, then, belongs to God because God made it. At the very least this reminds us that if the earth is God's, it is not ours. We do not own this planet, even if our behaviour tends to boast that we think we do. No, God is the earth's landlord and we are God's tenants. God has given the earth into our resident *possession* (Psalm 115:16), but we do not hold the title deeds of ultimate ownership. So, as in any landlord–tenant relationship, God holds us accountable to himself for how we treat his property. Several dimensions of this strong creation affirmation of the divine ownership of the earth may be mentioned as having significant ethical and missional implications.
(Wright 2006, pp. 393–395 and 397)

Wright enlarged on this basis in a John Stott London lecture in 2013.

> Come and take a look with me at three great truths from the
> Bible about creation, as the foundation and motivation for our
> earthkeeping – both in the sense of our responsible and proper
> use of the resources of the earth for all the purposes God intend-
> ed and allows, and in the sense of our active concern and care
> for the earth itself as the environment that sustains our life.
>
> • **The goodness of creation** as we look back to its original
>   creation by God.
> • **The glory of creation** as we look around at the ongoing
>   present role and function of all creation in bringing praise
>   and glory to the Creator.
> • **The goal of creation** as we look forward to God's purpose
>   for the whole creation in and through Jesus Christ.

1 The goodness of creation

Creation is good. That is the unmistakable message of the
opening chapter of the Bible. Six times God declares what he
has just done to be 'good', and the seventh time 'very good'. We
can think of this goodness of creation in two ways – in relation
to God, and in relation to ourselves.

a) Creation is good in relation to God

i) The good creation reveals the good God

In other Ancient Near Eastern accounts, creation is the work
of multiple deities, in varying degrees of conflict and malevo-
lence. By contrast, in the Old Testament, creation is the work
of the one single living God and therefore bears witness to
his existence, power and character. Creation reveals its Creator, though he is not part of it (in the way gods were often
intrinsically part of the world itself in other cosmologies). Just
as you can 'hear' Beethoven in his symphonies (though a

symphony is not the composer), or 'see' Rembrandt in his paintings (though a painting is not the artist), so we encounter the living God in creation (though the creation is not God). For example:

- **Psalm 19** the glory of God
- **Psalm 50:6** the righteousness of God ('the heavens proclaim his righteousness, for he is a God of justice)
- **Psalm 65:9** the care of God ('you care for the land and water it')
- **Psalm 104:27–30** the provision of God ('all creatures look to you . . .')
- **Acts 14:17** the kindness of God ('giving you rain . . . and Crops . . . food . . . joy')
- **Romans 1:20** the power of God.

ii) Creation has intrinsic value to God

The repeated affirmation, 'God saw that it was good', is made quite independently of us human beings. It is not initially *our* response to the beauty or benefits of creation (though it certainly should be), but God's evaluation of God's own handiwork. It is the seal of God's approval on the whole universe in all its functioning. So creation has intrinsic value because it is valued by God, who is the source of all value. To speak of the goodness of creation is not, first of all, to say that it is valuable to us (which of course it is), but to say that it is valued by God and was created 'fit for purpose' – God's purpose.

Thus, e.g., Psalm 104 celebrates not only those aspects of creation which serve human needs (crops and domestic animals), but also those that have no immediate connection with human life – the wild places and wild creatures that live there – simply being and doing what God created them to be and do.

iii) Creation is God's property

'The earth is the Lord's' (Psalm 24:1). 'To the Lord your God belong the heavens, even the highest heavens, the earth and everything in it' (Deuteronomy 10:14 [NIV]). These are staggering universal affirmations that we easily slip past. The whole universe (including planet earth) is God's property. It belongs to him. So the earth is first and foremost owned by God, not by us. God is the supreme landlord. We are God's tenants, living by God's permission in God's property. This generates huge ethical implications that cannot be explored here, but at the very least it reminds us that we are accountable to God for how we treat his property.

iv) Creation is God's temple

It is increasingly recognized that in the thought of the ancient world generally, and in Old Testament Israel specifically, temples were envisaged as (literally) 'microcosms' – i.e. small representations on earth of the shape and order of the cosmos itself. Meanwhile the cosmos could be seen as a 'macrotemple' – i.e. the dwelling place of the gods (or in Old Testament terms, of course, of the one true living Creator God) (*q.v.* Beale 2004; Walton 2009).

From this perspective, God's declaration that his work of creation was 'good' is a way of saying that he saw and approved the whole creation, functioning in all its ordered complexity both as the place prepared for him to install his 'image' (humankind), and as the place for his own dwelling ('heaven is my throne and the earth is my footstool', Isaiah 66:1–2 – temple language).

The Bible constantly speaks of the natural world in relation to God. The created order obeys God, reveals his glory, benefits from his provision, serves his purposes (in judgment or salvation), and is filled with his presence. So we honour creation as 'sacred' in that sense – not that it is 'divine' in itself, nor as something we are to worship (that is explicitly forbidden – Deuteronomy 4:15–20; Job 31:26–28; Romans 1:25), but because of its God-relatedness.

b) Creation is good in relation to us, human beings

So it is God's earth, then. But it is also our earth. 'The highest heaven belongs to God, but the earth he has given to the children of Adam' (Psalm 115:16). The earth is the place of human habitation. It is God's property, but it is also our responsibility. The earth is, in some sense, 'given' to human beings in a way that it is not 'given' to other animals.

So what makes us humans special or unique? At first sight, the Bible stresses much more what we have in common with the rest of the animals than anything different from them.

- We were blessed and told to multiply – but so were they, and before us!
- We were created 'on the sixth day' – after the other wild and domestic animals.
- We were created 'from the ground' – as they were, or rather 'from the dust of the ground' – 'hardly superior!'
- We were given the 'breath of life' – but so were all the living creatures that breathe (1:30; 6:17; 7:18, 22; Psalm 104:29–30).
- We were provided with food by God – but so are they (1:29–30).

In fact it is a matter of wonder and rejoicing that we share with all the other animals in the love, care and provision of God (Psalm 104:14–30). We are 'adam from the 'adamah. We are creatures of the Creator God, and that is wonderful!

What then makes us different? Two things are affirmed in Genesis: we were created in the image of God in order to be equipped to exercise dominion within creation (Genesis 1:26–28), and we were placed in the earth (initially in the garden in Eden), in order to serve and care for it (Genesis 2:15).

i) Created to rule (Genesis 1:26–28) – 'kings', in the image of God

The grammar of these verses implies that God created human beings *with the intention* that they should exercise rule over the rest of the animal creation, and that he created us in the image of God in order to equip us for that function. The two things (image of God and dominion over creation) are not identical with each other, but they are closely related: the first enables the second.

We were created to exercise the delegated kingship of God within creation. Just as emperors set up statues (images) of themselves in the countries they ruled to indicate their authority over those realms, so human beings as the image of God represent the authority of the real king.

But how does God exercise his kingship within creation?

- **Psalm 104** by caring and providing for all his creatures, wild, domestic and human.
- **Psalm 145** (which is addressed to 'my God the King'), by being gracious, good, faithful, generous, protective and loving, towards all he has made.

That is how *God* is king. Therefore, human rule in creation was never a licence to dominate, abuse, crush, waste or destroy. That is tyranny modelled on fallen human arrogance, not kingship modelled on God's character and behaviour. The true model of kingship is summarized in 1 Kings 12:7 – mutual servanthood. The people would serve the king – yes, provided he would serve and care for them without injustice. The earth will serve our needs – yes, provided we exercise our kingship in God's way by serving and caring for it.

ii) Located to serve (Genesis 2:15) – 'priests', in the service of creation

This follows naturally from the point above. God took the man he had created and put him in the garden (lit.) 'to serve and keep it'. Human rule within creation (Genesis 1) is to be exercised by human servanthood for creation (Genesis 2). The pattern of servant-kingship is very clear, and it was modelled perfectly of course by Jesus himself – the perfect human – when he deliberately demonstrated his status as Lord and Master by washing the disciples' feet. Kingship exercised in servanthood.

But the language of 'serving and keeping' has another resonance. It is the language of priesthood. Repeatedly in Leviticus it is said that the task of the priests and Levites was to serve God in the tabernacle/temple, and to keep all that God had entrusted to them there. We have, then, a priestly role as well as a kingly role within creation – significant language in view of how God will later speak of the role of Israel among the nations, and how Revelation will describe the role of redeemed humanity within the new creation.

So the language of God placing his image within creation has temple overtones as well, for that is where the images of the gods were indeed placed – in their temples. So with the cosmos functioning as the macro-temple of its Creator, God places his own image – the living human being – in his temple to dwell with him there. Creation functions as the dwelling place of God and human beings function as the image of God, ruling and serving creation on his behalf.

Summarizing this section, then, we may say that the goodness of creation is a way of affirming that it is God's earth and it is our earth – and in both senses it is good.

2 The glory of creation

a) God's glory expressed through the praise of creation

The first question in the Shorter Catechism of the Westminster Confession of Faith (as I recall from childhood!), is 'What is the chief end of man?' To which the answer is: 'The chief end of man is to glorify God and enjoy him for ever.' I believe the same question and the same answer could be applied to creation as a whole. Creation exists for the praise and glory of God, for God's enjoyment of his creation and its enjoyment of him.

So the ultimate purpose of *human* life (to glorify God) is not something that *distinguishes* us from the rest of creation – but rather something we share in common with the rest of creation. Of course, we must immediately agree that we as human beings glorify God in uniquely human ways – with our rationality, language, emotions, poetry, music, art – 'hearts and hands and minds and voices, in our choicest psalmody', as the hymn says. We know what it is for us to praise and glorify God.

But the Bible affirms that *all creation* already praises God and can be summoned repeatedly to do so (Psalms 145:10, 21; 148; 150, etc.). Indeed, John's vision of the whole universe centred around the throne of God reaches its climactic crescendo of praise when he says, 'Then I heard every creature in heaven and on earth and under the earth and on the sea and all that is in them' bringing worship 'to him who sits on the throne and to the Lamb' (Revelation 5:13).

Now, we may not be able to grasp or explain *how* creation praises God, or how God receives the praise of his non-human creatures. I have a feeling (no more than that), that creatures praise and glorify God simply by being and doing what they were created for, and God is pleased and glorified when they do. The non-human creation brings glory to God simply by existing, for it exists only by his sustaining and renewing power. But simply because we cannot understand *how* creation praises and glorifies God, we should not deny what the Bible so often affirms – namely that it does!

b) God's glory seen in the fullness of creation

The glory of God is sometimes linked to the fullness of the earth (literally in Hebrew, 'the filling of the earth'). The rich abundance of bio-diversity itself is celebrated in Genesis 1 as creation moves from 'functionless and empty' to ordered and full. Here are some more examples:

- Psalm 24:1 'The earth is the LORD's and everything in it' (lit) 'its fullness';
- Psalm 50:12 'The world is mine and all that is in it' (lit) 'its fullness' (after listing animals of the forest, cattle, birds and insects);
- Psalm 104:31 'May the glory of the LORD endure for ever; may the LORD rejoice in all his works' (after a psalm celebrating the diversity of creatures).

This gives an interesting perspective on the cry of the seraphim during Isaiah's vision of God in the temple. What they cry out is literally: 'Holy, Holy, Holy [is] YHWH Sebaoth. The fullness / filling of all the earth [is] his glory'. This is usually translated, 'the whole earth is full of his glory', and that is true of course. But reading the sentence in English in that way can marginalize the word 'full', as if the earth is just a receptacle full of glory. But the word 'fullness' stands emphatically first in the Hebrew sentence as a noun. And the fullness of the earth, as we can see in several psalms, is a shorthand expression for the abundance of life on earth in all its wonderful forms. Accordingly, it would be possible to translate, 'The abundance of life that fills the earth constitutes the glory of God' – that is to say, 'the glory of God can be seen in the abundance of God's own creation'.

Of course, we need to be careful not to read pantheism into such a statement, as if there were nothing more to God and his glory than the sum of creation itself. God's glory transcends creation ('you have set your glory above the heavens', is a way of expressing that truth). But having said that, we can certainly affirm that the glory of God is mediated to us through creation itself, not only in the awesome majesty of the heavens (Psalm 19:1) but also including the abundance of life on earth. We live in a glory-filled earth – one reason why Paul says that we are without excuse when we fail to glorify God and give thanks to him (Romans 1:20-21).

Proverbs 14:31 says: 'Whoever oppresses the poor shows contempt for their Maker, but whoever is kind to the needy honours God.' The principle is that since human beings are made in God's image, whatever we do to other people, in some sense we are doing to God (Jesus extended the principle in relation to himself in Matthew 25). I would argue that it is a legitimate extension of this same principle to conclude that, since the fullness of created life on earth in some sense constitutes God's glory (at least in one of the ways we experience it), whatever fulfils Genesis 1 and 2, by developing, enhancing, and properly using the resources of the earth while at the same time serving and caring for it, acknowledges and contributes to the glory of God. Conversely, whatever needlessly destroys, degrades, pollutes and wastes the life of the earth diminishes God's glory. How we treat the earth reflects how we treat its Creator and ours.

3 The goal of creation

At this point we are no longer just looking back to the original creation and our role within it, or looking around at the glory of God expressed in the praise of creation and the fullness of the earth. We now look forward to God's ultimate purpose for creation. And it is a very encouraging place to look!

a) Creation is included in the scope of God's redemptive purpose

The first thing we need to say is that creation *needs* redemption. From the very beginning of the Bible it is made clear that sin and evil have affected the natural order as well as human and spiritual life. 'Cursed is the earth because of you', said God to Adam. I think the primary focus of that statement is on the earth as soil, ground (*'adamah*, rather than *'erets*) in relation to human work, rather than on the geological structures and functioning of the planet. That is, I do not personally believe that we should attribute all natural phenomena that are potentially destructive (the shifting of tectonic plates, earthquakes, tsunamis, volcanic eruptions etc.) to the curse. Nevertheless, Paul does make the clear theological affirmation that the whole of creation is frustrated, subjected to futility in some sense, including 'decay and bondage' – and will remain so until it is liberated by God and 'brought into the freedom and glory of the children of God' (Romans 8:19–21).

The truth is, then, that just as creation shares in the effects of our sin, so we will share in the fullness of creation's redemption. For God's ultimate purpose is 'to bring unity to all things in heaven and earth under Christ' (Ephesians 1:10 – one of the most astonishingly universal and cosmic affirmations in the Bible). We are not going to be saved *out of* the earth, but saved *along with* the earth.

Where did Paul get such an idea from? Clearly from the Scriptures, the Old Testament. For the prophets certainly included ecology in their eschatology.

- **Isaiah 11:6–9** The messianic era will include environmental harmony.
- **Isaiah 35** The restoration of God's people will herald creational abundance.
- **Isaiah 65:17–25** Here we have God's explicit affirmation that he is 'creating' (the word is participial) 'new heavens and new earth'. The picture that follows depicts life on earth that is full of joy, free from tears, life-fulfilling, with deep satisfaction and fruitfulness in ordinary labour, free from the curses of frustration and injustice, and with environmental peace and harmony. It is a glorious picture that provided the images and vocabulary for Revelation 21–22.
- **Psalm 96:10–13** The whole of creation is called to rejoice because God is coming to put things right.

This is not a case of 'Old Testament earthiness' – an earthbound materialism that gets transcended by the more spiritual message of the New Testament. Not at all.

Paul speaks of a new redeemed creation being brought to birth within the womb of this creation – whose groanings are the labour pains of creation's future as well as our own (Romans 8:18–25). For we will inhabit the new creation in our redeemed bodies, modelled on the resurrection body of Jesus (Romans 8:23; Philippians 3:21; 1 John 3:2). That is a very important reason why the bodily resurrection of Jesus is so vitally important. They thought he was a ghost, but he deliberately demonstrated to his disciples that he was fully physical – with body parts, flesh and bones, and the ability to eat food (Luke 24:37–43). The resurrection is God's Yes! to creation. The risen Jesus is the first-fruits of the new creation.

b) Purging, not obliteration

Some people struggle with the whole idea of the redemption of creation because they believe that the future of the universe is total obliteration in a cosmic conflagration. This is sometimes linked to an unbiblical dualism in which matter itself is seen as inferior, tainted and temporary, whereas only the spiritual realm is pure and eternal. They envisage the future then in terms of ultimate release from the shackles of physicality on earth into the enjoyment of a spiritual heaven with God. However, even those who are not infected by that kind of dualism still want to take seriously the language of destruction by fire in 2 Peter 3:10–12. Surely, they argue, the picture of the Day of the Lord given here portrays final destruction, not redemption and renewal.

However, we need to see the context and argument of the whole chapter. Peter is arguing against those who scoff at the idea of a coming future judgment, complacently believing that everything will go on just as it always has for ever (vv. 3–4). What they forget, however, says Peter, is that such an attitude was around before the Flood, but God did intervene and act in judgment. So God will assuredly and finally do in the future what he prefigured in the past. What he did then by water, he will in the end do by fire.

Now the key thing to observe here is that the language of *destruction of the world* is used of both events. Look at the parallel points in verses 6–7.

> By these waters also the world of that time was deluged and destroyed. By the same word the present heavens and earth are reserved for fire, being kept for the day of judgment and the destruction of the ungodly.

What was destroyed in the Flood? Not the whole planet or creation itself, but the ungodly human society on the earth at that time – 'the destruction of the ungodly', as Peter says. The apocalyptic language of fire in the second part of the chapter, then, should be understood in its biblical sense of purging, cleansing judgment. The universe will be purged of all evil and 'the earth and everything done in it will be laid bare' – i.e. to the all-seeing eyes of our Creator and Judge. And after that fiery cleansing, after the destruction of 'the world as we know it' – in the sense of the world in its sinful rebellion against God – then Peter continues with the wonderful verse 13, 'in keeping with his promise we are looking forward to a new heaven and a new earth where righteousness dwells.'

c) Reconciled to God through the cross and resurrection of Christ

But how will all this be accomplished? In fact, it already has been! We may not be able to imagine with our finite brains what the new creation will be like or 'how will God do it?' But Paul assures us that it is already guaranteed, accomplished in anticipation, through the cross and resurrection of Jesus Christ.

Colossians 1:15–23 must be one of the most breathtaking passages Paul ever wrote about Jesus Christ. He paints in truly cosmic colours and dimensions. Five times he uses the phrase 'all things' (*ta panta*), and makes it clear by the addition of 'in heaven and earth', that he means the whole of creation at every possible level. And he tells us that the whole creation:

- was created by Christ and for Christ
- is sustained in existence by Christ
- and has been reconciled to God by Christ – specifically 'by making peace through his blood shed on the cross'.

That last phrase is vitally important. We must 'lift up our eyes' and see the truly cosmic scope of Christ's death. Paul says that through the cross God has accomplished the reconciliation of creation. And in that vast context he then goes on to add 'And you also . . .' (v. 21). We tend to start at the personal level (Christ died to atone for our sins and grant us eternal life – wonderfully true), then we might go on to the ecclesial level (all of us who are redeemed by Christ are part of the church, the people of God, the body of Christ). And just possibly we might go on to the rest of creation (we have to live here on earth until Christ returns to 'take us home'). In this text Paul moves in the exact opposite direction. He starts with Christ's cosmic, creational Lordship over all creation (which incidentally is where Jesus himself also starts in the so-called Great Commission, Matthew 28:18), moves on to speak about the church of which he is head, returns to the redemption of all creation through the cross, and finally comes to individual believers who have heard the gospel and responded in faith. 'This is the gospel', he says (Colossians 1:23). And it is the biblical gospel that includes creation within the redeeming, saving, reconciling plan of God accomplished through the death and resurrection of Christ.

d) 'A gospel issue'?

This helps us to understand a phrase in the Cape Town Commitment (CTC) that has raised the eyebrows of some. It speaks of creation care as 'a gospel issue'. There are some who have said that, while they agree that it is an important issue, a biblically grounded responsibility, and even a legitimate part of Christian mission, they would not agree that it is 'a gospel issue'.

Let's first of all quote the full context of that phrase, since it is theologically important.

> The earth is created, sustained and redeemed by Christ (Colossians 1:15–20; Hebrews 1:2–3). We cannot claim to love God while abusing what belongs to Christ by right of creation, redemption and inheritance. We care for the earth and responsibly use its abundant resources, not according to the rationale of the secular world, but for the Lord's sake. If Jesus is Lord of all the earth, we cannot separate our relationship to Christ from how we act in relation to the earth. For to proclaim the gospel that says 'Jesus is Lord' is to proclaim the gospel that includes the earth, since Christ's Lordship is over all creation. Creation care is thus a gospel issue within the Lordship of Christ.
> (CTC I1.7a)

The whole context of the words 'gospel issue' is important, since it defines 'gospel' in relation to Jesus Christ as Lord of all creation, not just in relation to our human need for salvation. That points to another lengthy part of the CTC, which expounds a biblical understanding of the gospel (CTC I.8). It speaks of the gospel not just as a personal salvation plan, but in its full biblical richness as the good news of all that God has done through Christ and the imperative that it addresses to us. So it speaks of the story the gospel tells, the assurance the gospel brings and the transformation the gospel produces. Here is the full summary of the first of those:

> *We love the story the gospel tells.* The gospel announces as good news the historical events of the life, death and

resurrection of Jesus of Nazareth. As the son of David, the promised Messiah King, Jesus is the one through whom alone God established his kingdom and acted for the salvation of the world, enabling all nations on earth to be blessed, as he promised Abraham. Paul defines the gospel in stating that 'Christ died for our sins according to the scriptures, that he was buried, that he was raised on the third day, according the scriptures, and that he appeared to Peter and then to the Twelve.' The gospel declares that, on the cross of Christ, God took upon himself, in the person of his Son and in our place, the judgment our sin deserves. In the same great saving act, completed, vindicated and declared through the resurrection, God won the decisive victory over Satan, death and all evil powers, liberated us from their power and fear, and ensured their eventual destruction. God accomplished the reconciliation of believers with himself and with one another across all boundaries and enmities. God also accomplished his purpose of the ultimate reconciliation of all creation, and in the bodily resurrection of Jesus has given us the first fruits of the new creation. 'God was in Christ reconciling the world to himself' (Mark 1:1, 14–15; Romans 1:1–4; Romans 4; 1 Corinthians 15:3–5; 1 Peter 2:24; Colossians 2:15; Hebrews 2:14–15; Ephesians 2:14–18; Colossians 1:20; 2 Corinthians 5:19). How we love the gospel story!

(CTC I.8b)

i) More than the means of personal salvation

Now, first of all, if you reduce 'the gospel' to mean only 'a mechanism by which you can ensure your personal salvation', you will necessarily consider that the phrase 'a gospel issue' can be applied only to matters that affect how you get saved, or whether you get saved. But the biblical gospel is not just a means of personal salvation (though of course it assuredly provides that). The gospel is the good news that is contained in the grand story of God's good purpose for all creation, a purpose in which, by God's grace, we can have a share. 'Gospel issues' are broader than individual salvation.

ii) 'Obeying the gospel'

Furthermore, secondly, if you reduce the gospel to something that has to do only with what you think in your head and assent to by faith (primarily a cognitive matter), then you will consider 'gospel issues' to be only those things that have to do with faith, or the lack of faith, or anything that might threaten the essential message of salvation by grace through faith. But Paul speaks of 'the obedience of faith', and of 'obeying the gospel'. That is, the gospel is something that we respond to not only by believing it, but by acting upon it and living in the light of it. We must live *now* in the light of the whole biblical story as *the* story – the story that begins with creation and ends with new creation and summons us to live in the first in preparation for the second. That is gospel living – living in faith and obedience in response to the good news, living 'worthy of the gospel'. And such gospel *living* includes creation within its scope since the gospel *message* does.

iii) The gospel of the kingdom of God

And thirdly, if you see the gospel as primarily to do with 'me and my needs', or 'others and their needs', you will see 'gospel issues' as only those things that either contribute to, or militate against, the solution to our greatest need, namely our sin and rebellion against God and our consequent need for forgiveness – a very serious issue indeed. There are real gospel issues at stake when we are dealing with people's eternal destinies. However, while such concern is entirely valid, it can easily overlook the fact that the New Testament (including Jesus himself) presents the gospel as the good news, not first of all about us and our destiny (though of course including that), but about the reign of God. In a world that calls Caesar Lord, the gospel declares 'there is another king – King Jesus'. The gospel proclaims the Lordship of Jesus Christ and the fact that he exercised that Lordship through his self-emptying incarnation, earthly life, atoning death, victorious resurrection, glorious ascension and ultimate return, and calls us to respond in repentance and faith to that proclamation. From that point of view, 'gospel issues' take on a wider level of meaning and scope. The essence of our responding to the gospel is that we choose to submit to Jesus of Nazareth as Lord. The gospel calls me to recognize Jesus as Lord not just of my personal discipleship, but of the whole environment in which I live, for 'all authority in heaven and on earth (i.e. in all creation) is given to me', said Jesus. If the gospel declares Jesus to be truly Lord of all creation, then how I live out my discipleship to Jesus must also include creation. It is, as the CTC says, 'a gospel issue *within the Lordship of Christ*' (that defining phrase is intentional and crucial).

Or to put it bluntly, for someone to claim to be a Christian, to be a follower and disciple of Jesus, to be submitting to Jesus as Lord, and yet to have no concern about the creation, or even to reject with hostility those who do act on such concern, seems to me to be a denial of the biblical gospel which proclaims that Jesus Christ is the creator, sustainer and redeemer of creation itself. I cannot claim Christ as *my* Lord and Saviour while at the same time denying (or acting as if I denied) what the biblical gospel proclaims, that he is *creation's* Lord and Saviour. It is, for that reason, a gospel issue.

e) Our final destination

What, then, is our final destination? It is amazing (and regrettable) how many Christians believe that the world ends with us all leaving the earth behind and going off to heaven to live there instead. It may well be the influence of countless hymns that use that kind of imagery, but it is decidedly not how the Bible ends.

There is, of course, an important truth that gives great comfort and hope in saying that when believers die in faith and in Christ, they go to be with him – safe and secure and at rest, free from all the perils and suffering of this earthly life. But the Bible makes it clear that that 'intermediate state' (as it is sometimes called) is just that – 'intermediate' – it is not our final destination to 'stay in heaven'. The Bible's final great dynamic movement (Revelation 21–22) is not of us all going off up to heaven, but of God coming down here, bringing the city of God, establishing the reunification of heaven and earth as his dwelling place with us for ever. Three times the loud voice from the throne of God says '*with* mankind, . . . *with* them, . . . *with* them'. We should remember that Immanuel does not mean 'Us with God', but 'God with us'. We do not go somewhere else to be with God; God comes to earth to be with us – as the psalmists and prophets had prophesied and prayed for. 'O that you would rend the heavens and come down!' (Isaiah 64:1).

And in that new creation, with God dwelling at last in the cleansed temple of his whole creation (so that no microcosmic temple will be needed, as John saw), the tribute of the nations will be brought into the city of God – the 'glory of kings', purged and purified and contributing to the glory of God (Revelation 21:22–27).

Conclusion

What does all this mean for our ecological thinking and action in the here and now? It means that in godly use of, and care for, the creation we are doing two things at the same time. On the one hand we are exercising the created role God gave us from the beginning, and in so doing we can properly be glorifying God in all our work within and for creation. And on the other hand we are anticipating the role that we shall have in the new creation, when we shall then assume fully our proper role of kings and priests – exercising the loving rule of God over the rest of his creation, and serving it on God's behalf as the place of God's temple dwelling.

This is what gives wonderful resonance to that song of praise to the crucified and risen Christ (the Lamb who was slain who sits on the throne), sung by the four living creatures who represent all creation and the twenty-four elders who represent the whole people of God:

> You are worthy to take the scroll and to open its seals because you were slain, and with your blood you purchased for God persons from every tribe and language and people and nation. You have made them to be a kingdom and priests to serve our God, and they shall reign on the earth. (Revelation 5:9–10 [NIV 2011])

Ecological action now is both a creational responsibility from the Bible's beginning, and also an eschatological sign of the Bible's ending – and new beginning. Christian ecological action points towards and anticipates the restoration of our proper status and function in creation. It is to behave as we were originally created to, and as we shall one day be fully redeemed for.

The earth is waiting with eager longing for the revealing of its appointed kings and priests – redeemed humanity glorifying God in the temple of renewed creation under the Lordship of Jesus Christ.

(Wright 2013)

Wright's lecture is amplified by David Bookless of A Rocha in, '"Let everything that has breath praise the LORD": The Bible and biodiversity':

> What gives nature its value? Anthropocentric views (which see the world as here to serve human interests) and ecocentric views (which aim to value all species equally) compete but are flawed. In contrast, a biblical perspective emphasises that both human and non-human creatures are made for the glory of God and have value directly in relation to God. This has significant implications for Christian attitudes to biodiversity conservation and for the conservation movement.

In secular Western cultures, where religion is often relegated to the private sphere, it is unusual to encounter scientists requesting assistance from people of faith. Yet, in the field of wildlife conservation, recent years have seen a growing stream of such approaches. Beginning with a gathering of global faith leaders at Assisi for the 25th anniversary of the World Wildlife Fund in 1986, this process has gathered momentum. It includes a major five-year programme on 'World Faiths and the Environment', sponsored by the World Bank working with the WWF; partnerships or discussions initiated by major conservation bodies such as Conservation International, BirdLife International, the RSPB and the Sierra Club; and serious academic engagement with the place of world faiths in conservation at Yale and Oxford Universities.

The reasons why secular conservationists are engaging with world faiths are various. They include the significant overlap between specific faith communities and the world's biodiversity hotspots (the 2 per cent of global land containing 60 per cent of the world's plant and animal species) and significant landholdings of faith groups. However, the most significant reason is the recognition that the biodiversity conservation movement faces a crisis, and many within it believe the ethical resources of world faiths can help . . .

At the heart of the crisis within biodiversity conservation is a simple question which divides the global conservation movement: What gives nature its value? Is conservation's raison d'être purely instrumental, preserving habitats and species because of the 'ecosystem services' (Millennium Ecosystem Assessment 2005) they provide for human thriving, or can we speak of intrinsic or inherent values within species and ecosystems and, if so, on what are these values based? Can Christianity help with the search for ethical values or, as some assert (White 1967; Stuart et al. 2005), has the doctrine of humanity as 'the image of God' caused such a divide between people and the rest of nature that Christianity is part of the problem? . . . The issue before us, then, may be simply expressed:

are animals created purely for human use, or do they have independent value to God, and if so, how should humans treat them? . . .

Genesis 1 and 2 [emphasize] humanity's commonality with other creatures, but also draw out the unique privileges and responsibilities incumbent on being human. Our first 'great commission' is directly related to how we treat the birds, animals, sea-creatures and the earth itself, along with which we were created. Our vocation as human creatures is to glorify God in assisting in the flourishing of the whole good creation. Thus, biodiversity conservation becomes a missional task and a key means of reflecting God's image . . .

The Noah account in Genesis 6 – 9 deserves more serious theological attention than it has often received. It reveals a God who cares not only about the salvation of human beings but who is passionate about biodiversity conservation. The ship of salvation contains four pairs of humans, up to seven pairs of some species, and at least one breeding pair of each, 'So that their kind might continue upon the earth' (Genesis 7:1–4). In other words all these creatures, including presumably those that were unclean, harmful or irrelevant to human beings, have value rooted in how God sees them. This ancient text cuts across contemporary conservationists' talk of 'natural capital', 'ecosystem services', and 'putting a price on nature', all of which are based on instrumental value and economy viability. From Noah we learn that the value of the creatures resides neither in their value to humanity nor in some absolute intrinsic value. Their value, as with the value of every human being, is contingent. It lies in terms of their importance to God . . .

[T]here are theologically important passages about creation in the Psalms and Wisdom literature. Many psalms affirm that, according to their kind, non-human creatures worship and praise God and also that God cares and provides for all creatures (e.g., Psalms 65:5–13; 69:34; 96:11–13; 98:7–9; 145:13–21; 148:1–13). Psalm 145:9 [NIV], for instance, states 'The Lord is good to all; he has compassion on all he has made.' This is the God whose character humanity is to reflect . . .

In Psalm 104, humans are but one of the many works of God and no mention is made of any privilege or authority with regards to other creatures . . . Yet, neither is the Psalm eco-centric. The earth does not belong to any or all created species. It belongs in its totality to God, a God who provides for all creatures and rejoices in all his works (verse 31). The natural world is to provide for all species and, by implication, its riches are to be shared by all, not accumulated by one at the expense of all others.

In the Old Testament Wisdom literature, wisdom arises out of the 'fear of the Lord' (Proverbs 9:10) and a close study of the world. This examination of the world around us includes the natural world: witness Solomon's nature-based wisdom (1 Kings 4:33) and Proverbs' injunction to observe wise but small creatures such as ants (Proverbs 30:24–28).

Job 38 – 41 is the longest passage in the Bible about creation, with a particular focus on phenomena and creatures beyond human understanding and control. God mocks Job's, and humanity's, inability to comprehend the scale and scope of nature's vastness. God delights in wild, weird and wonderful creatures: the lion, raven, mountain goat, wild ass (onager), wild ox (auroch), ostrich, warhorse, hawk, eagle or vulture, Behemoth and Leviathan (perhaps respectively hippopotamus and crocodile). Some of these species threaten human life; others live beyond the orbit of human concerns; even the war-horse, used by humanity, cannot be controlled. Job 38:25–27 is explicit that God's purposeful action extends beyond providing natural resources for humanity's use, watering and providing grazing 'on a land where no one lives, on the desert, which is empty of human life'. The world is overseen and cared for by God, who takes interest and delight in creatures and happenings that, from a human perspective, appear irrelevant or even threatening . . .

Although the New Testament says less about animals and their place in God's purposes, to conclude that the Bible's concern for the natural world disappears with Jesus would be mistaken. Firstly, the New Testament does not destroy but fulfils and builds upon the Old: the covenant with Noah was an everlasting covenant and remains intact.

Secondly, Jesus' parables, his references to fig trees, foxes and flowers, arise from and model a deep attentiveness to the natural world. He urged the disciples to 'consider' the birds and flowers (Matthew 6:25–34) . . . [I]n the wilderness Jesus is described as being 'with the wild animals' (Mark 1:13), which probably references Isaiah 11's vision of the peaceful Kingdom and 'indicates Jesus' peaceable presence with the animals' (Bauckham 2011, p. 76).

Thirdly, Christ's death and resurrection not only demonstrate God's grace in the redemption of human beings, but also encompass the restoration of a broken creation. Colossians 1:15–20 and Romans 18:19–28 are amongst several Pauline passages which make explicit the continuity between God's work in creation and consummation. All things, people and animals, were made very good, have been damaged by sin, are included in the scope of Christ's reconciling work on the cross, and can potentially be incorporated in the final renewal and reintegration of heaven and earth. On the role of redeemed humanity within God's purposes, as N. T. Wright says, 'The whole creation is waiting in eager longing . . . for God's children to be revealed: in other words, for the unveiling of those redeemed humans through whose stewardship creation will at last be brought back into that wise order for which it was made' (in Bauckham 2011, p. 213).

Fourthly, the biblical vision of new creation incorporates human and animal life (Isaiah 11:6–9; 65:17–25; Hosea 2:14–23) in harmonious coexistence. Wolves, lambs, leopards, goats, calves, lions, cows, bears, snakes and small children are pictured living side-by-side in peace. It is described as a 'holy mountain' (Isaiah 11 and 65), a 'new Jerusalem' (Isaiah 65), and a creation-wide covenant where weapons of war will be destroyed (Hosea 2). The four living creatures of Revelation 4:6–11 represent the whole of creation worshipping the risen Christ in this new realm. They are heavenly creatures with multiple eyes and wings but also symbolize wild animals (lion), domesticated animals (ox), humanity and birds (eagle). They . . . add their 'Amen' to the worship of 'every creature in heaven and on earth and under the earth and on the sea, and all that is in them' (Revelation 5:13).

Thus, the new creation envisaged in Revelation 21 – 22 is not exactly a return to Eden, nor human artifice, nor Divine novelty, but a perfect combination of elements of all three . . . With Revelation 22's constant references back to Eden's rivers and the tree of life, this is a radical renewal of the original paradise, in which the very best of human work is incorporated harmoniously into the natural world and yet in the centre, radiating light and life, is the heavenly city, a new creation all of God's. Within this vision, care for and conservation of wildlife is not a romantic ideal or a pointless task, but an anticipatory sign of the Kingdom of God, where all creation will be renewed and restored . . .

[A] biblical response to the crisis of biodiversity loss will be essentially theocentric rather than not anthropocentric or eco-centric. Such a perspective avoids both ecolatry (eco-idolatry) and ecophobia (hatred of ecological concerns). The Bible, from Genesis to Revelation, reveals that God's purposes for humanity must be seen within the context of God's care and concern for every living creature. [We conclude] with biblical principles based on the material discussed.

1 This world and all its creatures (human and non-human) belong to God and exist to bring glory to God.
2 The value and purpose of every species derives from God alone, and is tied to God's plans in creation, covenant, redemption and reconciliation.

3 Species have value independently of their usefulness to humanity, so ecological decisions should not be made on anthropocentric or economic grounds alone.

4 Every species matters, irrespective of its usefulness to humanity. Avoidable extinctions damage the integrity of God's world, erase something of God's self-revelation in creation, and silence elements of creation's worship of God.

5 Humanity has a divine vocation in reflecting God's character towards the animal kingdom through encouraging the flourishing of biodiversity and resisting its depletion. This is both a missional task to be fostered as a special vocation for some, and part of the wider calling of all Christ's disciples.

6 In an age of ecological depletion, Christianity offers ultimate hope both for people and biodiversity, rooted in the redeeming work of Christ for all creation.

Evangelical Christians urgently need to recover a biblical vision of caring for other creatures. Early evangelicals including Wesley, Spurgeon, Wilberforce, Shaftesbury and Carey were each active in animal welfare or conservation (Bookless 2014b). Their examples demonstrate that environmental concerns need not dilute Christian priorities in evangelism, loving our neighbours and seeking justice for the poor. Rather, an integral biblical world-view loves and cares for everything that God created and sustains in love and is included in Christ's redeeming work. If, as the Lausanne Movement's Cape Town Commitment (I.7a) states, creation care is 'a gospel issue within the Lordship of Christ', it cannot be ignored or marginalised but must be fully integrated into Christian discipleship and mission. This includes challenging the idols of consumerism and materialism which not only drive species towards extinction, but exploit the poor and damage us spiritually. It means recognising that our resource use, energy consumption, food ethics, and purchasing power all need to become subject to the Lordship of Christ. In all these areas, Christians should

work with others to seek ways of living which give witness to a sustainable and biodiverse future for God's world. As evangelicals recover their lost heritage in witnessing to a biblically theocentric worldview and supporting practical initiatives for biodiversity conservation, they will discover that Christ's Lordship is proclaimed, and creation's worship is magnified as everything that has breath praises the Lord.
(Bookless 2014a)

The default position for most Christian (and most secular) approaches to conservation is that we are called to be 'stewards'. Other words are sometimes used, but they express the same idea. There are those who decry the concept, on the grounds that it implies subordination and hierarchy, but it is widely and usually uncritically accepted. It could be regarded as uncontroversial. The idea that humanity was responsible to God for the use of the earth was an integral part of Judeo–Christian thought for many centuries. It was implicit in the Benedictine rule, which held sway over large tracts of Europe before the Reformation; it was expressed formally by Sir Matthew Hale, a distinguished seventeenth-century Chief Justice of England in a book *The Primitive Origination of Mankind*:

In relation to this inferior World of Brutes and Vegetables, the End of Man's Creation was, that he should be the ViceRoy of the great God of Heaven and Earth in this inferior World; his Steward, Villicus, Bayliff, or Farmer of this goodly Farm of the lower World . . . if we observe the special and peculiar accommodation and adaptation of Man, to the regiment and ordering of this lower World, we shall have reason, even without Revelation, to conclude that this was one End of the Creation of Man, namely, to be the Vice-gerent of Almighty God, in the subordinate Regiment especially of the Animal and Vegetable Provinces.
(Hale 1677, p. 370)

In Hale's view there was clearly no escape from humanity's responsibility to God for the proper management of the earth, with the task to control the wilder animals and to protect the weaker, to preserve and improve useful plants and to eliminate weeds and, interestingly, to maintain the beauty as well as the productivity of the earth.

Three centuries later the UK Government, in a White Paper that formed its submission to the 1992 Earth Summit, declared:

> The starting point for this government [to determine policies and priorities for environmental care] is the ethical imperative of stewardship, which must underlie all environmental policies ... It was the Prime Minister (Margaret Thatcher) who reminded us that we do not hold a freehold on our world, but only a full repairing lease.
>
> (Government White Paper 1990)

Notwithstanding, the concept of stewardship needs critical examination, and this has been done by Richard Bauckham in a series of lectures originally called 'Beyond stewardship: The Bible and the community of creation', and published as *The Bible and Ecology* (Bauckham 2010). He notes that secular use of the stewardship concept excludes reference to God, which empties the term of theological meaning. Bauckham describes multiple limitations of this paradigm, including its absurd hubris regarding human capacity to understand complex ecosystems well enough to manage them positively, and disregard for our own relationships within the rest of creation. Additionally, 'stewardship' can fail to recognize God's ongoing involvement in sustaining creation, overestimate the appropriateness or goodness of human intervention in the whole of creation, and fail to acknowledge humanity's own embeddedness within – rather than outside or above – the created world, a position that obscures our creaturely interdependence with other species and created elements.

Bauckham develops these criticisms in detail in *The Bible and Ecology*, but sets out the positive aspects of creation care in an essay giving an overview of the major ecological themes of the Bible (Bauckham 2011), showing the way to a proper biblical understanding of our place in creation, not as detached and superior managers but as fellow members of a cosmos of creatures all orientated towards glorifying and worshipping God.

Scientists Warners and Heun (2019) have provided a noteworthy addition to reconsidering the 'Christian environmental stewardship' paradigm which has long dominated evangelical creation care. They note additional limitations of the stewardship concept: a sense of individual duty rather than joyful and loving collective care, overemphasis on separation of both God and humans from creation, the impression that human stewards are left in charge of creation in God's absence, and a sometimes simplistic proprietary relationship that misses God's immanence and deep love for creation. These considerations are prompting new attention to additional dimensions of creation care in biblical studies.

The Third Lausanne Congress was held in Cape Town in October 2010. It brought together 4,200 evangelical leaders from 198 countries, with the declared goal being to bring a fresh challenge to the global church to bear witness to Jesus Christ and his teaching – in every nation, in every sphere of society and in the realm of ideas. There was no possibility that Stott could travel to Cape Town. He was almost ninety years of age, living in St Barnabas College in Lingfield, Surrey, and very weak. His final public appearance had been at the Keswick Convention three years previously, but he was very conscious of what was happening in Cape Town. Stott's advance audio greetings to the Cape Town Congress opened by noting new challenges, such as 'the spectre of global warming, which adds new urgency to our evangelism' (2010a). He sent a message to Cape Town: 'I shall be very sorry to miss being with you. But I will be with you all each day in prayer, expectation and confidence as you plan to make known the uniqueness of Jesus Christ all over the world.'

The fruit of the Congress was set out in a Cape Town Commitment. Stott received a copy in March 2011. His eyesight had almost gone and he asked friends to read it to him. All the matters that he had yearned for evangelicals to address were clearly laid out – not merely in the document itself but also in a commitment to act. He rejoiced to learn of the plans to take forward the major areas in a series of global consultations. The first of these consultations was organized and hosted by Las Newman, entitled 'Creation care and the gospel'. It took place in Jamaica in October 2012 – a week after Hurricane Sandy travelled from the Caribbean up the Atlantic Coast to Canada, killing at least 285 people in 7 countries, destroying 305,000 homes, and causing around US$75 billion damage. The Jamaica Consultation produced the 'Jamaica call to action' with the following two major convictions.

Creation Care is indeed a 'gospel issue within the lordship of Christ' (CTC I-7-A). Informed and inspired by our study of the Scripture – the original intent, plan, and command to care for creation, the resurrection narratives and the profound truth that in Christ all things have been reconciled to God – we reaffirm that creation care is an issue that must be included in our response to the gospel, proclaiming and acting upon the good news of what God has done and will complete for the salvation of the world. This is not only biblically justified, but an integral part of our mission and an expression of our worship to God for his wonderful plan of redemption through Jesus Christ. Therefore, our ministry of reconciliation is a matter of great joy and hope and we would care for creation even if it were not in crisis.

We are faced with a crisis that is pressing, urgent, and that must be resolved in our generation. Many of the world's poorest people, ecosystems, and species of flora and fauna are being devastated by violence against the environment in multiple ways, of which global climate change, deforestation, biodiversity loss, water stress, and pollution are but a part. We can no longer afford complacency and endless debate. Love for God, our neighbors and the wider creation, as well as our passion for justice, compel us to 'urgent and prophetic ecological responsibility' (*CTC* I-7-A).
(Lausanne/WEA Creation Care Network 2012)

The documents behind the Jamaica Consultation and its 'Jamaica call to action' have been published as *Creation Care and the Gospel* (Bell and White 2016). The idea that creation care is a 'gospel issue' is not yet accepted by some evangelicals. For that reason, it was important that the biblical basis for creation care should be spelt out in detail. This was done by Jonathan Moo (2016, pp. 28–42). It is an appropriate witness to continue and conclude the legacy of John Stott. Moo begins by recapitulating the reasons for creation care in Scripture: the 'good earth' created by God, described in the early chapters of Genesis and in many psalms (especially 104 and 148), and rejoiced in by its Creator as related in the book of Job. He points out that God has committed this good earth to our care, and illustrates this by using the 'triangle' concept of Chris Wright (see pages 214 and 215) portraying how God, humankind and the rest of creation are linked, but with the linkages distorted by our disobedience, as expounded by Isaiah, Hosea and Paul. Despite all this, Moo goes on to insist that there is hope both for us and the creation as a whole.

> The good news is that despite our unfaithfulness, God is faithful. This is why Paul can say in Romans 8 that the subjection of creation was done 'in hope' (v. 20). It was God's intention that all of creation should share not only in the results of the fall of humankind but also in our redemption. Creation, Paul says, will one day be freed from its slavery to ruin and enter into the glory that accompanies the redemption of the children of God (Romans 8:21). In Christ, the new Adam and true image of God, the future full healing of all of creation is secured.
>
> Paul does not give us any details about what creation's freedom will look like apart from suggesting that it means the undoing of its present futility. It will reach the purpose for which God always intended it. It will be liberated from corruption and ruin, because the children of God will finally fulfil the role in Christ for which they were created. The brokenness that marks life in this age – brokenness in the relationship

between humankind and God, and between humankind and the rest of creation – is healed in Christ. In Christ, God's *shalom*, peace and wholeness, is secured. More expansive pictures of what this looks like are found in other biblical texts, where this hope is described as the reconciliation or renewal of all things (Matthew 19:28; Acts 3:21; Colossians 1:20); a new heaven and new earth (Isaiah 65:17; 66:22; 2 Peter 3:13; Revelation 21:1); or the kingdom of this world becoming the kingdom of God and of his Messiah (Revelation 11:15). In all such texts, the glorious future of creation so exceeds human imagination that only symbol and metaphor can begin to describe it. What Romans 8 makes unmistakably clear is that this very same creation that is now groaning has a future in God's purposes. Whatever else we might conclude about the details of biblical hope, we must affirm in the light of Romans 8 that this creation, this very earth, will not be left behind.

It has sometimes been suggested that other biblical texts – notably the book of Revelation and 2 Peter 3 – teach that this earth will be left behind or destroyed and discarded in the end. If this world is going to be tossed aside, so the argument goes, then perhaps we ought not to spend time and effort in caring for the present creation; it would be as futile as polishing the railings of a ship that is destined to sink. But in the light of the whole of the biblical story of God's faithfulness to creation, the *Titanic* analogy is simply wrong. Such a negative conception of the earth's future is most obviously contradicted by Paul's portrayal of an entire creation that anticipates sharing in the freedom and glory that attends our resurrection, the 'children of God to be revealed' and the 'redemption of our bodies' (Romans 8:19–23). Whatever discontinuity there may be between the present age and the age to come, this same creation finds the creator's intentions for it fulfilled, its future secured, and its healing accomplished in the new creation. Yet even if Scripture did suggest that there was no continuity between this world and the next, the command to love God and neighbour would still compel us to care well for the world as it has been entrusted to us now, for the sake of future generations.

Consider 2 Peter 3, a text that more than any other emphasizes discontinuity, the break between this age and the age to come. The 'day of the Lord' is described in this passage as coming at an unknowable and unpredictable time, 'like a thief' (2 Peter 3:10), and it will involve God's fiery judgement of 'the present heavens and earth' (v. 7), the disappearance of the 'heavens' and the destruction by fire of the 'elements' (v. 10). Due to some textual confusion among original manuscripts, some readers might think that 2 Peter 3:10 also describes the burning up and destruction of the earth itself. The King James Version, for example, renders the end of the verse as 'the earth also and the works that are therein shall be burned up'. But, as recent commentators have recognized, and as is reflected in most contemporary translations, the best Greek manuscripts attest to a reading that has the earth and the works done being 'found' or 'laid bare' before God (Bauckham 1983, pp. 303 and 316–321; Moo, 2014, p. 155, n. 18). The emphasis of 3:10 is on the impossibility of anything being hidden from God's final judgement and on the concomitant importance of how life is lived now. This serves as a direct challenge to the false teachers, dealt with throughout 2 Peter, who deny the coming of the Lord and encourage the heedless pursuit of greed and pleasure without regard for the priorities of God's kingdom.

The 'elements' which 2 Peter 3:10 says are 'destroyed by fire' may well refer to the heavenly elements, the *stoichea* that later texts associate with the stars, sun and moon. The scenario described in 2 Peter 3:10 would then best be understood as a picture of God coming to his creation, the heavens that symbolically separate his throne-room from the earth disappearing with a roar, the elements in between dissolving before his fiery presence, and the earth and all the works of humanity being 'found' before him, laid bare and discovered for what they really are. This is a cosmic picture of what 1 Peter describes as the testing of our faith by fire, which will be 'found [the same

Greek verb as is used for 'laid bare' in 2 Peter 3:10, NIV] to result in praise and glory and honour when Jesus Christ is revealed' (1 Peter 1:7; cf. 1 Corinthians 3:13). The emphasis of 2 Peter 3 is thus on the enduring value and significance of present life, and perhaps even of the earth itself, which is finally 'laid bare' or 'found' on the day of the Lord in the midst of the fire of his 'judgement and destruction of the ungodly' (2 Peter 3:7 [NIV 2011]).

The analogy that 2 Peter uses in the immediate context is telling: the future judgement by fire is compared to the Flood of Noah's day, when 'the world of that time was deluged and destroyed' (3:6). The reference to the Flood narrative should remind readers of God's 'everlasting covenant' with all the creatures of the earth (Genesis 9), of his faithfulness and commitment to his creation, of the promise anticipated in his call of Noah to save all non-human life through the waters of judgement. The waters of the Flood, like the fire of final judgement, certainly mean 'destruction' for a world corrupted by injustice and polluted by evil. But it is not a destruction into nothingness, a rubbishing of this earth and a starting over with something else (all anachronistic ideas for first-century readers) (Adams 2007, p. 226). The earth that Noah and his family discovered after the waters receded was the same earth they had stood upon before the Flood, yet it was also a new world, cleansed of the human evil and violence that had been corrupting and destroying it (cf. Genesis 6:11–12). The 'new' world that emerges on the other side of judgement is quite clearly *this* world made new, a world purified and reclaimed: 'a new heaven and a new earth, where righteousness dwells' (2 Peter 3:13 [NIV 2011]). The challenge to Peter's readers is to live now as those who belong to this coming earthly realization of God's kingdom, to embody the godly ways of living that pertain to new creation life and to be 'found' to be at 'peace with him' (v 14) on the day of the Lord's visitation. The comfort of 2 Peter 3 is found in the reminder that God's purposes will prevail no matter what. In the end, the new heavens and new earth is granted by the grace of God, and does not finally depend on us. God, by his grace, enables and ennobles our efforts, even using them to speed on the day of the Lord (v. 12), yet the transcendent hope presented us in this text both humbles and frees us from the burden and despair of thinking that the future ultimately depends only on our own successes or failures. As Paul reminds readers at the end of his magnificent description of resurrection hope in 1 Corinthians 15, the certainty of the future resurrection means that our labour is not in vain (1 Corinthians 15:58), for the results are finally in God's hands.

Romans 8 and 2 Peter 3 provide tantalizing hints of God's purposes for this earth, of a creation liberated from futility and ruin, where evil is vanquished and righteousness makes its home. But it is especially in the cosmic visions of John's Apocalypse that we find a canvas large enough to begin to glimpse the beauty and wonder of the new heaven and new earth. Revelation reminds us from the beginning that the hope of God's people is not finally to escape to heaven but to 'reign on the earth' (5:10), and this reign is not confined to a temporary millennial period but encompasses the 'for ever and ever' of the new creation (22:5) when the New Jerusalem will have come down from heaven to earth (21:2). This reign is only possible because of the redemption and victory obtained through the blood of the lamb (5:9), in whose reign we are made able to share: 'the kingdom of the world has become the kingdom of our Lord and of his Messiah, and he will reign for ever and ever' (11:15). Read in the context of the rest of Scripture (as Revelation demands to be read), we find here the restoration of the image of God (cf. Colossians 1:15; 3:10) and of the role originally intended for us as 'kings and priests' (Revelation 1:6, KJV) within creation. This renewal begins now for all of those in Christ, yet the last chapters of Revelation point beyond merely present realities to the future hope of 'a new heaven and a new earth' (21:1) when all things are made new (21:5). This is not a making of *all new things,* but a restoration and renewal of everything; a bringing to fulfilment of God's purposes for creation from the beginning. God dwells intimately with his people (21:3) as he did in the garden, and the tree of life is restored, now serving to heal the nations of the world.

The new creation to come is not merely a return to Genesis, however. Christ's resurrected body yet bears the wounds of his crucifixion and, though transformed, it is recognizably continuous with his body before the resurrection. In the same way, the new creation entails the gathering up and the renewal of all of the first creation and its history. The new heaven and new earth is thus described as both the Garden of Eden and the city of the New Jerusalem, and the kings and the nations enter it with their splendour. The glory they contribute is perhaps a sign of the endurance of all that is best of human culture and civilization – with art, science, and all human striving now freed from captivity to sin, evil, and injustice. The new creation is a place where all of the results of humankind's rebellion are no more – death, mourning, crying, pain (21:4), the curse (22:3) – but it is not merely a resetting of the clock to day one, but rather the fulfilment of God's original intentions for this creation. The latent threat symbolized by the sea (21:1) and night (22:5), the 'waters' and 'darkness' of Genesis 1:2, are not even present in the new creation, as the world has been taken beyond all threat, with God's purposes for humanity and all of creation brought to fruition (Moo 2009).

A biblical environmental ethos finds its driving vision here, in this hope for the liberation and renewal of creation itself. This cosmic hope reaffirms the value of all of creation in God's ultimate purposes. It calls upon those who claim to be in Christ to begin to live like it – to begin to live as those who have been adopted as God's children, in whom the image of the creator is being renewed, and whose lives now reflect the priorities of God's new creation.

To return to Romans 8, Paul implies in this passage that the revelation of the children of God awaits the future resurrection (v. 23), but he also affirms in the very same chapter that we have *already* been adopted as God's children and already are expected to live like it (vv. 14–17). If the entire creation longs to see us become who we are – to have our status as God's children revealed – then our lives even now ought to begin to be orientated towards creation in a way that is in keeping with God's ultimate purposes. We ought to live in a way that is consistent with creation's eventual freedom from futility and ruin when all things are made new. God's new creation breaks into the present in Christ and in all of those who have been made God's children in Christ. Our work is not to *save* the planet, or to bring about the kingdom of God by our own efforts. We are rather called to live as instantiations of the kingdom of God, members of a resistance movement against all that would destroy God's creation, trusting in his grace for the future.

When we take seriously the cosmic breadth of Christian hope and our call to live as God's children now, we find that the scope of our love and of our ethics extends beyond our fellow human creatures to embrace all of God's creation. Our casual selfishness in how we use the earth's resources, in how we treat our global neighbours, and in how we treat creation itself is seen in this light to be an affront to God, an abrogation of our responsibility, and a rejection of our identity as his children in Christ.

We may be tempted to avoid the radical implications of a biblical theology of creation care. We might claim that our calling is to care for our human neighbours and not to get caught up in misanthropic *green* concerns. Or we might plead ignorance, claiming that we cannot know precisely how to reflect God's love in the way we relate to non-human creation. If there are difficult ethical questions for Christians about interpersonal ethics, it may be all the more difficult to agree on what it means to live ethically in relation to non-human creation. Where are we to go for guidance in weighing trade-offs, and in making detailed, difficult decisions as individuals, communities, churches, and missions agencies?

Scripture is not a manual to give us all of the answers. But we *are* given an ethos, a set of principles. We have seen that these include the recognition of the value that all of creation has before God; of the particular and distinctive value of human beings as members of the community of creation; and of the call to reflect the sacrificial love of Christ in all of our relations. We must use the abilities God has given us to study creation, and to make the best decisions we can in caring for it and for its human inhabitants; indeed, as has become clear, it is impossible to care for our human brothers and sisters without caring for the environment in which they, and we, live. We must be wary, however, of our predilection to find answers that fit comfortably within our societies and cultures; of our temptation to evade the challenges of radical discipleship (Stott 2010b). We must be wary, for example, of the language of *prioritization* of human welfare versus the environment. Such language, especially as it is used in wealthier parts of the world, is too often rooted in false trade-offs that ignore longer-term consequences or reflect unexamined commitments to conducting business as usual. It too often represents assimilation to a world where money and Western notions of development and success reign unchallenged. In short, it represents a failure of the imagination. We must also remember, based on the testimony of Scripture, that non-human creation, in all its wonderful diversity, has value before God. Wherever possible, we are therefore compelled to work towards solutions that enhance the health of both human and non-human communities (*q.v.* Moo and White 2014; Bauckham 2016).

We must also be wary of the language of prioritization of gospel proclamation versus care for the poor and care for the earth, as if one did not enrich the other. It is obviously possible to care for the needy and to care for the environment without proclaiming the gospel. Plenty of non-Christian organizations and even many Christian organizations and churches attest to that. But is it possible to proclaim the gospel, to be faithful witnesses to the God who reveals himself to us through the

Spirit in the incarnate Christ and in his written word without caring for the poor and caring for his earth? The *good news* revealed to us in the New Testament is that in Jesus, the Son of God and Messiah of Israel, God has defeated the powers of sin and death and inaugurated his restored rule over all of his creation. He has made provision through the incarnation, death, resurrection, and ascension of Jesus for all people to receive forgiveness of sins and new life in the Spirit, enabling them to live for ever as his children under the Lordship of Christ. This good news is for the whole of the earth, because it reveals the way in which God's purposes for all of creation are accomplished in Christ – the means by which a world wracked by sin and corruption is renewed and restored to its creator. Thus, as the Cape Town Commitment expresses it, 'to proclaim the gospel that says Jesus is Lord is to proclaim the gospel that includes the earth, since Christ's Lordship is over all creation. Creation care is thus a gospel issue within the Lordship of Christ'.

. . . [W]e groan alongside the rest of creation as we long for the return of Christ our king, for the making of all things new (Revelation 21:5). Often, in fact, it may be only in lament and groaning alongside all of creation, in concert with the Holy Spirit, that we are enabled to persevere and keep from giving up.

God has not left us alone. He is present with us by his Spirit, granting us – as Peter says – 'times of refreshing . . . from the Lord' as we await the renewal of all things (Acts 3:19–21). We have our hope in Christ as an anchor for our soul (Hebrews 6:19). So we are also hopeful and joyful as we plant trees, as we restore wetlands, as we grow food more sustainably, as we teach and we research, as we support and get involved with those who are working on the front lines to transform our communities and our world, as we seek to reshape the priorities of our societies and to live as signposts to God's kingdom, as we engage in all of the hard work of caring well for creation, and also as we celebrate and enjoy the world of God's creation, glorifying our creator and redeemer.

In the biblical hope of new creation, we are given the gift of seeing this world with new eyes. We are freed to love and find joy in *nature* as God's good creation – just as the psalmists did; and we are enabled to join alongside all of creation in its praise of God in Christ . . .

I conclude with the story of Jeremiah. When Jerusalem was under siege by the king of Babylon and the prophet was imprisoned by his own king for predicting that the Babylonians would destroy the city, that the world as the king of Judah knew it was about to come to an end, Jeremiah did an odd thing. He bought a field and ensured the deed for the field would be stored for a long time to come (Jeremiah 32). Why? Because Jeremiah had a confident hope in God's promise that one day in the future, houses, fields, and vineyards would once again be bought and sold in the land. One day, the Lord would gather his people back from exile, make an everlasting covenant with them and plant them securely in the land. So Jeremiah invested in God's future. He expected the end of the world as he knew it; but he was joyful because he had considered *all* the facts. For us too, in the face of what sometimes seems like the end of the world as we know it, we can go on joyfully caring for creation and engaging in all of the gospel work that God calls us to, because we know all the facts – or at least as many facts as we need. We know the challenges that are facing God's creation; we know what God demands of us; and we know that he is faithful.

(Moo 2016, pp. 35–42)

John Stott's biographer Timothy Dudley-Smith wrote the hymn 'The God who set the stars in space' for Berry's *The Care of Creation*. It encapsulates many of the ideas in the foregoing pages.

The God who set the stars in space
   and gave the planets birth
created for our dwelling place
   a green and fruitful earth;

a world with wealth and beauty crowned
    of sky and sea and land,
where life should flourish and abound
    beneath its Maker's hand.

A world of order and delight
    God gave for us to tend,
to hold as precious in his sight,
    to nurture and defend;
but yet on ocean, earth and air
    the marks of sin are seen,
with all that God created fair
    polluted and unclean.

O God, by whose redeeming grace
    the lost may be restored,
who stooped to save our fallen race
    in Christ, creation's Lord,
through him whose cross is life and peace
    to cleanse a heart defiled
may human greed and conflict cease
    and all be reconciled.

Renew the wastes of earth again,
    redeem, restore, repair;
with us, your children, still maintain
    your covenant of care.
May we, who move from dust to dust
    and on your grace depend,
no longer, Lord, betray our trust
    but prove creation's friend.

Our God, who set the stars in space
    and gave the planets birth,
look down from heaven, your dwelling place,
    and heal the wounds of earth;
till pain, decay and bondage done,
    when death itself has died,

creation's songs shall rise as one
    and God be glorified!
(Dudley-Smith in Berry 2000, pp. 184–185)

Conclusion

John Stott was well aware of the damage we do (and have done) to the environment. Impressed by Rachel Carson's *Silent Spring* and convinced by the reasoning of the Brundtland report (World Commission on Environment and Development, 'Our common future', 1987), he fully accepted the need for sustainability of resource use; was aware of the problems of pollution and the environmental stresses of and on a growing population; and had seen for himself the problems that climate change was already causing for those least able to cope with it, but these were not overriding considerations for him. The normal rhetoric of environmentalists was not Stott's way.

Too often the Christian response is merely to add a gloss about the need for grace in a bad situation. This was not Stott's approach either or his purpose. As with everything in his life, his ambition was to proclaim Christ and his written word. And this was his distinctive and crucial contribution to creation care. His lifelong love of the natural world meant that he had integrated his birdwatching with his theology. He argued as strongly as he could that evangelicals have a defective doctrine of creation, although it was not until he was in his mid-fifties that he went public on this. In his first sermon on the environment in 1977, he asked the All Souls congregation:

> I wonder if you would agree with me that many of us Christians – particularly, those who call ourselves or are called by others evangelical Christians – tend to have a good doctrine of redemption and a bad doctrine of creation. Indeed some of us don't have a doctrine of creation at all.
> (Stott 1977b)

He repeated this charge in his introduction to *The Birds Our Teachers* in 1999. He planned to proclaim to US students at Urbana (2003b):

'although we have a good doctrine of redemption, we tend to have a bad doctrine of creation. This is all the more regrettable because the same God is the author of both, and both are called the "works of the Lord"'. He repeatedly used the thought picture of God as the author of two books – one of words, the other of works, quoting Francis Bacon, 'let no man think or maintain that he can search too far or be too well studied in either – let all men endeavour proficiency in both.' He summed up his frustration at the blindness of Christians in his final instruction to the church about creation care in *The Radical Disciple*, using the words of his chosen successor, Chris Wright:

> It seems quite inexplicable to me that there are some Christians who claim to love and worship God, to be disciples of Jesus and yet have no concern for the earth that bears his stamp of ownership. They do not care about the abuse of the earth, and indeed by their wasteful and over-consumptive lifestyles, they contribute to it.
> (Wright 2006, p. 414)

Is there any way he could have been clearer? Is the root problem the failure to understand the biblical message about creation? Stott wrote, 'God intends . . . our care of creation to reflect our love for the creator' (in Berry 2000, pp. 8–9), and reminded his readers of Moses' words, 'To the Lord your God belong the heavens, even the highest heavens, the earth and everything in it' (Deuteronomy 10:14 [NIV 1984]).

It seems fitting to conclude with a prayer, written by John Stott and included in his book *Christian Basics*:

> Almighty God, you created the planet earth, you make peace, and you love justice. Give your own concern for the environment to those who are destroying it, your peace to the violent places of the world, and your justice to the deprived and the oppressed. And show us what we can do to forward your purposes of love, through Jesus Christ our Lord.
> (Stott 1991, p. 160)

Afterword

Planetary gardening
A shared Christian vocation

> Remain in me, as I also remain in you. No branch
> can bear fruit by itself; it must remain in the vine.
> Neither can you bear fruit unless you remain in me.
> (John 15:4, NIV 2011)

Right, fruitful relations are part of an organic whole. Let us explore together the place of human beings in an organic system that transcends humanity and includes the entire created order, and reflect on what cultivating fruitful relations within that living community can look like. Planetary gardening: this is a shared Christian vocation. We focus here on the urgent need for Christians to recognize our place within the creation story in order for us to live out our creational vocation as responsible care-takers of the planet. I propose that the joint search for incarnational missional responses to the ecological crisis will naturally draw followers of Christ together across historic divides, and further God's intended *shalom* in the creation-community.

We begin with a snapshot from northern Argentina and the plight of the indigenous *Wichi* people, faced with the rampant exploitation of the biotic community of which they have been a part for thousands of years. I became personally familiar with their situation because my sister, her husband and several close friends worked for many years with *Wichi* leaders.

'The forest swallowers'

The forest has been far more than a source of food and livelihood for the *Wichi* people. It has been their home and defined their culture in all its dimensions, including their cosmology and their political, judicial, educational and health systems ever since they settled there, thousands of years ago (Leake and Andrade 2012, p. 76). In recent years, however, as Argentina has struggled to keep a foot in the global economic system, the soy business has been taking over the entire region. Bulldozers, which the *Wichi* call 'forest swallowers', are tearing through millennial forest, clearing the land for the soy monoculture, and creating a 'locust effect' of devastation. Deprived of their livelihood, as their precarious jobs are taken over by machines, and exiled from their forest-home as land continues to be expropriated by agroindustry while governments turn a blind eye, 'the indigenous people live as shipwrecked people in a landscape dominated by monoculture' (Leake and Andrade 2012, p. 76). Leaders who dare to protest and defend their land and environment are frequently murdered. Says a *Wichi* leader, 'The policy of deforestation is destroying the biodiversity on which we depend without proposing any alternative for our life. The elimination of the native forest means our annihilation . . . It is genocide and the final blow of Conquest' (Leake and Andrade 2012, p. 83).

What story?

What is our place as created beings in relation to the rest of the biotic system, the web of life of which humanity is but a part? I suggest that our response is dependent on the story in which we see ourselves embedded. Says sociologist Christian Smith:

> For all our science, rationality, and technology, we are no less the makers, tellers, and believers of narrative construals of existence, history and purpose than were our forebears at any other time . . . We not only continue to be animals who make stories but also animals who are made by our stories.
> (Smith 2003, p. 64)

In our globalized world, meaning-making stories abound, stories that compete, merge and clash with one another. Stories of conquest and submission, of progress and development, of fatalism and despair. Stories about how we were created and for what. Stories about how the world should run, about what is valuable and what is not, about who is valuable and who is not. Stories about this world and the world to come, or no world to come. Stories into which and out of which we live. A necessary question for all who identify as followers of Jesus Christ in the world is this: given the broad repertoire of stories available, in which of them do we recognize ourselves and from which of them must we struggle to extricate ourselves?

The most prevalent and all-encompassing current global story is capitalism. In this story, acquisition and accumulation of capital are sought as supreme goals. Economic growth, limitless progress and development justify slavery, oppression and exclusion of people as well as the rape of nature. Ecuadorean Roman Catholic bishop, the late Leonidas Proaño, paints the picture (in Tamayo 2017, p. 214): 'Capitalism is cold . . . It is unconcerned with people. All it cares about is profit. People only matter inasmuch as they yield profit. In order to devour profit, it devours people.'

Capitalism also devours our planet, humanity's only home. The reports of the United Nations Intergovernmental Panel on Climate Change indicate that our planet is diving head-long into an even larger planetary crisis than scientists had predicted (IPCC n.d.).

The plight of the *Wichi* is not an isolated case. Sadly, it is representative of the impact of the current global story on indigenous and poor communities and their habitats around the world. Says Argentine economist Alfredo Salibián:

Latin America is the creditor of the enormous ecological debt contracted by old and 'new invaders', in both cases with their local associates. The economic policies based on this 'new' philosophy of 'conquest' has profaned the land: they have turned it into an instrument that marginalizes its legitimate owners, and they have the potential capacity of displacing or determining the environmental conditions for the extermination of

entire populations – mostly indigenous – and to degrade or totally destroy the environment.
(Salibián 2012, p. 212)

Though European exploitation of the Americas began more than 500 years ago and though the commodification of people, land and its fruits is as old as human rebellion against our Creator, never in history has the dictatorship of the market been as global, absolute and all-encompassing as it is today. Everything – and everyone – is susceptible to being bought and sold. When the gears of global capitalism smash the great majorities; when the aridity of consumption calcifies hearts and incinerates consciences; when the agro-industrial machinery grinds down forests, commodifies water and enslaves entire people groups; when structures of repression fabricate a world of superficial make-believe and ignore the crude reality, we need to heed the artists, those poets, painters, singers of life, denouncers of death, who shake the sleeper and awaken dreams. Prophets who name and, in naming, discover, uncover and reveal the heart of darkness under the varnish of our 'developed' world.

One of the original callings of humanity is caring for creation (Genesis 1:26–28). I suggest that a first necessary step towards living out our vocation as care-takers of our planetary garden is the acknowledgement of our personal and communal entanglement in historic and present stories of greed and systems of exploitation. Jesus' warning to his followers was strong: 'Watch out! Be on your guard against all kinds of greed; life does not consist in an abundance of possessions' (Luke 12:15, NIV). Even so, through the ages, Christianity has justified and even promoted imperialisms of different sorts, the genocide of people and the destruction of local ecologies – often for the sake of profit. Still today, the drive to consume, to sustain privileged lifestyles, to insulate from the impact of environmental degradation continues, hardly unchecked by churches, which all too often must be named as complicit culprits.

In light of this prevailing story, in the midst of global warming, rising waters, intense pollution, loss of species, critical human indifference and other such hopeless realities, we must ask: is there any good news? Are we condemned to live in a world of scarcity, competition, violence, plunder and hopelessness? Is life possible this side of heaven? How can Christianity be part of the solution rather than just part of the problem? Can we live into another story?

Lesslie Newbigin proposed that Christian faith is not only a matter of 'dwelling in a tradition of *understanding*; it is also a matter of dwelling in a *story* of God's activity' (Newbigin 1989, p. 51, italics added). As Kevin Vanhoozer wrote:

> The primary story from which Christians derive their sense of what the world is like and of who they are is the story of God in Christ reconciling the world to himself (2 Corinthians 5:19) . . . Our deepest truest identity is thus discovered in the biblical narrative, not the so-called foundational narratives of this or that culture or this or that nation.
> (Vanhoozer 2006, p. 113)

The Christian community is called to 'indwell the story the Bible tells' and, in so doing, it develops a new way of reading Scripture and a new way of being in the world (Newbigin 1989, pp. 97, 98). Let us turn, then, to the biblical story.

A new way of being in the world

The women and men who first heard the words of the biblical book we know as Genesis were people in exile. Torn away from their loved ones. Uprooted from their land. Enslaved under imperial rule. The social order of Babylon that held the ancient Israelites subservient to the king and the gods of Babylon was reinforced by a creation story called the *Enuma Elish*. According to that mythology, the world was the product of a bloody battle between selfish and vengeful gods. The Jewish exiles had no place in it. They were nobodies. There was no good news.

Into that hopeless scene a notably contrasting story erupted, a story of generosity and abundance, of community and celebration.

It was the poetic creation song we know as Genesis 1. In this plot, God, in an uncontested and serene manner, brought creation into being. The process was harmonious, one of opening up space and then filling it with abundant diversity. The product was good. Good. Beautiful. Whole. Naturally holding together. Each part manifesting the will of the Creator: Good. And where did they, those battered people, fit into that story? Let's turn to the familiar passage that is Genesis 1:26–28 (NRSV):

> Then God said, 'Let us make humankind in our image, according to our likeness; and let them have dominion over the fish of the sea, and over the birds of the air, and over the cattle, and over all the wild animals of the earth, and over every creeping thing that creeps upon the earth.'
> So God created humankind in his image,
>   in the image of God he created them;
>   male and female he created them.
> God blessed them, and God said to them, 'Be fruitful and multiply, and fill the earth and subdue it; and have dominion over the fish of the sea and over the birds of the air and over every living thing that moves upon the earth.'

According to the story revealed by God and retold for generations and recorded by the writer of Genesis, those suffering people at the bottom of the Babylonian heap were anything but nobodies. Truly, their backs were bent by oppression and after long years of disobedience and exile they could hardly remember who they were. The writer of Genesis powerfully reminded them that they had been amazingly created by the sovereign ruler of the universe so they were full of dignity. Yet, further, they had been created in the very image of God! As such, they were blessed to thrive and to rule as God's representatives within the created order. Rather than being trod underfoot, they could stand tall. Knowing their true identity could strengthen them to resist the false identity imposed on them by the empire of the day. As beings granted life by a generous God who created out of love, not out of violence, nor out of necessity, they had direct access to God and could live into their vocation as care-takers, gardeners, of the creation community.

In addition to reminding the exiled Jews about their true identity, the writer of Genesis reminded them of their true vocation. In Babylon, they might not have been valued as anything more than insignificant cogs in the imperial machinery and their lives might have been absorbed in menial service to the purposes of their oppressors. Yet, made as they were in God's image, they shared in God's good rule over the whole earth and all its creatures. Amazingly good news! Enslaved exiles as rulers?!

A key issue here, however – and a live one for Christians to this day – is the nature of that rule. In the imagination of the exiled people of God, rule equalled violence and imposition. That is what their lived experience had taught them. They had been forced into exile by a foreign power. In the *Enuma Elish*, the rule of the gods was arbitrary and self-interested. In Babylon, power was wielded to suppress, repress, oppress. Imagination and energy were focused on consuming rather than on creating, on attaining comfort and individual achievement rather than on communal well-being, on plundering creation instead of caring responsibly for it. The author of Genesis depicted God's rule as one that radically contrasted with the one exercised in Babylon. The nature of God's rule challenged God's people to re-cast their definition of what it meant to have dominion. God, the community-of-love, exercises power in creative, generous, life-generating ways, and God celebrates the goodness of the work of God's hands. In the Genesis story, power is translated into creative work and responsible care. The connection is clear. Since that is how God exercises power, and human beings are created in the image of God, then power is delegated to them to be exercised through responsible work and creative care of the creation community, of which they are only a small part:

The LORD God took the man and put him in the Garden of Eden to work it and take care of it.
(Genesis 2:15, NIV)

Leonardo Boff, a Roman Catholic theologian from Brazil who has deep ecological concerns, affirms that 'care' has two dimensions: love, which involves devotion, commitment, attention; and work, which entails concern and intervention. Though both dimensions are necessary, the capitalist system has implanted, Boff says, 'the dictatorship of the way-of-being through work-domination . . . [and] opened the way to anthropocentrism, to androcentrism, to patri-archalism and to machismo' (Boff 2008, p. 65).

Boff encourages believers not to stop working but to 'renounce the hunger of power' and 'the obsession with efficacy' by 'organizing work in synchronicity with nature and its rhythms and mani-festations. We must recover the other dimension of care, the way of being that rescues our most essential humanity' (Boff 2008, p. 65). We will return to considerations of our most essential humanity in a moment.

Earlier we asked, can Christianity be part of the solution rather than part of the problem? I submit that it all depends on our under-standing and embodiment of the Christian story. Christendom, the meshing of political, cultural and religious power, is incapable of breaking the cycle of plunder in which it is so deeply complicit. In contrast, radical Christian communities which divest from power and recognize that they have been brought together by God's grace and purposed for mutual grace as part of the creation-community in which they belong can play a crucial role in the world. This process demands multiple and radical conversions, a turning back to God's gracious purposes and away from the anxious striving of our exploitative society. For each of those con-versions, indigenous traditions, values and practices can lead the way if we have eyes to see and ears to hear. Space only allows for the mention of a few.

1 From individualism to creation-community.
2 From silent complicity to prophetic denunciation and embodied annunciation.
3 From illusions of growth to acknowledgment of limits and de-growth.

From individualism to creation-community

Planetary gardening requires a conversion from individual striving to the recognition of belonging in the creation-community. God's self-revelation through the story in Scripture makes God known as Father, Son and Holy Spirit, existing eternally in ever-mutual love, as the perfect community. Daniel Groody states:

> God is more than an idea to which intellectual assent is made; God is a profound and primary relationship to which a commitment is made.
> (Groody 2007, p. 191)

When the Community-of-Love chose to mark humanity with God's image, God rooted God's communal identity at the core of our being. We are made *by* community and *for* community. We are made by love and for love, and full realization as human beings – abundant life – is found in being bound in love to God, to one another and to the entire creation-community.

In the story of our 'developed' society, individual achievement is the aspired to goal and success is measured exclusively in monetary terms. When our self-consuming society feeds off and nurtures selfishness, plunders nature and engenders an unquenchable thirst that urges everyone to compete with everyone else because there is not enough room at the top, God's communal image is effaced in the race. Indigenous people, many of whom continue to live into another story, can remind the rest of humanity of our relational nature. For example, in the Quechua, *uyway*, the value of caring upbringing, there is recognition that 'I bring you up and you bring me up.' Mutuality includes deep respect, reciprocity, co-responsibility and solidarity with the rest of creation, which leads the *Wichis* and other indigenous groups to be preservers rather than exploiters of the earth and all that she grants them. My friend Terry LeBlanc, a First Nations person from what we know as Canada, has often reminded me, 'Ruth, was there ever a time in which you gave to the rest of creation more than she gave you?' And Boff reminds us:

We have Earth-elements in our bodies, blood, heart, mind and spirit. From this fact results the awareness of deep unity … To feel that we are Earth forces us to be down to earth, and to perceive ourselves within a complex community with other brothers and sisters, microorganisms, waters, plants, animals.
(Boff 2008, p. 48)

Non-indigenous people may need to explore new frontiers of creational belonging. Says Boff:

Each person needs to discover him- or herself as part of the local ecosystem and of the biotic community, with reference to both its natural aspect and its cultural dimension. One needs to get to know one's brothers and sisters who share the same atmosphere, the same scenery, the same soil, the same springs, the same nourishing sources; one needs to know the kinds of plants, animals and microorganisms that inhabit the common environmental niche; one needs to know the history of the scenery, to visit its rivers and mountains, to frequent its waterfalls and caves; one needs to know the history of the peoples who live there, their saga and who built their habitat, the way they worked with nature, the way they preserved or wrecked nature, who were their points and sages, heroes and heroines, saints, founding fathers and/or mothers of their local civilization.
(Boff 2008, p. 95)

Recognizing, as most indigenous people do, that we are part of the biotic community allows us to seek more just ways of living together, a creational conviviality.

From silent complicity to prophetic denunciation and embodied annunciation

Planetary gardening requires a conversion from silent complicity to prophetic denunciation and embodied annunciation. Prophetic denunciation. Truth about the responsibility of humanity in the environmental crisis must be faced, named, lamented, made known and remedied. The heart of darkness that beats under the mask of progress must be exposed. We must speak the inconvenient truth. We must advocate for policies that respect the integrity of creation. We must re-cast any theological articulation that spiritualizes faith and alienates people from the world God so loves while they await the day that they will be whisked away to some distant heaven and this world goes up in flames.

The second dimension of the prophetic role to which the church is called is the worshipful embodiment of the good news, prophetic annunciation. God is recognized as such through care for God's handiwork and proper use within the limits of a just and balanced coexistence. Even within the church there often operates a functional paganism, according to which worship is conceived as hardly more than an ingredient in religious services. Meanwhile, much energy, imagination, personal and community longing are focused on achieving and accumulating those things that consumer society identifies as goods. Wonder at who God is and at the intricate work of God's hands must translate into the search for more sustainable ways of living which respect that creation. The rule of the 5 Rs – to re-think before purchasing, discerning between needs and wants; reject the ruling myth that the value of people depends on their possessions; reduce consumption; reuse and repurpose or recycle – can help urbanites to recover communal indigenous practices of respectful conviviality as part of creation. All these are forms of worship of the Creator.

Prophetic mission is a risky business. It involves announcing, denouncing, renouncing and living alternatively. Around the world, an environmental activist or an eco-defender is being murdered every couple of days – an average of four per week worldwide in the past decade, and still increasing annually (Global Witness n.d; Global Witness and *The Guardian* 2017). Farmers are murdered by soldiers while defending their ancestral lands from coffee plantations in the Philippines; wildlife rangers are slain by poachers in multiple countries. Widely known cases of indigenous leaders include the murder in 2016 of Honduran Berta Cáceres, who opposed a dam's construction on indigenous territory, and the murder in 2017 of Mexican Isidro Baldenegro López, who resisted illegal logging; both had received the Goldman Environmental Prize. In 2019, Bribri leader Sergio Rojas Ortiz was murdered for defending the land of his ancestors in Costa Rica (Surcos Digital 2019).

Agribusiness and mining were linked to 60 per cent of 2017's eco-defenders' deaths (Platt 2018). How many of these, we might ask, were Christians putting their own skin in the fray, not out of a political ideology or partisan commitment, but out of a burning desire to care for every last corner and inhabitant of God's world, especially for the most vulnerable and for indigenous people?

From illusions of growth to acknowledgment of limits and de-growth

Finally, planetary gardening requires a conversion from illusions of growth to the acknowledgement of limits and intentional de-growth:

> Degrowth is a rejection of the illusion of growth and a call to repoliticize the public debate colonized by the idiom of economism. It is a project advocating the democratically led shrinking of production and consumption with the aim of achieving social justice and ecological sustainability.
> (D'Alisa, Demaria and Kallis 2015, p. i)

The issue is that current global capitalism, based as it is on the exploitation of people and of nature, and depending on the production and consumption of more things, is not only unjust and exclusionary but it is also unsustainable. Every year, by overfishing and overharvesting forests, we use up the annual available ecological resources and services earlier than the year before and far sooner than nature can regenerate them. We also emit more carbon dioxide into the atmosphere than ecosystems can absorb. In 1971, Earth Overshoot day fell on 21 December. In 2019, we passed the threshold on 29 July – the earliest date ever (SDG Knowledge Hub, IISD 2019).

When growth is the majority goal, the *Wichi* and other indigenous people can hardly afford to stay out of the game. Even so, many of them still live far more sustainably than dominant majorities and have inspired studies and proposals for what is now known as the 'de-growth movement'. Drawing on learnings from indigenous communities, this movement, which is gaining strength around the world, is calling for the use of fewer natural resources and for society to be organized and live differently:

> Caring in common is embodied in new forms of living and producing, such as eco-communities and cooperatives and can be supported by new government institutions, such as work-sharing or a basic and maximum income, institutions which can liberate time from paid work and make it available for unpaid communal and caring activities.
> (D'Alisa, Demaria and Kallis 2015, p. 4)

The *Wichi* sense of the good life, *el buen vivir*, the Quechua *allincausay* or the Zulu *ubuntu* all rest on a sense of sufficiency achieved by sharing and mutual care. And returning to the biblical story, the law given to the ancient Israelites was also designed to ensure the health of the land, the livelihood of all members of the community and even the sustenance of outsiders. Both Sabbath rest and jubilee restitution worked together to counter accumulation and restore right relations between people and of those with the natural world.

Gardening together

A few years ago, the intentional Christian community in Costa Rica to which my husband and I belong, Casa Adobe, engaged with our working-class neighbourhood, asking in what ways we could accompany them. They asked us to expand our internal community garden beyond our walls, and we responded with workshops on urban gardening, sustainability and food security. Today, two community gardens are thriving in the neighbourhood and have become an intergenerational gathering place, where young and old, women and men work, laugh, exchange seeds and celebrate the fruits of the earth together. As people from the local Roman Catholic parish, Protestant/evangelical members of Casa Adobe and neighbours who do not attest to any particular faith worked jointly, mutual trust grew. In our experience, gardening together draws people closer to one another, across many of the fabricated barriers that separate people, and allows the cultivation of relationships for the common good. On a larger scale, common concern and action for the well-being of our planetary garden, in addition to being an act of worship to God, can draw us back into the story of shared humanity and open up opportunities for followers of Jesus to point others to the Creator.

Conclusion

Truly, the news regarding the state of our planet is not good and, as humanity, we are utterly unable to breathe life into the dry bones of our disintegrated society or our depleted ecosystem. Yet not all is lost. That is because God continues to embrace the creation-community, making possible our embodiment of our true identity and vocation. The same Spirit who hovered over the waters in the beginning is still breathing life into every living being. The same Lord, through whom and for whom all that is was created, stepped into our world, gave himself away in order to reconcile all things and is present among us as our risen Lord (Colossians 1:15–20). The same Creator who walked in the garden with the first humans is still dwelling among God's people today. The presence of God's word and God's Spirit in the Christian community nurtures an alternative story. Within that story, Jesus – not the emperor of the day nor the global market – is acknowledged as the only Lord, one who is worshipped more fully not through mere religious rites, but through truth-filled countercultural living as part of the creation-community. We need not live imprisoned by a spirit of scarcity and competition, fear and violence. Thanks to God's generosity and against all odds, we can celebrate goodness, beauty, community and abundance even here and now. We can learn from and engage with communities such as the *Wichi*, who are far more connected to the rest of creation than most of us urbanites are. We can rest assured that God's image will one day be fully restored in us and the whole created order will once again be good. Meanwhile, may we step out in hope to care for the Earth and all that is in it, as the planetary gardeners we are called to be.

Ruth Padilla DeBorst

Note: This text is adapted from a presentation at 'All things new: Creation, community, and vocation', Human Needs and Global Resources, a symposium held at Wheaton College, Illinois, USA, in March 2019.

Appendix 1

An evangelical declaration on the care of creation (1994)

This declaration was produced in 1994, largely out of frustration among evangelicals with the conclusions of the World Council of Churches 'Justice, peace and the integrity of creation' programme (Thomas 1993; Berry 2000). It was endorsed by several hundred evangelical leaders, including Stott. He was key to obtaining the support of influential US evangelical pastor Rick Warren for the 'Evangelical climate initiative' in 2006 and, because of this, endorsement by many evangelical leaders (Wilkinson 2012, p. 44). Berry noted:

The earth is the LORD's, and the fullness thereof (Psalm 24:1)

As followers of Jesus Christ, committed to the full authority of the Scriptures, and aware of the ways we have degraded creation, we believe that biblical faith is essential to the solution of our ecological problems.

- Because we worship and honour the Creator, we seek to cherish and care for the creation.
- Because we have sinned, we have failed in our stewardship of creation. Therefore we repent of the way we have polluted, distorted, or destroyed so much of the Creator's work.
- Because, in Christ, God has healed our alienation from God and extended to us the first fruits of the reconciliation of all things, we commit ourselves to working in the power of the Holy Spirit to share the Good News of Christ in word and deed, to work for the reconciliation of all people

in Christ, and to extend Christ's healing to suffering creation.

- Because we await the time when even the groaning creation will be restored to wholeness, we commit ourselves to work vigorously to protect and heal that creation for the honour and glory of the Creator – whom we know dimly through creation, but meet fully through Scripture and in Christ.

We and our children face a growing crisis in the health of the creation in which we are embedded, and through which, by God's grace, we are sustained. Yet we continue to degrade that creation.

- These degradations of creation can be summed up as: 1) land degradation; 2) deforestation; 3) species extinction; 4) water degradation; 5) global toxification; 6) the alteration of atmosphere; 7) human and cultural degradation.
- Many of these degradations are signs that we are pressing against the finite limits God has set for creation. With continued population growth, these degradations will become more severe. Our responsibility is not only to bear and nurture children, but to nurture their home on earth. We respect the institution of marriage as the way God has given to ensure thoughtful procreation of children and their nurture to the glory of God.
- We recognize that human poverty is both a cause and a consequence of environmental degradation.

Many concerned people, convinced that environmental problems are more spiritual then technological, are exploring the world's ideologies and religions in search of non-Christian spiritual resources for the healing of the earth. As followers of Jesus Christ, we believe the Bible calls us to respond in four ways.

- First, God calls us to confess and repent of attitudes which devalue creation, and which twist or ignore biblical revelation to support our misuse of it. Forgetting that 'the earth is the Lord's', we have often simply used creation and forgotten our responsibility to care for it.
- Second, our actions and attitudes towards the earth need to proceed from the centre of our faith, and be rooted in the fullness of God's revelation in Christ and the Scriptures. We resist both ideologies which would presume the Gospel has nothing to do with the care of non-human creation and also ideologies which would reduce the Gospel to nothing more than the care of that creation.
- Third, we seek carefully to learn all that the Bible tells us about the Creator, creation, and the human task. In our life and words we declare that full good news for all creation which is still waiting 'with eager longing for the revealing of the children of God' (Romans 8:19).
- Fourth, we seek to understand what creation reveals about God's divinity, sustaining presence, and everlasting power. And what creation teaches us of its God-given order and the principles by which it works.

Thus we call on all those who are committed to the truth of the Gospel of Jesus Christ to affirm the following principles of biblical faith, and to seek ways of living out these principles in our personal lives, our churches, and society.

- The cosmos, in all its beauty, wildness and life-giving bounty, is the work of our personal and loving Creator.
- Our creating God is prior to and other than creation, yet intimately involved with it, upholding each thing in its freedom, and all things in relationships of intricate complexity. God is *transcendent*, while lovingly sustaining each creature; and *immanent*, while wholly other than creation and not to be confused with it.

- God the Creator is relational in very nature, revealed as three persons in One. Likewise, the creation which God intended is a symphony of individual creatures in harmonious relationship.
- The Creator's concern is for all creatures. God declares all creation 'good' (Genesis 1:31); promises care in a covenant with all creatures (Genesis 9:9–17); delights in creatures which have no human apparent usefulness (Job 38 – 41); and wills, in Christ, 'to reconcile all things to himself' (Colossians 1:20).
- Men, women, and children, have a unique responsibility to the Creator; at the same time we are *creatures*, shaped by the same processes and embedded in the same systems of physical, chemical, and biological interconnections which sustain other creatures.
- Men, women, and children, created in God's image, also have a unique responsibility for creation. Our actions should both sustain creation's fruitfulness and preserve creation's powerful testimony to its Creator.
- Our God-given, stewardly talents have often been warped from their intended purpose: that we know, name, keep, and delight in God's creatures; that we nourish civilization in love, creativity and obedience to God; and that we offer creation and civilization back in praise to the Creator. We have ignored our creaturely limits and have used the earth with greed, rather than care.
- The earthly result of human sin has been a perverted stewardship, a patchwork of garden and wasteland in which the waste is increasing. 'There is no faithfulness, no love, no acknowledgement of God in the land . . . because of this the land mourns, and all who live in it waste away' (Hosea 4:1, 3). Thus, one consequence of our misuse of the earth is an unjust denial of God's created bounty to other human beings, both now and in the future.
- God's purpose in Christ is to heal and bring to wholeness not only persons but the entire created order. 'For God was

pleased to have all his fullness dwell in him, and through him to reconcile to himself all things, whether things on earth or things in heaven, by making peace through his blood shed on the cross' (Colossians 1:19–20).

- In Jesus Christ, believers are forgiven, transformed and brought into God's kingdom. 'If anyone is in Christ, there is a new creation' (2 Corinthians 5:17). The presence of the kingdom of God is marked not only by renewed fellowship with God, but also by renewed harmony and justice between people and the rest of the created world. 'You will go out with joy and be led forth in peace; the mountains and the hills will burst into song before you, and all the trees of the field will clap their hands' (Isaiah 55:12).

We believe that in Christ there is hope, not only for men, women and children, but also for the rest of creation, which is suffering from the consequences of human sin.

- Therefore we call upon all Christians to reaffirm that all creation is God's; that God created it good; and that God is renewing it in Christ.
- We encourage deeper reflection on the substantial biblical and theological teaching which speaks of God's work of redemption in terms of the renewal and completion of God's purpose in creation.
- We seek a deeper reflection on the wonders of God's creation and the principles by which creation works. We also urge a careful consideration of how our corporate and individual actions respect and comply with God's ordinances for creation.
- We encourage Christians to incorporate the extravagant creativity of God into their lives by increasing the nurturing role of beauty and the arts in their personal, ecclesiastical and social patterns.
- We urge individual Christians and churches to be centres of creation's care and renewal, both delighting in creation

as God's gift, and enjoying it as God's provision, in ways which sustain and heal the damaged fabric of the creation which God has entrusted to us.

- We recall Jesus' words that our lives do not consist in the abundance of our possessions, and therefore we urge followers of Jesus to resist the allure of wastefulness and overconsumption by making personal lifestyle choices that express humility, forbearance, self-restraint and frugality.

- We call on Christians to work for godly, just and sustainable economies which reflect God's sovereign economy and enable men, women and children to flourish along with all the diversity of creation. We recognize that poverty forces people to degrade creation in order to survive; therefore we support the development of just, free economies which empower the poor and create abundance without diminishing creation's bounty.

- We commit ourselves to work for responsible public policies which embody the principles of biblical stewardship of creation.

- We invite Christians – individuals, congregations and organizations – to join with us in this evangelical declaration on the environment, becoming a covenant people in an ever-widening circle of biblical care for creation.

- We call upon Christians to listen to and work with all those who are concerned about the healing of creation, with an eagerness both to learn from them and also to share with them our conviction that the God whom all people sense in creation (Acts 17:27) is known fully only in the Word made flesh in Christ the living God, who made and sustains all things.

- We make this declaration knowing that, until Christ returns to reconcile all things, we are called to be faithful stewards of God's good garden, our earthly home.

(Berry 2000, pp. 17–22)

Appendix 2

'Reasons for environmental concern', excerpt from *Issues Facing Christians Today* (2006)

The chapter 'Caring for creation' in the fourth edition of *Issues Facing Christians Today* (2006) had four main sections: 'Reasons for environmental concern', 'The biblical perspective', 'The conservation debate' and 'Contemporary awareness'. The first of these is dependent on current and changing knowledge and for that reason is not included in the main text of this book, but it is reproduced here for completeness (Stott 2006, pp. 136–146). That it has been reproduced in an appendix should not be taken to imply that it is unimportant, merely that it is subject to amendment in a way that biblical texts and their interpretation are not. This is a section that Stott expanded and updated with each revised edition of the book first published in 1984 (in 1990, 1999 and 2006). It illustrates both his own engagement with developing scientific knowledge and the gathering public environmental concerns. Stott, characteristically, was keen to include contemporary matters to prompt and to guide faithful action as 'Christians have a second commitment, namely to the world in which God has placed us', rather than giving in to the temptation to withdraw (Stott 1984, preface; p. 10 in 2006 edition). It gives a snapshot of the framing of the principal issues from that time, as well as the range of expertise and resources that Stott consulted in the process of seeking to 'think Christianly, that is, to apply the biblical revelation to the pressing issues of the day' (Stott 1984, preface; p. 9 in 2006 edition) and to better understand how to care for God's world. The other sections from the chapter are given on pages 169–179. (Note that many of the footnotes and old Internet citations in the original chapter are not reproduced here.)

Reasons for environmental concern

Population growth

The first is population growth. It has been known for centuries that the world population is growing. Only since World War II, however, has the accelerating growth rate been clearly perceived and the potential for disaster in the aftermath of an unchecked population explosion predicted. It is said that in the year AD 1800 there were about 1,000,000,000 people on earth. By 1900 this had doubled to 2,000,000,000, and by 1974 it had doubled again to 4,000,000,000. It is estimated that we currently rely on the equivalent of 1.2 planets to supply our annual needs, and yet, despite a decelerating growth rate, world population is still increasing such that the current 6,100,000,000 will grow to a probable 11,000,000,000 by the middle of this century according to UN figures.

Out of 4,000,000,000 people in the 1980s, one fifth of them (800,000,000) were destitute, and it is being anxiously asked how more than 7,000,000,000 people can possibly be fed thirty-five years later. This is a special problem in the developing world where 90% of population growth is taking place. The earth cannot sustain a larger population which, owing to poverty and even starvation, is forced to use its resources with only short-term gain in mind, often making long-term destruction inevitable. But this is not just a Majority World problem. In Britain, for example, the population is growing at the comparatively slow rate of 116,000 people per year. However, each new Briton uses more than thirty times the amount of fossil fuel consumed by the average Bangladeshi. Thus it takes a population growth of 3,390,000 Bangladeshis to equal the environmental impact of just over 100,000 Britons (Prance 1996, p. 31). The wealthy consume too much and are wasteful, while the poor are preoccupied with their immediate survival, rather than with the long-term care of the planet. Worldwide, sickness through crowded urban conditions and rural land degradation are pushing millions to the brink of starvation.

There are varying opinions even among Christians about the extent of the population problem and what should be done in response to it. In his Grove booklet entitled *Population Growth and Christian Ethics*, Roy McCloughry argues that the population problem is primarily neither economic nor environmental but moral, because it is basically about relationships. He pleads for 'a positive vision for human life', in which (1) human beings are seen to have an intrinsic value because they are made in God's image; (2) access to education, especially by women and children, enables them to develop their full potential and to enjoy a quality of life compatible with their human dignity; and (3) the limiting and spacing of children is determined not by coercive governments but by the free decision of the parents (McLoughry 1995). Any discussion of population must begin by reaffirming the dignity of all human life, and the rights of human beings to live out their full potential. As Professor John Guillebaud has argued, if the vicious spiral of poverty and population is not to continue – where poverty leads to families having more children in order to increase family income and yet they find they are unable to cope with the numbers – then both planned parenting and social justice will be needed. The former enables them to take responsible decisions about family size; the latter enables poor people to climb out of their poverty (Guillebaud, in Berry 2000, pp. 155–160).

It is this concern that people should be able to live out their full potential which causes us great concern when we consider the impact of AIDS on so many countries. In some a generation has been so affected that every area of society has suffered.

Resource depletion

The second cause for concern is resource depletion. It was the so-called 'Club of Rome' which in 1972 drew the world's attention to the finite nature of the earth's resources. Until then Western leaders had confidently been predicting an annual growth rate of 4%. Now continuous growth and finite resources were seen to be incompatible. It was E. F. Schumacher who in 1973 popularized the unpalatable truth in his famous book *Small Is Beautiful*, subtitled *A study of economics as if people mattered*. He wrote of 'the failure to distinguish between income and capital where this distinction matters most … namely the irreplaceable capital which man has not made, but simply found'. His first example of this 'natural capital' was fossil fuels: 'Fossil fuels are not made by men; they cannot be recycled. Once they are gone they are gone for ever.' In 2003 the Association of Peak Oil (ASPO) predicted that world demand for oil would outstrip the ability of the world's oilfields to produce economically before 2015. This is not an issue of how much oil there is in the ground, but the increasingly limited rate at which it can be extracted. Much of the 'easy oil' has been produced (Aleklett 2003).

Schumacher's other example was 'living nature' (the plankton of the oceans, the green surface of the earth, clean air, etc.), much of which was being destroyed by pollution. 'If we squander our fossil fuels, we threaten civilization,' he wrote, 'but if we squander the capital represented by living nature around us, we threaten life itself.' The folly of 'the modern industrial system', he continued, is that it 'consumes the very basis on which it has been erected. To use the language of the economist, it lives on irreplaceable capital, which it cheerfully treats as income' (Schumacher 1973, pp. 11–16; Newbigin 1986, p. 114).

One of the scarce resources which is a focus of concern is water. It has long been said that water will be even more important than oil as a threatened scarce resource in the next fifty years. Some have even predicted that violence between nation states will take place over access to water and rights to rivers which cross boundaries between countries. Access to clean water and adequate sanitation were declared to be a 'human right' in 2002. The United Nations Committee on Economic, Cultural and Social Rights stated in a 'general comment' that 'water is fundamental for life and health. The human right to water is indispensable for leading a healthy life in human dignity. It is a prerequisite to the realization of all other human rights.'

Two other aspects of environmental degradation are extremely important and could have their own sections. The first is deforestation and the second is land degradation.

Deforestation has been happening for many years, but not at the current rate, and its impact is now global rather than local. If the current rate continues, the world's rainforests are predicted to disappear within 100 years, causing an incalculable impact on climate and on plant and animal species. Much clearing is done for agricultural purposes such as grazing cattle and planting crops by poor farmers in the process called 'slash and burn'. But in the case of intensive agriculture many square miles can be deforested at a time, to graze cattle. Commercial logging can also cut hundreds of square miles of trees. The causes of deforestation and its impact are very complex. As the need for products grows in a consumer-orientated world, more wood is needed to meet the demand. In other cases forests are cut down to build towns, and the construction of dams causes areas of forest to be flooded. The impact on the climate is due to the fact that forests are 'the lungs of the planet'. According to the earth observatory at NASA, the plants and soil of tropical forests hold 460–575,000,000,000 metric tons of carbon worldwide, with each acre of tropical forest storing about 180 metric tons of carbon. When a forest is cut and burned to establish cropland and pastures, the carbon that was stored in the tree trunks (wood is about 50% carbon) joins with oxygen and is released into the atmosphere as CO_2. The destruction of tropical rainforests also has the potential for making many millions of species of flora and fauna extinct.

Vast areas of America, Africa and Asia, once fertile agricultural land, are now through misuse irrevocable deserts or dustbowls. Worldwide, deserts have increased by 150% during the past 100 years, so that almost 50% of the earth's land surface is now desert or semi-desert. The Aral Sea, once the most productive fishing site in central Asia and the fourth largest inland sea in the world, is now at half its volume of thirty years ago. A poorly conceived irrigation scheme to channel water away from the rivers that feed the sea resulted in its virtual drying out. In some places the coast has moved thirty miles, replaced by a desert of sand and salt deposits (Matthews 1993, p. 36). Deforestation leads to severe soil erosion. It is estimated that 25,000,000,000 tons of topsoil are lost each year. Soil has been so abused in parts of the world that 11% of the world's vegetated soil is now beyond recovery. This is an area the size of China and India (Matthews 1993, pp. 48–49). Some of this destruction of the environment undoubtedly happens as a result of human ignorance (e.g., the early dust bowls). Nevertheless, the Church of England's Board for Social Responsibility were not exaggerating when they said that 'despoiling the earth is a blasphemy, and not just an error of judgement, a mistake' (Board for Social Responsibility 1970, p. 61). It is a sin against God as well as humankind.

Reduction in biodiversity

Biodiversity is a term that, according to Sir Ghillean Prance, Director of the Royal Botanic Gardens at Kew, London, encapsulates 'the diversity of species of living organisms on earth, the genes or genetic information which they contain and the complex ecosystems in which they live' (Prance 1996, p. 45). Estimates for the number of different living species on earth range from 5,000,000 to 50,000,000, with conservative estimates generally around the 10,000,000 mark (Prance 1996, p. 45). Each species contains a unique genetic code and lives in a certain habitat, often requiring very specific conditions for life. Extinction is a daily part of normal life in a world where species exist in a surprising amount of flux. The concern in the biodiversity discussion, however, is not simply with the natural extinction of species, but with the rate at which human intervention in the natural environment has accelerated those extinctions since humans have been the main cause of extinction. Habitat loss, introduced species and overexploitation are the main threats, with human-induced climate change becoming an increasingly important problem. According to the World Conservation Union (IUCN), the largest and most prestigious conservation network, current extinction rates are at least 100–1,000 times higher than background or 'natural' rates.

The reason why scientists are worried about the loss of biodiversity is not only that individual species become extinct, but that when they do, the delicate balance of their ecosystem is disturbed. And when a so-called 'keystone' species becomes extinct, large-scale problems are quickly encountered. A well-known example is the near extinction of sea otters off the west coast of the United States. Stephen Schneider, a professor in biological sciences at Stanford University, describes what happened. 'After their decline, a major disturbance propagated through the offshore marine community. Sea urchins, normally a principal food for otters, multiplied rapidly and in turn decimated the kelp forests leading to biologically impoverished, desert-like stretches of sea floor known as sea-urchin barrens. Only after controversial political pressures to restore the otter were successful did the urchin populations decline, the kelp grow back, and a new community of fish, squid, and lesser organisms reestablish themselves' (Schneider 1998, p. 107).

According to the 2004 IUCN Red List of Threatened Species, a total of 15,589 species face extinction. One in three amphibians and almost half of all freshwater turtles are threatened, on top of the one in eight birds and one in four mammals known to be in jeopardy falling into the Critically Endangered, Endangered or Vulnerable categories. This line-up has now been joined by one in three amphibians (32%) and almost half (42%) of turtles and tortoises. With amphibians relying on fresh water, their catastrophic decline is a warning about the state of the planet's water resources. Even though the situation in freshwater habitats is less well known than for terrestrial habitats, early signs show it is equally serious. More than half (53%) of Madagascar's freshwater fish are threatened with extinction. The vast ocean depths are providing little refuge to many marine species which are being overexploited to the point of extinction. Nearly one in five (18%) of assessed sharks and rays are threatened. Many plants have also been assessed, but only conifers and cycads have been completely evaluated, with 25% and 52% threatened respectively. There is good news with a quarter of threatened bird species benefiting from conservation measures, but the number of species threatened with extinction is an underestimate as so few have been assessed.

Waste disposal

A third reason for concern is waste disposal. An increasing population brings an increasing problem of how to dispose safely of the undesirable by-products of production, packaging and consumption. The average person in the UK throws out his or her body weight in rubbish every three months. The average American's waste output has nearly doubled in the last forty years, and although the US recycles more than a third of its waste, this still represents more than most other countries' total waste output. In the mid 1990s Organization for Economic Cooperation and Development (OECD) countries were producing almost two tons in household and industrial waste per person each year. Although Africans generate less, more than two thirds of their rubbish is not formally disposed of at all, but up to 96% of a typical family's waste in poor countries is made up of food and biodegradable products. Most of the rubbish from wealthy economies could be reprocessed, but instead it is sent to incinerators or landfill sites. A glaring example of the problem occurred in 1987 when the so-called 'garbage barge' left Long Island, New York, and spent six months searching for a port that would take its 3,000-plus tons of garbage. Having been declined entry to numerous ports in the USA and elsewhere, the barge eventually returned to New York where the problem had begun.

In January 1994 the British government published an extensive report entitled *Sustainable Development: The UK Strategy*. It recommended a four-fold 'hierarchy of waste management', namely 'reduction', 'reuse', 'recovery (including recycling and energy recovery)' and 'disposal without energy recovery by incinerator or landfill'. The last of these options, although the commonest, is the least environmentally friendly. It is still unavoidable, however, whenever 'the environmental costs of recycling waste, in terms of energy consumption and emissions, are higher than for disposal'. Clearly the best option in the hierarchy is to reduce the waste which we produce and so have less to dispose of. The implications of poor waste disposal can be disastrous for natural resources. Calvin B. DeWitt cites an example of the presence of DDT in the fatty tissue of penguins in Antarctica as well as the presence of pesticides in a remote lake on Isle Royale in Lake Superior, which are far removed from the places where these chemicals were used (DeWitt in Berry 2000, p. 62).

Climate change

A fourth major environmental concern, which has been at the forefront of discussion since the 1980s, is our damaged atmosphere, owing to a combination of ozone depletion and climate change.

The depletion of the protective ozone layer exposes us to ultraviolet radiation, which causes skin cancers and upsets our immune system. In consequence, the discovery in 1985 of a continent-sized hole in the ozone over the Antarctic caused widespread public alarm. By 1991 this hole had reached a record size, extending over 21,000,000 square kilometres, and by 1993 the concentration of Antarctic ozone was the lowest ever registered. The neighbouring countries of Argentina and Chile, Australia and New Zealand have been reporting damage to animals and vegetation as well as to humans, and by the mid 1990s serious ozone depletion was recorded in the more temperate regions of the Northern Hemisphere as well (Prance 1996, p. 41). In the spring of 2005, the ozone depletion in the Northern Hemisphere was the most severe so far recorded.

Soon after the discovery of the Antarctic ozone hole, its cause was traced to chlorofluorocarbons (CFCs), chemicals which are used in aerosol propellants, air conditioners and refrigerators. Recognizing the gravity of the crisis, the United Nations Environmental Programme took action. The Montreal Protocol (1987) called for the halving of CFC use by 1999, while several amendments in the 1990s resolved that industrialized nations should phase out CFCs completely by 1996 and non-industrialized nations by 2006. By 2006, when asked whether the Montreal Protocol had been successful in reducing ozone-depleting gases in the atmosphere, the National Oceanic and Atmospheric Administration (NOAA), a branch of the US Department of Commerce, could state (WMO/UNEP 2007):

> Yes, as a result of the Montreal Protocol, the total abundance of ozone-depleting gases in the atmosphere has begun to decrease in recent years. If the nations of the world continue to follow the provisions of the Montreal Protocol the decrease will continue throughout the 21st century. Some individual gases such as halons and hydrochlorofluoro-carbons (HCFS) are still increasing in the atmosphere, but will begin to decrease in the next decades if compliance with the Protocol continues. By mid-century, the effective abundance of ozone-depleting gases should fall to values present before the Antarctic 'ozone hole' began to form in the early 1980s.

The issue of climate change is a different, though related, problem (see Houghton 1994). The warmth of the earth's surface (which is essential for the planet's survival) is maintained by a combination of the radiation it absorbs from the sun and the infrared radiation it emits into space. This is the so-called 'greenhouse effect'. Atmospheric pollution by 'greenhouse gases', methane, nitrous oxide and especially carbon dioxide, results in reducing the infrared emission and so increasing the earth's surface temperature.

With some notable exceptions, there is widespread agreement among scientists about the seriousness of the human contribution to the greenhouse effect. Nor is the public's reaction uniform. It ranges from the fear of an imminent catastrophe to a dismissal of the threat as a fiction. There is general agreement, however, that by the year 2100 the average global temperature is likely to rise between 2° and 6° centigrade. The Arctic is warming at twice the global average and nearly all mountain glaciers are shrinking. Mount Kilimanjaro will lose its ice cap over the next twenty years, having survived all climate fluctuations experienced over the last 9,000 years. The long-term effects could include substantial climatic changes, including further thermal expansion of the oceans, the flooding of many islands, port cities and low-lying countries like Bangladesh, the drying out of previously fertile regions, and the regional extinction of plants which cannot adjust to the changes.

The year 2005 saw hurricanes added to the list of indications that climate change was taking place. 'This hurricane season shattered records that have stood for decades – most named storms, most hurricanes and most category five storms. Arguably, it was the most devastating hurricane season the country has experienced in modern times,' said Conrad C. Lautenbacher Jr, NOAA administrator. Hurricane Katrina, which devastated the town of New Orleans, is likely to be the costliest US hurricane on record, and the final tally for damage is likely to be the greatest in US history, breaking a record set only the previous year. Katrina was also the deadliest US hurricane since 1928, claiming at least 1,200 lives. Examination of such extraordinary weather conditions shows that there is at least a case to answer as to whether such hurricanes are here to stay as a consequence of climate change and not just, as some have suggested, an aberration which will eventually go away.

Ocean acidification is also a serious problem. According to a report from the Royal Society (2005), oceans are absorbing carbon dioxide at an unsustainable rate. They help stave off climate change and over the past 200 years have absorbed about half of the carbon dioxide produced by humans, primarily through the burning of fossil fuels. They are currently taking up one ton of this carbon dioxide for each person on the planet every year, but with acidity rising their ability to do this will decrease and the finely balanced and complex mechanisms which sustain ocean life are being affected. This is yet another reason for reducing emissions of greenhouse gases into the atmosphere and particularly carbon dioxide.

We need to reduce greenhouse gas emissions globally at an incremental rate to 60% below year 2000 levels by 2050 (Royal Commission on Environmental Pollution 1998). To achieve 60% reduction, multilateral action by the global community will have to deliver significant reductions by 2025 (World Energy Outlook 2004). However, to date there is a reticence about being held to targets.

In December 1997 negotiators from all over the world met in Kyoto, Japan, to discuss setting limits and reducing greenhouse gas output. After eleven days of intense debate and multiple compromise by all sides, those attending reached a tentative agreement. Thirty-eight industrialized nations, including the USA, the EU, Russia and Japan, all agreed to reduce emissions to 6–8% below 1990 levels by 2008–2012. Developing countries are not required to meet these same reductions, but have been given the option to comply and receive technological and material aid in return. As part of reaching their individual reduction goals the industrialized nations are able to 'trade' emissions between themselves. Thus if the EU, having pledged to reduce emissions to 8% below 1990 levels, were to achieve a 12% reduction, they could then sell the surplus reduction to another country that had been unable to reach its own goal. The country buying the surplus would then be able to apply it towards its own reduction goal. In this way, a potential for economic incentive was worked into the reduction process.

The Kyoto Protocol became a legally binding treaty on 16 February 2005, having fulfilled two conditions. Firstly, it was ratified by at least fifty-five countries. Secondly, it had been ratified by nations accounting for at least 55% of emissions from 'Annex 1' countries, plus thirty-eight industrialized countries given targets for reducing emissions, plus Belarus, Turkey and now Kazakhstan. However, Australia and the USA did not ratify the treaty and in 2001 the USA, which is responsible for about a quarter of the world's emissions, pulled out with President George W. Bush saying that implementing it would gravely damage the US economy. His administration said that the treaty was 'fatally flawed' because it does not require developing countries to commit to emissions reductions and the rapidly developing economies of China and India fall into this category. However, President Bush did say that he backed emissions reductions by voluntary action and new energy technologies. China and India, however, have ratified the protocol. Environmental groups commented that at the world summit of the G8 in 2005 the agreement on climate change was weakened by the decision to opt for consensus between the eight nations, when in fact only seven had ratified the protocol. One indication of this is that a draft of the communiqué used the word 'threat' of climate change, but the official version talked of a 'serious long-term challenge'. Dialogue with the United States and broad consensus across all nations came at the price of definitive targets and a united stance on the urgency of the problem.

These five major reasons for concern – population growth, resource depletion, loss of biodiversity, waste disposal and climate change – are integrally related to one another and together constitute a single 'interlocking global crisis'. This expression was used in *Our Common Future*, the official report of the 1987 UN World Commission on Environment and Development. The central notion of the report was that the various environmental, development and energy problems which plague the world are all aspects of the same crisis, the solution to which lies in 'sustainable development'. This was reaffirmed at the 1992 Earth Summit in Rio, and given sweeping endorsement in *Agenda 21: A blueprint for action for global sustainable development into the 21st century*. One of the official papers to come out of Rio, *Agenda 21*, is a wide-ranging document which has been adopted by 178 governments. It sets environmental, development and economic goals covering a whole spectrum of human and national activities. It does not have the power of a fully legal document, but it has been called 'international soft law', meaning that it carries moral authority and that all nations should adhere to it to the best of their ability. Although the term 'sustainable development' has been variously interpreted, it was defined in *Our Common Future* as development which 'meets the needs of the present without compromising the ability of future generations to meet their own needs' (World Commission on Environment and Development 1987). Indeed, the intergenerational responsibility implicit in the word 'sustainable' has been captured in the popular expression 'not cheating on our kids'.

Bibliography

Adams, E. (2007) *The Stars Will Fall from Heaven: Cosmic catastrophe in the New Testament and its world*. London: T&T Clark.

Aleklett, Kjell (2003) 'A revolutionary transformation', *The Lamp Magazine*, 85(1), 5 October, Peak Oil (available online at: <www.peakoil.net/TheLamp/TheLamp.html>).

Anderson, J. N. D. (1968) *Into the World: The needs and limits of Christian involvement*. London: Falcon.

Anderson, J. N. D. (1985) *An Adopted Son: The story of my life*. Leicester: IVP.

Armstrong, P. (2000) *The English Parson-Naturalist*. Leominster: Gracewing.

Atherstone, A. (2011) 'The Keele Congress of 1967: A paradigm shift in Anglican evangelical attitudes', *Journal of Anglican Studies*, 9, pp. 175–197.

Barclay, O. R. (1970) See Triton, A. N.

Barclay, O. R. and Horn, R. M. (2002) *From Cambridge to the World*. Leicester: IVP.

Barlow, N. (1958) *The Autobiography of Charles Darwin 1809–1882*. London: Collins.

Barr, J. (1993) *Biblical Faith and Natural Theology*. Oxford: Oxford University Press.

Bauckham, R. (1983) *Word Bible Commentary: Volume 50: Jude, 2 Peter*. Waco, TX: Word Books.

—— (2010) *The Bible and Ecology: Rediscovering the community of creation*. Waco, TX: Baylor University Press.

—— (2011) *Living with Other Creatures: Green exegesis and theology*. Waco, TX: Baylor University Press.

—— (2016) 'Ecological hope in crisis?', in Bell, C. and White, R. S., *Creation Care and the Gospel*. Peabody, MA: Hendrickson, pp. 43–52.

Beale, G. (2004) *The Temple and the Church's Mission: A biblical theology of the dwelling place of God*. Leicester: Apollos.

Bear, C. (2003) 'Caring for creation' seminar at InterVarsity Urbana Student Missions Conference (available online at: <https://urbana.org/seminar/caring-creation>).

Bell, C. and White, R. S. (eds) (2016) *Creation Care and the Gospel: Reconsidering the mission of the church*. Peabody, MA: Hendrickson.

Berry, R. J. (1972) *Ecology and Ethics*. London: IVP.

—— (ed.) (2000) *The Care of Creation: Focusing concern and action*. Leicester: IVP.

—— (ed.) (2006) *Environmental Stewardship*. London: T&T Clark.

—— (2008) 'The research scientist's psalm', *Science & Christian Belief*, 20, pp. 147–161.

—— (2013) 'Disputing evolution encourages environmental neglect', *Science & Christian Belief*, 25, pp. 113–130.

Blamires, H. (1963) *The Christ Mind: How should a Christian think?* London: SPCK.

Bliss, L. (2013) *Environmental Missions: Planting churches and trees*. Pasadena, CA: William Carey Library.

Blocher, H. (1984) *In the Beginning*. Leicester: IVP.

Board for Social Responsibility (1970) 'Man in his living environment: An ethical assessment'. London: Church Information Office. See also 'Our responsibility for the living environment,' a report from the Board for Social Responsibility's Environmental Issues Reference Panel (1986). London: Church House Publishing.

Bockmühl, K. (1975) *Conservation and Lifestyle*, Grove Booklet on Ethics No. 20. Cambridge: Grove Books.

Boff, L. (2008) *Essential Care: An ethics of human nature*. Waco, TX: Baylor University Press.

Bookless, D. (2008) *Planetwise: Dare to care for God's world.* Nottingham: IVP.

—— (2014a) '"Let everything that has breath praise the Lᴏʀᴅ": The Bible and biodiversity', Cambridge Paper 23(3), September.

—— (2014b) 'Why should I care? Evangelical perspectives on earthcare', in Kaoma, J. (ed.), *Ecology and Mission.* Oxford: Regnum Books.

Brooks, D. (2004) 'Who is John Stott?', *New York Times*, 30 November (available online at: <www.nytimes.com/2004/11/30/opinion/who-is-john-stott.html>).

Broomhall, M. (1929) *The Man who Believed God.* London: China Inland Mission.

Cape Town Commitment (2010) See under Lausanne Congress on World Evangelization, Third.

Cameron, J. (2012) *The Humble Leader: John Stott.* Fearn, Ross-shire: Christian Focus.

—— (2020) 'John R. W. Stott: A biographical sketch', in Wright, C., Brown, L., Newman, L. et al.; Cameron, J. (series ed.), *John Stott: Pastor, leader and friend.* (Expanded and updated 2021.) Oxford: Dictum Press, pp. 3–6. Used by permission of Dictum Press.

Carson, R. (1962) *Silent Spring.* Boston, MA: Houghton Mifflin.

Catherwood, C. (1984) *Five Evangelical Leaders.* London: Hodder & Stoughton.

Cavanaugh, W. T. and Smith, J. K. A. (eds) (2017) *Evolution and the Fall.* Grand Rapids, MI: Eerdmans.

Chapman, A. (2012) *Godly Ambition: John Stott and the evangelical movement.* New York: Oxford University Press.

Cranfield, C. E. B. (1975) 'A critical and exegetical commentary on the epistle to the Romans', in *The International Critical Commentaries: Volume I.* London: T. & T. Clark.

Crosby, C. (2008) 'Essays in orni-theology', review of Stott, J. R. W., *The Birds, Our Teachers*, in *Christianity Today*,

13 November (available online at: <www.christianitytoday. com/ct/2008/novemberweb-only/146-41.0.html>).

D'Alisa, G., Demaria, F. and Kallis, G. (eds) (2015) *Degrowth: A vocabulary for a new era*. New York: Routledge.

Darwin, C. R. (1839) *The Voyage of the Beagle*. London: John Murray.

DeWitt, C. B. (2000) 'Creation's environmental challenge to evangelical Christianity', in Berry, R. J. (ed.) (2000) *The Care of Creation*. Leicester: IVP, pp. 60–74.

DeYoung, K. and Gilbert, G. (2010) *What Is the Mission of the Church?* Wheaton, IL: Crossway.

Dudley-Smith, T. (1995a) *John Stott: A comprehensive bibliography*. Leicester: IVP.

—— (ed.) (1995b) *Authentic Christianity*. Leicester: IVP.

—— (1999) *John Stott: The making of a leader*. Leicester: IVP.

—— (2000) 'The God who set the stars in space', in Berry, R. J. (ed.), *The Care of Creation*. Leicester: IVP, pp. 184–185. 'The God who set the stars in space' by Timothy Dudley-Smith (b. 1926). © Timothy Dudley-Smith in Europe and Africa. © Hope Publishing Company in the United States of America and the rest of the world. Reproduced by permission of Oxford Publishing Limited (Music) through PLSclear. All rights reserved.

—— (2001) *John Stott: A global ministry*. Leicester: IVP.

Echlin, E. (1989) *The Christian Green Heritage: World as creation*, Grove Ethical Studies No. 74. Cambridge: Grove Books.

Elsdon, R. (1981) *Bent World*. Leicester: IVP.

Elsdon, R. (1992) *Greenhouse Theology*. Tunbridge Wells: Monarch.

Evangelical Environmental Network (n.d.) 'On the care of creation' (available online at: <https://creationcare.org/ what-we-do/an-evangelical-declaration-on-the-care-of-creation.html>

Geldenhuys, J. N. (1953) *Supreme Authority*. Grand Rapids, MI: Eerdmans.

Global Witness (n.d.) 'Land and environmental defenders', available online at: <www.globalwitness.org/en/campaigns/environmental-activists>).

Global Witness and *The Guardian* (2017) 'The defenders: 207 environmental defenders have been killed in 2017 while protecting their community's land or natural resources' (available online at: <www.theguardian.com/environment/ng-interactive/2017/jul/13/the-defenders-tracker>; see also Gnanakan, K. (1999) *God's World: A theology of the environment*. London: SPCK.

Gnanakan, K. (2014) *Responsible Stewardship of God's Creation*. New York: World Evangelical Alliance.

Goheen, M. W. (2014) *Introducing Christian Mission Today: Scripture, history and issues*. Downers Grove, IL: IVP.

González, J. L. (2015) *Creation: The apple of God's eye*. Nashville, TN: Abingdon.

Government White Paper (1990) 'This common inheritance: Britain's environmental strategy', Department of the Environment. London: HMSO.

Graham, B. (2005) 'John Stott', in 'The 2005 Time 100', *TIME*, 18 April (available online at: <http://content.time.com/time/specials/packages/article/0,28804,1972656_1972717_1974108,00.html>).

—— (2012) Tribute included in the order of service produced for the service of thanksgiving for John Stott at St Paul's Cathedral, 13 January (available online at: <https://markmeynell.files.wordpress.com/2012/01/jrws-memorial-service.pdf>).

Greene, M. (2020) 'A vision for whole-life discipleship', in Wright, C., Brown, L., Newman, L. et al.; Cameron, J. (series ed.), *John Stott: Pastor, leader and friend*. Oxford: Dictum Press, pp. 68–71. Used by permission of Dictum Press.

Groody, Daniel (2007) *Globalization, Spirituality and Justice: Theology in global perspective*. New York: Orbis.

Guillebaud, J. (2000) 'Population numbers and environmental degradation', in Berry, R. J. (ed.), *The Care of Creation*. Leicester: IVP, pp. 155–160

Hale, Sir M. (1677) *The Primitive Origination of Mankind, Considered and Examined According to the Light of Nature.* London: William Shrowsbery.

Halton, C. (ed.) (2015) *Genesis: History, fiction, or neither?* Grand Rapids, MI: Zondervan.

Harris, P. (1983) *Under the Bright Wings.* London: Hodder & Stoughton. Used by permission of Regent College Publishing.

—— (2008) *Kingfisher's Fire.* Oxford: Monarch.

—— (2011) 'Birding before dawn around the world', in Wright, C. J. H. (ed.), *John Stott: A portrait by his friends.* Nottingham: IVP, pp. 155–161.

Harris, P. and L. (2012) 'Bliss' podcast.

Harrison, P. (1998) *The Bible, Protestantism and the Rise of Natural Science.* Cambridge: Cambridge University Press.

Henry, C. (1947) *The Uneasy Conscience of Modern Fundamentalism.* Grand Rapids, MI: Eerdmans.

Higgins, R. (1978) *The Seventh Enemy: The human factor in the global crisis.* London: Hodder & Stoughton.

Hindson, J. (2016) *Consider the Lilies.* Malton: Gilead.

Hodson, M. J. and Hodson, M. R. (2015) *A Christian Guide to Environmental Issues.* Abingdon: BRF.

—— (2017) 'An introduction to environmental ethics', Grove Ethics Series 184. Cambridge: Grove Books.

Hollow, M. (2008) *A Future and a Hope.* Toronto: Monarch.

Houghton, J. T. (1994) *Global Warming: The complete briefing.* Oxford: Lion.

Hunt, K. and Hunt, G. (2011) 'A double portion of language skills', in Wright, C. J. H. (ed.), *John Stott: A portrait by his friends.* Nottingham: IVP, pp. 99–103.

IPCC (n.d.) 'Global warming of 1.5°C', Special Report (available online at: <www.ipcc.ch/sr15>).

—— (2001) 'Climate change 2001: The scientific basis' report (available online at: <www.ipcc.ch/site/assets/uploads/2018/07/WG1_TAR_FM.pdf>).

Isaac, M. (2015) *From Land to Lands, from Eden to the Renewed Earth*. Carlisle: Langham.

Keswick Classics (2008) *John Stott at Keswick*. Milton Keynes: Authentic.

Kirk, A. (2011) 'The London Institute – founded by that funny man in the floppy hat', in Wright, C. J. H. (ed.), *John Stott: A portrait by his friends*. Nottingham: IVP, pp. 173–178.

Khua Hnin Thang, R. (2014) *The Theology of the Land in Amos 7–9* . Carlisle: Langham.

Labberton, M. (2021) 'Between two worlds? The gospel in the life of John Stott', in Meitzner Yoder, L. S. (ed.), *Living Radical Discipleship*. Carlisle: Langham, pp. 3–14.

Lausanne Committee for World Evangelization (1980) 'An evangelical commitment to simple lifestyle', Lausanne Occasional Paper 20 (available online at: <https://lausanne.org/content/lop/lop-20>).

Lausanne Committee for World Evangelization and World Evangelical Fellowship (1982) 'Evangelism and social responsibility: An evangelical commitment', Lausanne Occasional Paper 21 (available online at: <https://lausanne.org/content/lop/lop-21>).

Lausanne Congress on World Evangelization, First (1974) The Lausanne Covenant and other selected official documents from the event are available online at: <https://web.archive.org/web/20101227142306/http://www.lausanne.org/lausanne-1974/lausanne-1974-documents.html>.

Lausanne Congress on World Evangelization, Second (1989) The Manila Manifesto and other selected official documents from the event are available online at: <https://web.archive.org/web/20101228181919/http://www.lausanne.org/manila-1989/manila-1989-documents.html>.

Lausanne Congress on World Evangelization, Third (2010) The Cape Town Commitment and other related resources from the event are available online at: <https://lausanne.org/content/ctcommitment>.

Lausanne/WEA Creation Care Network (2012) 'Jamaica call to action' (available online at: <https://lausanne.org/content/statement/creation-care-call-to-action>).

Leake, A. P. and Andrade, V. S. (2012) *'La deforestación del Chaco Salteño: ¿Crónica de un genocidio anunciado?'*, in Scott, L. (ed.), *El cuidado de la creación y el calentamiento global: perspectivas del Sur y del Norte*. Buenos Aires: Kairós, pp. 65–94.

Lewis, C. S. (1953) *Introduction to St Athanasius on the Incarnation*. London: Mowbrays. Quotes by C. S. Lewis © copyright CS Lewis Pte Ltd. Used with permission.

—— (1958) *Reflections on the Psalms*. London: Geoffrey Bles. Quotes by C. S. Lewis © copyright CS Lewis Pte Ltd. Used with permission.

Linzey, A. (1988) *Christianity and the Rights of Animals*. London: SPCK.

Lomberg, B. (2002) *The Sceptical Environmentalist*. Cambridge: Cambridge University Press.

Lovelock, J. (1979) *Gaia: A new look at life on Earth*. Oxford: Oxford University Press.

Luther, M., Pelikan, J. (trs) ([1521] 1956) *The Sermon on the Mount*, Vol. 21 of *Luther's Works*. Saint Louis, MO: Concordia.

McCloughry, R. (1995) *Population Growth and Christian Ethics*. Grove Ethical Studies no. 98. Cambridge: Grove Books.

McHarg, I. L. (1969) *Design with Nature*. New York: Natural History.

—— (1972–1973) Dunning Trust lectures, quoted in the *Ontario Naturalist*, March 1973.

Manila Manifesto (1989) See under Lausanne Congress on World Evangelization, Second.

Manning, B. (1942) *The Hymns of Wesley and Watt*. London: Epworth.

Matthews, J. T. (1993) 'Nations and nature: A new view of security, in Prins, G. and Tromp, H. (eds), *Threats without Enemies*. London: Earthscan, pp. 36–49.

Maxwell, G. (1963) Article in *The Observer*, 13 October.

Meitzner Yoder, L. S. (ed.) (2021) *Living Radical Discipleship*. Carlisle: Langham.

Micah Declaration on Integral Mission (2001) See Cape Town Commitment, paragraph I.10.b (available online at: https://lausanne.org/content/ctcommitment#p1-10. See also: <https://live-micah-global.pantheonsite.io/wp-content/uploads/2020/10/integral_mission_declaration_en.pdf>).

Millennium Ecosystem Assessment (2005) *Ecosystems and Human Well-Being: Synthesis*. Washington DC: Island Press.

Moo, J. A. (2009) 'The sea that is no more: Revelation 21.1 and the function of sea imagery in the apocalypse of John', *Novum Testamentum*, 51, pp. 148–167.

—— (2014) 'New Testament hope and a Christian environmental ethos', in Moo, J. A. and Routledge, R. (eds), *As Long as the Earth Endures: The Bible, creation and the environment*. Nottingham: Apollos, pp. 149–169.

—— (2016) 'The biblical basis for creation care', in Bell, C. and White, R. S. (eds), *Creation Care and the Gospel: Reconsidering the mission of the church*. Peabody, MA: Hendrickson, pp. 28–42. Extracts from *Creation Care and the Gospel: Reconsidering the mission of the church* by C. Bell and R. S. White (eds), copyright 2016 by Hendrickson Publishers, Peabody, Massachusetts. Used by permission. All rights reserved.

Moo, J. A. and White, R. S. (2014) *Hope in an Age of Despair: The Gospel and the future of life on earth*. Nottingham: IVP.

Moss, R. (1982) *The Earth in Our Hands*. Leicester: IVP.

Moule, C. F. D. (1964) *Man and Nature in the New Testament: Some reflections on biblical ecology*. London: Athlone.

Newbigin, L. (1986) *Foolishness to the Greeks*. London: SPCK.

—— (1989) *The Gospel in a Pluralist Society*. Grand Rapids, MI: Eerdmans.

Northcott, M. (2014) *A Political Theory of Climate Change*. London: SPCK.

Oreske, N. and Conway, E. (2010) *Merchants of Doubt*. New York: Bloomsbury.

Padilla, C. R. (2010) *Mission between the Times*. Carlisle: Langham.

Padilla DeBorst, R. (2019) 'Planetary gardening: A shared Christian vocation'. Adapted from presentation at the 'All things new: Creation, community, and vocation' March 2019 symposium, Human Needs and Global Resources, Wheaton College, Illinois (available online at: <https://wheaton.edu/academics/academic-centers/human-needs-and-global-resources-hngr/symposium/2019-symposium/2019-video-page>).

Platt, John R. (2018) 'At least 197 eco-defenders murdered in 2017', Global Justice Ecology Project, 5 February (available online at: <https://globaljusticeecology.org/at-least-197-eco-defenders-murdered-in-2017>).

Prance, G. T. (1996) *The Earth under Threat*. Glasgow: Wild Goose Publications.

Rawles, K. (2012) *The Carbon Cycle*. Uig: Two Ravens Press.

Reed, R. L. and Ngaruiya, D. K. (eds) (2019) *God and Creation*. Carlisle: Langham.

Research Scientists' Christian Fellowship Conference statement (1973) 'Man has a positive responsibility to manage nature', *Journal of the American Scientific Affiliation*, 25(1), March, pp. 3–4 (available free online at: <https://asa3.org/ASA/PSCF/1973/JASA3-73Complete.pdf>). This document first appeared in *Perspectives on Science and Christian Faith*. Used by permission of *Perspectives on Science and Christian Faith*.

Richter, S. L. (2008) *The Epic of Eden: A Christian entry into the Old Testament*. Downers Grove, IL: IVP Academic.

Richter, S. L. (2020) *Stewards of Eden: What Scripture says about the environment and why it matters*. Downers Grove, IL: IVP Academic.

Ringgren, H. (1962) *The Faith of the Psalmists*. London: SCM Press.

Rokhum, K. (2021) 'Loving our neighbour in God's world', in Meitzner Yoder, L. S. (ed.), *Living Radical Discipleship*. Carlisle: Langham, pp. 79–92.

Royal Commission on Environmental Pollution (1998) '21st report: Setting environmental standards', Command Paper 4053. London: TSO.

Royal Society (2005) 'Ocean acidification due to increasing atmospheric carbon dioxide', 30 June (available online at: <https://royalsociety.org/topics-policy/publications/2005/ocean-acidification>).

Ruse, M. (2001) *Can a Darwinian be a Christian?* Cambridge: Cambridge University Press.

Russell, C. A. (1994) *The Earth, Humanity and God*. London: UCL Press.

Salibián, Alfredo (2012) '*Reflexiones sobre la problemática ambiental latinoamericana*', in Scott, L. (ed.), *El cuidado de la creación y el calentamiento global: perspectivas del Sur y del Norte*. Buenos Aires: Kairós, pp. 205–240.

Schaeffer, F. A. (1970) *Pollution and the Death of Man: The Christian view of ecology*. London: Hodder & Stoughton.

Schneider, S. (1998) *Laboratory Earth: The planetary gamble we can't afford to lose*. New York: Basic Books.

Schumacher, E. F. (1973) *Small Is Beautiful: A study of economics as if people mattered*. London: Blond & Briggs.

SDG Knowledge Hub, IISD (2019) '2019 Earth Overshoot Day reaches earliest date ever', 1 August (available online at: <https://sdg.iisd.org/news/2019-earth-overshoot-day-reaches-earliest-date-ever>).

Sider, R. J. (ed.) (1980) *Living More Simply: Biblical principles and practical models*. Downers Grove, IL: IVP.

—— (ed.) (1982) *Lifestyle in the Eighties: An evangelical commitment to simple lifestyle*. Philadelphia, PA: Westminster.

Singer, P. ([1975] 1990, 2nd edn) *Animal Liberation*. New York: Random House.

Smail, T. (2001) *The Forgotten Father*. Eugene, OR: Wipf & Stock.

Smith, C. (2003) *Living Narratives: Moral, believing animals: Human personhood and culture*. New York: Oxford University Press.

Solano Miselis, J. R. (2016) 'In defense of life and harmony', *Journal of Latin American Theology*, 11(2), pp. 169–184.

Spurgeon, C. H. (1960) *An All-Round Ministry: A collection of addresses to ministers and students*, quoted in Stott, J. ([1999] 2007).

Stanley, B. (2013) *The Global Diffusion of Evangelicalism: The age of Billy Graham and John Stott*. Nottingham: IVP.

Steer, R. (2009) *Inside Story: The life of John Stott*. Nottingham: IVP.

Stott, J. R. W. (1966) *The Canticles and Selected Psalms*. London: Hodder & Stoughton, pp. 30–34. Used by permission of the Excecutors of John Stott's Literary Estate.

—— ([1967] 1997) *Our Guilty Silence: The gospel, the church and the world*. London: Hodder & Stoughton; 1997, reprinted, Leicester: IVP.

—— (1974a) *Basic Christianity*. London: IVP.

—— (1974b) 'The biblical basis of evangelism', opening address for part three, First Lausanne Congress on World Evangelization (available online at: <https://web.archive.org/web/20101229051510/http://www.lausanne.org/documents/lau1docs/0065.pdf >).

—— (1975) 'The Lausanne Covenant: An exposition and commentary by John Stott', 'The nature of evangelism', Lausanne Occasional Paper 3, section 4, Lausanne Committee for World Evangelization (available online at: <www.lausanne.org/content/lop/lop-3?_sf_s=the+results+of+evangelism+include+responsible+service+in+the+world&_sfm_wpcf-select-gathering=1974+Lausanne>).

—— ([1975] 2016) *Christian Mission in the Modern World*. London: Falcon. (Updated and expanded by Wright, C. J. H., 2016. London: IVP.)

—— (ed.) (1977a) *Obeying Christ in a Changing World* (3 volumes). London: Collins.

—— (1977b) Sermon 'God and the environment', 14 August, All Souls Langham Place, London (available online at: <www.allsouls.org/Groups/317295/Sermons/Sundays/ZA007_

All_Life/ZA007_All_Life.aspx?show_media=216474&show_file=229826>). Used by permission of the Executors of John Stott's Literary Estate.

—— ([1978] 1984, 2000) *Christian Counter-Culture*. Leicester: IVP. (Republished in 1984 as *The Message of the Sermon on the Mount* and revised, with additions, in 2020.)

—— (1982) *I Believe in Preaching*. London: Hodder & Stoughton.

—— (1984) 'Am I supposed to love myself or hate myself?', *Christianity Today*, 20 April, 28(7).

—— (1988a) *Favorite Psalms*. London: Three's Company, pp. 10–13, 21–25, 95–97, 98–101. Copyright © 1988, 2021, used by permission of the Executors of John Stott's Literary Estate.

—— (1988b) Sermon on 'creation', 25 September, All Souls Langham Place, London. Edited transcript used by permission of the Executors of John Stott's Literary Estate.

—— (1989) 'Learning how to fly kites', *World Christian*, October. Quoted in Dudley-Smith, T. (2001) *John Stott: A global ministry*. Leicester: IVP.

—— (1990) 'The biblical imperative', A Rocha Occasional Paper No. 2. (Presented at 'Caring for God's world' conference, sponsored by A Rocha and the London Institute for Contemporary Christianity, in Reading, on 28 October 1989.)

—— (1991) *Christian Basics*. Ada, MI: Baker.

—— (1992) *The Contemporary Christian: Applying God's word to today's world*. Leicester: IVP.

—— (1993) Foreword, in Harris, P., *Under the Bright Wings*. London: Hodder & Stoughton, pp. ix–xi.

—— ([1994] 2020) *The Message of Romans: God's good news for the world* (revised edition). London: IVP. *Note:* Abbreviation 'BAGD' stands for Walter Bauer, *A Greek–English Lexicon of the New Testament and Other Early Christian Literature*, translated and adapted by William F. Arndt and F. Wilbur Gingrich, 2nd edition, revised and augmented by F. Wilbur Gingrich and Frederick W. Danker from Bauer's 5th edition, 1958 (University of Chicago Press, 1979). (NB: Now 'BDAG'.)

—— (1996) 'The works of the Lord', in LeQuire, S. (ed.), *The Best Preaching on Earth: Sermons on caring for creation.* Valley Forge, PA: Judson, pp. 78–83. Extracts reprinted from *The Best Preaching on Earth: Sermons on caring for creation*, edited by Stan L. LeQuire, copyright © 1996 by Judson Press. Used by permission of Judson Press.

—— (1999) Sermon, 'The feeding of ravens: faith', 1 August, All Souls Langham Place, London (available online at: <www.allsouls.org/Media/AllMedia.aspx?show_media=51682&show_file=53869>). Transcript used by permission of the Executors of John Stott's Literary Estate.

—— ([1999] 2007) *The Birds Our Teachers: Essays in ornitheology.* London: Three's Company, pp. 7–10, 20–22, 23–25, 31–32, 57, 60–66, 94–95. Extract taken from *The Birds Our Teachers* by John Stott. Text copyright © 1999 John Stott. This edition copyright © 2007 ZipAddress Ltd. Used by permission of Lion Hudson Ltd.

—— (2000) Foreword, in Berry, R. J. (ed.), *The Care of Creation.* Leicester: IVP, pp. 7–9.

—— (2002) *People My Teachers.* London: Three's Company, pp. 108–114. Extract taken from *People My Teachers* by John Stott. Text copyright © 2002 John Stott. This edition copyright © 2002 ZipAddress Ltd. Used by permission of Lion Hudson Ltd.

—— (2003a) *Why I Am a Christian.* Leicester: IVP.

—— (2003b) Unpublished manuscript. Notes from seminar, 'Caring for creation', written to be presented at InterVarsity Urbana Student Missions Conference 2003. Lambeth Palace papers. Used by permission of the Executors of John Stott's Literary Estate.

—— (2003c) John Stott message read by Joshua Wathanga, InterVarsity Urbana Student Missions Conference (available online at: <https://urbana.org/message/john-stott-message-read-joshua-wathanga>).

—— (2004) Sunday Worship 'Let the little birds be your theologians' on BBC Radio 4, broadcast from the Hookses,

Pembrokeshire, Wales, 18 April. Used by permission of the Executors of John Stott's Literary Estate.

—— (2006) *Issues Facing Christians Today*. Basingstoke: Marshall, Morgan & Scott, pp. xi–xii, 9, 10, 119–120, 135–146, 151–157. (First published in 1984. Revised editions 1990, 1999 and 2006.) Extracts taken from *Issues Facing Christians Today* by John Stott. Copyright © 1984, 1990, 1999, and 2006 by John Stott. Used by permission of Zondervan. <www.zondervan.com>

—— (2007) 'The model: Becoming more like Christ", John Stott's final public address, Keswick Convention, 17 July, *Knowing & Doing*, Fall 2009 (available online at: <https://www.cslewisinstitute.org/Becoming_More_Like_Christ_Stott>).

—— (2010a) An audio greeting from John Stott, Cape Town (available online at: <https://www.youtube.com/watch?v=EU2jqP08bzo>).

—— (2010b) *The Radical Disciple*. Downers Grove, IL: IVP.

Stuart, S. N., Archibald, G. W., Ball, J., Berry, R. J., Emmerich, S. D., et al. (2005) 'Conservation theology for conservation biologists: A reply to David Orr', *Conservation Biology*, 19, pp. 1689–1692.

Sunquist, S. W. (2013) *Understanding Christian Mission: Participation in suffering and glory*. Grand Rapids, MI: Baker.

Surcos Digital (2019) '*Asesinado Sergio Rojas Ortiz dirigente indígena de Salitre*', 19 March (available online at: <https://surcosdigital.com/asesinado-sergio-rojas-ortiz-dirigente-indigena-de-salitre>).

Tamayo, J. J. (2017) *Teologías del Sur: el giro descolonizador*. Madrid: Trotta.

Thomas, J. M. (ed.) (1993) 'Evangelicals and the environment', *Evangelical Review of Theology*, 17(2), pp. 115–286.

Thomas, K. (1983) *Man and the Natural World: Changing attitudes in England 1500–1800*. London: Allen Lane.

Times, The (2011) 'The Rev Jon Stott', 29 July (available online at: <www.thetimes.co.uk/article/the-rev-john-stott-23j3mkjdfr3`>).

Triton, A. N. (1970) *Whose World?* London: IVP.

UCCF (1973) 'Man has a positive responsibility to manage nature', *Journal of the American Scientific Affiliation*, 25(1), March, pp. 3–4 (available free online at: <https://asa3.org/ASA/PSCF/1973/JASA-73Complete.pdf>). This document first appeared in *Perspectives on Science and Christian Faith*. Used by permission of *Perspectives on Science and Christian Faith*.

United Nations Committee on Economic, Social and Cultural Rights (n.d.) for information on implementation of the International Covenant on Economic, Social and Cultural Rights, visit the committee's website at: <www.ohchr.org/en/hrbodies/cescr/pages/cescrindex.aspx>.

Valerio, R. ([2004, revised editions 2008, 2019] 2019) *L is for Lifestyle: Christian living that doesn't cost the Earth*. London: IVP.

Vanhoozer, K. (2006) '"One rule to rule them all?" Theological method in an era of world Christianity', in Ott, C. and Netland, H. A. (eds), *Globalizing Theology: Belief and practice in an era of world Christianity*. Grand Rapids, MI: Baker Academic, pp. 85–126.

Visser 't Hooft, W. A. (1968) 'The mandate of the ecumenical movement', address given at the presentation of the report of the Central Committee, in Goodall, N. (ed.), 'The Uppsala report 1968: Official report of the Fourth Assembly of the World Council of Churches, Uppsala, July 4–20 1968'. Geneva: World Council of Churches. Appendix V, pp. 312, 317–318.

Walton, J. (2009) *The Lost World of Genesis One: Ancient cosmology and the origins debate*. Downers Grove, IL: IVP Academic.

—— (2015) *The Lost World of Adam and Eve*. Downers Grove, IL: IVP Academic.

Ward, B. and Dubos, R. (1972) *Only One Earth: The care and maintenance of a small planet*. Harmondsworth: Penguin.

Warners, D. P. and Heun, M. K. (eds) (2019) *Beyond Stewardship: New approaches to creation care*. Grand Rapids, MI: Calvin.

Welsby, P. A. (1984) *A History of the Church of England, 1945–1980*. Oxford: Oxford University Press.

White, L. (1967) 'The historical roots of our ecologic crisis', *Science*, 155, pp. 1203–1207. (Reproduced in White, L. (1968) *Machina ex Deo: Essays on the dynamism of Western culture*. Cambridge, MA: MIT Press.)

Wilkinson, K. (2012) *Between God and Green*. New York: Oxford University Press.

Winter, P. (1996) *The Adventures of a Birdwatcher*. St Louis, MO: privately printed.

Wirzba, N. (2015) *From Nature to Creation: A Christian vision for understanding and loving our world*. Grand Rapids, MI: Baker Academic.

—— (2019) *Food and Faith: A theology of eating* (2nd edn). New York: Cambridge University Press.

WMO/UNEP (2007) 'Scientific assessment of ozone depletion: 2006', Global Ozone Research and Monitoring Project, Report No. 50. Geneva: WMO (available online at: <https://csl.noaa.gov/assessments/ozone/2006>).

Woodley, R. S. (2012) *Shalom and the Community of Creation: An indigenous vision*. Grand Rapids, MI: Eerdmans.

World Commission on Environment and Development (1987) *Our Common Future*. Oxford: Oxford University Press.

Wright, C. J. H. (2006) *The Mission of God*. Nottingham: IVP.

—— (2009) *The God I Don't Understand: Reflections on tough questions of faith*. Grand Rapids, MI: Zondervan.

—— (ed.) (2011) *John Stott: A portrait by his friends*. Nottingham: IVP. Published in the USA in 2011 as *Portraits of a Radical Disciple: Recollections of John Stott's life and ministry*. Downers Grove, IL: IVP.

—— (2013) 'The goodness, the glory and the goal of creation', John Stott London lecture, 23 October (available online at: <www.theearthkeepers.org/wp-content/uploads/2018/02/Creation-goodness-glory-goal-TEXT.pdf>). Used by permission of C. J. H. Wright, A Rocha and Regnum Books. A shorter, modified version of this lecture was printed as

'The care of creation, the gospel, and our mission', in Kaoma, K. J. (ed.) (2015) *Creation Care and Christian Mission.* Oxford: Regnum Books, pp. 183–197.

—— (2020) 'Abrahamic and apostolic ministry', in Wright, C., Brown, L., Newman, L. et al.; Cameron, J. (series ed.), *John Stott: Pastor, leader and friend.* (Expanded and updated 2021.) Oxford: Dictum Press, pp. 31–40. Used by permission of Dictum Press.

Wright, C., Brown, L., Newman, L. et al.; Cameron, J. (series ed.) (2020) *John Stott: Pastor, leader and friend.* (Expanded and updated 2021.) Oxford: Dictum Press. Used by permission of Dictum Press.

Wright, N. T. (2008) 'Jesus is coming – plant a tree!', in *The Green Bible.* New York: HarperCollins, pp. I-72–I-85.

Wright, Tom (2013) *Creation, Power and Truth: The gospel in a world of cultural confusion.* London: SPCK.

—— (2014) *Surprised by Scripture: Engaging contemporary issues.* London: SPCK.

Yeo, K. K. and Green, G. L. (eds) (2021) *Theologies of Land: Contested land, spatial justice, and identity: Crosscurrents in Majority World and Minority Theology Series.* Eugene, OR: Cascade.

Index of Scripture references

Index of Scripture references

Index of Scripture references